ISBN 978-1-330-06577-8
PIBN 10017081

# Similar Books Are Available from
# www.forgottenbooks.com

"MY GARDEN" SERIES
EDITED BY . . . . .
R. HOOPER PEARSON
EDITOR OF THE . . . .
GARDENERS' CHRONICLE

My Garden in Summer

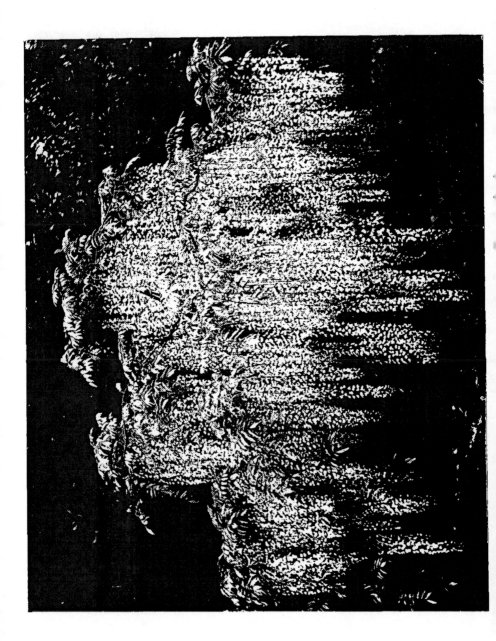

# My Garden in Summer

By E. A. Bowles, M.A.

London : T. C. & E. C. Jack
67 Long Acre, W.C.
And Edinburgh
1914

# CONTENTS

CHAP.                                                                    PAGE

   I. THE MERGING OF SPRING AND SUMMER . 

  II. THE IRIS BEDS . . . . . . . . . 14

 III. BEARDLESS IRISES OF SUMMER . . . . . 30

  IV. ROSES . . . . . . . . . . . 46

   V. SINGLE ROSES . . . . . . . . . 62

  VI. GERANIUMS . . . . . . . . . . 92

 VII. A JUNE STROLL . . 116

VIII. A JUNE AFTERNOON . . . . . . . . 134

  IX. AQUATICS . . . . . . . . . . 157

   X. SUCCULENTS . . . . . . . . . 180

  XI. HOW JULY BEGINS . . . . . . . . 202

 XII. GRASSES . . . . . . . . . . 219

XIII. DAISIES . . . . . . . . . . 237

XIV. BEDDING OUT . . . . . . . . . 252

 XV. FLOWERS FOR CUTTING . . . . . . . 263

XVI. AS JULY ENDS . . . . . . . . . 273

XVII. AUGUST . . . . . . . . . . 292

    INDEX . . . . . . . . . . 303

# ILLUSTRATIONS

## BLACK AND WHITE PLATES

Wistaria multijuga as a standard . . . . . *Frontispiece*

FACING
PAGE

Rosa xanthina . . . . . . . . . . . 66

Meconopsis heterophylla . . . . . . . . . 130

Adenocarpus anagyrus . . . . . . . . . 144

The Vine Pergola and Viburnum tomentosum var. plicatum . 148

Dianthus arvergnensis and microlepis . . . . . . 156

Campanula Allionii in Moraine . . . . . . . 158

Yucca recurvifolia and Spiraea camtschatica . . . . 176

Gunnera chilensis . . . . . . . . . . 180

Cereus paucispinus . . . . . . . . . . 188

Agave Parryi . . . . . . . . . . . 190

Succulent plants on the Pond steps . . . . . . 194

Bed of Succulents on the Terrace . . . . . . 196

Sempervivums on Terrace wall . . . . . 198

Romneya trichocalyx . . . . . . . . 206

Campanula lactiflora . . . . . . . . . 208

Aira caespitosa . . . . . . . . . . . 224

Spiraea arborea . . . . . . . . . . 268

Eryngium serra by the Cactus bank . . . . . . 274

Potentilla davurica and Phormium tenax . . . . . 280

Linum arboreum . . . . . . . . . . 282

Ligustrum ovalifolium multiflorum . . . . . . 284

Convolvulus mauritanicus . . . . . . 286

Genista aethnensis . . . . . . 296

# My Garden in Summer

Spring is ever present in any garden, where tender young growth·and promise of flower are continually springing from the ground. Certain scents and sounds mean Summer to me; taken singly, like specific characters, they are insufficient, but in combination they spell a certain season. The snoring drawl of a contented greenfinch and the mowing machine whirring over the lawns, turning them into parallel-striped carpets of two shades of green, the scent of the bruised and cut grass drying in the sun, initiate the summer feeling, and constitute the prelude ; but the monotoned double croon of a turtle-dove, with its well-trilled R's, and the high-pitched rattle of the hay-cutter in the meadows, followed by the aroma of new-mown hay, with a whiff of the clean fragrance of a Dog Rose, build up the real article, and guarantee the presence of Summer as surely as the facts that you can cast clouts without missing them, and go out after dinner without further clothing than that meal demands.

There is so gradual a transition from Spring to Summer that one only notices the invasion of the warmer season here and there at first ; it is as though these sister-queens agreed to rule together for a spell, and their courtiers and servants mingled freely ; a Rose or a Lily appears among the tall, over-blown Tulips, which daily lay down some of their vernal banners as they drop their petals. A little later we must look in quiet, shady corners for the courtiers of Queen Spring, whilst everywhere may be seen those of Summer in rose-laden bushes and tropical flowers, returned with the

2

# Merging of Spring and Summer

reign of the new monarch from their exile to the greenhouses. It generally happens that the feeling that Spring has lost the upper hand comes over me when I get back to my garden after an arduous day's work on the first day of what was once the Temple, and is now, the Chelsea Show. The masses of Roses and Rhododendrons and Azaleas seen there under canvas are not somehow convincing arguments of Summer's rule, at least not sufficiently strong to overcome the display made by the banks of well-preserved Tulips that in most seasons come from the fields of two or three great growers. Even the presence of Sweet Peas and Chrysanthemums, Dahlias and forced fruit, produces no sensation of Summer, for they all have an untimely, forced appearance. But, on my return, a stroll in my own garden before it is time to dress for dinner, shows that the Tulips that looked respectable yesterday, are now shabby and faded, and disappointing at close quarters, and I go to look for bloom on summer-flowering plants that I have been reminded of by the forced specimens at the show. There is so much to be done, and to be looked at, in the garden at this time of the year that I often miss the show of buds appearing upon some treasure until reminded by flowers in an exhibit that I have not called upon mine this season, and I enjoy the visit of inquiry, especially if it is rewarded by a promise of abundance. It does one good to lift the leaves of *Paeonia lutea* and find clusters of plump buds hidden beneath them, or to discover a goodly number of flowering shoots just starting out sideways from the rosettes of *Gentiana Kurroo*, and so to be assured that both the

3

# My Garden in Summer

beginning and end of Summer will give their widely different charms.

The garden gave me a curious effect of the overlapping of Spring and Summer this season in an unusually early offering of Sweet Peas, from plants raised in pots and planted out betimes, while I was still able to gather a good bunch of Daffodils, and for over a fortnight I had these unusual companions side by side on a flower table. Of course the first Sweet Peas are generally the best; on the other hand these last Daffodils were the worst of the season, but were of great interest to me, for they represented an experiment I had undertaken to find out what is the best way to treat bulbs from New Zealand, and how soon they can be acclimatised to our seasons and fit for the show table.

I received some gloriously heavy, fat bulbs in january, that had been sent off from New Zealand as soon as lifting was possible, and I tried them in three ways, potted and stood in ashes, planted in a warm southern border, and in a cool one facing north in a moisture-retaining compost. The southern border showed the first leaves, but not until the middle of May, and then the poor Daffodils raced ahead, springing up as rapidly as mushrooms, and produced thin-textured miseries of flowers by the end of the month. With their short stalks and poor, starry segments they were caricatures of the beautiful things their labels proclaimed them: King Alfred was more like the herdsman's wife or one of the burnt cakes than his Majesty the Great. Any wild Pseudo-narcissus from the fields would have beaten

4

Pæonies and Zinnias. By H. Ackerman.

(See p. 3.)

# Merging of Spring and Summer

such a flower on the show table. The potted bulbs, even though stood under a north wall, as soon as the leaves began to lengthen, plainly showed they had been forced against their will, and so the most successful were those in the cool northern border, which flowered until the middle of June, and were less like caricature Daffodils than those that flowered earlier. Judging from these results I should not advise the importation of New Zealand Narcissi for the purpose of providing bloom in June, but from the leaves they made and retained till late Autumn, and a bulb I unearthed as a sample in the shaded bed, I have good hopes of acclimatising them by cool treatment during their two first years, and getting fine flowers from them in the third. I have also here a very late form of *N. poeticus* that I grubbed out of the hay meadows above Lanslebourg in the Haute Maurienne three years ago. There it flowers naturally in mid-June, and this year I left it still in flower here in the second week of that month when I started off to revisit its birthplace. It is a meanly-formed, skimpy flower and of a dull, unclean white, sometimes inclining to a distinct yellow tone, interesting but not beautiful, but if it will retain its June-flowering habit I shall continue to value it, and perhaps, some day, mated with a freshly-arrived New Zealander, it may produce a summer-flowering race.

When Spring is merging into Summer in the last days of May, I like to watch the daily progress of *Wistaria multijuga*, which increases almost hourly in beauty, until the full display of the lavender cascade of flowers is

# My Garden in Summer

reached in June. Many of the flower-clusters are by then a yard, or even more, in length, and the older flowers at the upper end do not fall until the last few buds are opening at the tips of the bunches, so that the effect is as striking as that produced by any flowering shrub that can be grown in the open air. I have often heard complaints that the *multijuga* forms are rather shy flowerers, and I think that is true of plants that are trained on walls or on anything that encourages the slender shoots to wander on and still find support, and that it is necessary to induce woody growths to stand away free from any support before a really profuse flowering can be expected. This habit fits them for use as standards, and I know of few things better for sheltered positions on lawns. My oldest specimen was turned out of its pot into its present position some dozen of years ago, and it soon threw out wild arms seeking for something to twine around beyond its central stake. The aspirations of these tentacles were cut short ; they thickened into self-supporting branches about a yard in length, and after three seasons of this treatment commenced to bear flowers, and every year up to and including 1912 the flower display increased in wealth. Then it was so lavish that the foliage that followed was thinner than usual, and I half expected this season's flowering would be poor, but was sadly disappointed when I found no more than three flowering buds which dried up and fell off at an early stage of development. I hope and trust its absolute barrenness is of the nature of a rest cure, and that next season it will be strong and well again, and appear at Queen Summer's

6

# Wistarias

State Ball clad in a court train of greater length than ever.

When buying *W. multijuga* it is wise to see plants in flower, and choose those that please your taste in colour and form ; for it is raised very easily from seed, even in the warmer parts of this country, and seedlings vary enormously.  Further, we can hardly expect the altruism of the Japanese gardener to so thoroughly overpower his commercial instincts that he should export his largest and longest flowered and best coloured varieties at the same price as the ordinary seedlings ; so it is he who keeps a wary, wide-open eye in the show tent and nursery that will be best pleased with *Wistaria multijuga* in his garden.

This is especially true of the white variety, which in its best form is one of the loveliest things that can excite an optic nerve.  When the flowers of the racemes are open on rather more than half their length, that upper portion is snowy white, and the rest is a wonderfully shaded series of tints of the softest emerald green, of course deepest at the tapered tip, as though the paint had been allowed to run down.

I unfortunately bought the white one I wished to grow into a standard in unenlightened days, and I do not believe it will ever be a very startling object, for its racemes are short, and the unopened buds more nearly resemble aquamarines, or broken soda-water bottles, than the emeralds I had hoped for.  The poor plant stands higher up the gravelly bank than the lilac form, and is often thirsty about flowering time, and flings the baby

7

# My Garden in Summer

buds off the central rachis as crabs are said to do with their legs and claws unless packed too closely for kicking in the boiling pot.

A little disappointment such as this provides a text for a Jeremiad on the uncertainty of success in gardening, the a-gley-ganging tendency of your best-laid plans that comes so aft that, though it may enhance your rare triumphs, still lets you feel that you are gambling against all the forces of Nature with those of Chance thrown in.

I can see a fine allegorical picture in the subject. The keen, eager young gardener sits in the limelight beam that comes Rembrandt-wise from a hole in the roof; at his feet lie trowels and forks, baskets of soil, patent manures, and insecticides; Nicholson's *Dictionary of Gardening* lies open on his knee and shows marginal pencil notes and signs of frequent use; his chin rests on his left hand and his clear, frank eyes under slightly raised, puzzled eyebrows gaze anxiously at the faces of his opponents on the other side of the table, trying to read their intentions by their expressions. These figures are in half shadow, and grouped in friendly union to outwit the gardener: a ray of light falls on one side of the face of the Clerk of the Weather, and he looks benevolent enough as seen by his opponent, but the shadowy side of his face has a half-closed eye and a finger to his nose as he winks and signals to John Frost, Esq., who has laid his arm around the neck of the other, and though pretending not to be interested in the game is evidently, by a gentle hug, encouraging the bluff of his accomplice. Other figures are ranged behind, all with linked arms to denote their

8

# Wistarias

co-operation in the conspiracy. One recognises the personification of the Nurseryman's list by the trimming of laudatory adjectives bordering his garments: heavenly-blue, salmon-rose, very free flowering, and hardy-with-me are some that occur frequently. The Law of Averages is a stern-visaged ancient, clad in a grey surtout bearing a pattern of columns of figures and mathematical symbols, and so on and so on ; you can fill in the rest of the crowd, I expect. When this picture is painted, if it is given two stars in Baedeker and placed in Dresden or Amsterdam, crowds will take Cook's tickets to go and see it, but put it in our own National Gallery and they will still take the foreign tickets to see something else. But just so do we gamble with the soils and seasons and move our pawns or plant our Wistarias with a deal of thought, and some unforeseen move by an unknown Japanese or some undiscovered poverty of the lower soil cries check, the longed-for effect does not come off, and we are led to growling and sermonising in this sardonic strain. Take warning then, good reader, and choose your plant in bloom, and dig a deep enough hole to be sure the subsoil is good, then I hope you will escape the wait of several seasons ending in the discovery that your specimen is an inferior variety. Many people howled aloud when at last they flowered the much-belauded *W. multijuga rosea*, for they had not properly worked out the rule of three sum presented in the catalogues. Surely they should have known that as a tender, delicate rose is to three and sixpence, so would be their imagination of *W. multijuga rosea* to the slightly pink-tinted flowers of the pallid reality. If you allow a long bunch of its still unopened buds to trail on your white shirt cuff you will see it really is not white but quite sufficiently tinted with pinkish lavender to warrant the varietal name of rosea in a nursery list without the addition of superba or magnifica and the consequent charge of seven and sixpence. I am pleased with mine, however, for it grew from its own pergola post until it mixed with a *Clematis montana rubens* on the next one, and as the two plants flower together and the drooping racemes of the Wistaria are very long and freely produced, the soft pink of the Clematis backed by the pearly-rose shade of the Wistaria makes a delightful picture.

A second plant of this variety I intended should clamber up an old Scots Pine was planted at its foot, and long after the one in the pergola was providing us annually with a barrow full of trimmings, number two had not climbed a yard of its tree, and looked as sulky as a rolled-up hedgehog. So we moved it to form a third specimen standard *multijuga* on the lawn. In its first season there it flung out as many long feelers as an Anthea Sea-anemone, and the following June it flowered, and still further convinced me that *multijuga* forms are best as standards, unless one has room for an overhead trellis on which to train them as the Japanese do. I have also planted *W. chinensis*, both lilac and white, as standards in this group on the lawn, but they are much slower in growing into effective specimens, and are not more than a quarter of the size of the *multijuga* trees, but are beginning to make a

good annual show at flowering time. Perhaps it is the
method of propagation practised with **W. chinensis** that
makes it so slow to start. I was shown the process in one
of the great nurseries of Holland ; root cuttings are struck
in heat in a large house—thousands of them—and then the
long, slender growths from old plants are grafted on to
these newly-rooted babes, and by the next season a fairly
tall hobbledehoy Wistaria can be sent out into the world
before it has learnt manners or thought of flowering, but
many are plunged out in pots and twiddled round stakes
till they come to budding age, but by then their roots
must surely be sadly cramped and twisted. One thing is
necessary to guard against in a young specimen, that is
allowing two growths to twine round each other, for this
will end in one or both being more or less strangled, and
a checked flow of sap that may result in cast flower-buds
in dry seasons. Two other forms are being started as
standards here, but away from this older group and nearer
to the River. They came from Japan direct, and are the
sole survivors of a case of many plants. No one packs
more beautifully than the Japanese ; their very knots and
string and nails fill me with admiration ; but the last few
consignments I have received have had to contend with
ill-luck or bad judgment—one arrived soddened and more
closely resembling ensilage than living plants ; the next
was baked dry enough for a herbarium, probably having
had a seat next to an engine-room. In this last travelled
my Wistarias, and they had made some yards of growth,
the colour of boiled sea-kale, not much thicker than a

wasp's waist, and fragile as cheese-straws. What little of this tangle remained attached to the woody stems soon wilted in the light and air, and I thought bang had gone those sixpences laid out on them. But the plucky old stumps shot out new buds from most unexpected places, and by midsummer both of them were leafy enough to be planted out.

One of them, named fragrans, appears to be a good white form of *multijuga,* but not very long in the raceme so far. The other is ranked as a species, *W. brachybotrys,* and my plant is the white form of it. After two seasons of barrenness it produced a marvellous crop of flower buds, and promised to be a glorious spectacle, but did not live up to it, for the racemes, as its name implies, are short, not longer than six inches in fact, and the plant rushed into leaf just as the flowers opened and smothered up the display of snowy bloom with the yellow-green foliage ; but it is said to behave otherwise in Japan, being there the first species of the season to flower, and its tufts of blossoms completely cover the closely-pruned branches before any trace of a leaf appears. So it may be that with age, and pruning into close spurs, I may yet see its show without lifting the leaves to find it. *W. multijuga* in Japanese pictures seems to flower in a more leafless state than it does in English gardens ; but the trees most gene-rally depicted are either some centuries old or else spurred, dwarfed specimens, but in *multijuga* the presence of leaves does not matter, for owing to the length of the racemes, and especially where grown as a standard or on an over-head trellis, the pendant fringe of blossom is none the

# Wistarias

worse for a dome of golden-bronze coloured leaves. The Japanese call the Wistaria Fuji Niki-so, the plant of two seasons, as its flowering period connects Spring and Summer there as here, where the lilac-coloured *W. chinensis* often produces its first-fruit of floral offerings in early May if it is grown against a warm wall, especially if in some angle facing south and next to the kitchen chimney, while as a standard in the open it may lag behind in the procession, like the Sunday-school child whose ˙bootlace will come untied, until June and *W multijuga* are in full swing.

# CHAPTER II

## The Iris Beds

As *Wistaria brachybotrys* has brought us to the River bank let us walk along it and examine its flanking Iris beds under the ancient Yews, and this time make the journey in the opposite direction to that we took in the Spring volume, so that we may stop short before we reach the final bed, then a thick mass of *I. florentina* bloom, now of blue-grey leaves only relieved by a few Martagon Lilies. What strikes one as the greatest change since the last visit is the varied range of colouring now in the beds. Then the show consisted of the cool lavender grey of *florentina* and the deep blue purples of *germanica* forms, while the intermediate Iris Golden Fleece, and a few belated flowers of Leander and other dwarf Irises provided all there was of yellow. Now in some beds, where we have grouped yellow varieties together, there is a rich golden effect, and the mauves, lilacs, and pinks of forms of *I. pallida* contrast with white and purple *amoenas*, and the thunderstorm bronzes and lurid buffs of *squalens* varieties in other beds, to form the rainbow effect one expects in an Iris garden.

They are not grouped so systematically and brainily as I could wish, the result of playful habits of young her-

# The Iris Beds

ring gulls who have for many years lived in this part of
the garden, and alas, when old enough to give up silly
habits of playing with every label, wooden or zinc
(though the former are their better-loved toys, as they
float when placed in the River), some sad fate has over-
taken the veterans, and a younger generation has come to
play the dickens with the labels,—and I love their cry so
much that I forgive the label-removing nuisance.  The
needful work of sorting and regrouping has never yet
been achieved, and the Irises exist in repeated small clumps
instead of the broad masses my mind desires, but my
muscles shrink from the labour of planting.

Here at the corner facing the Lunatic Asylum beds and
the large Ivy-covered Yew, the mixture is mostly composed
of yellows, bronzes, and whites.  Of the former Gracchus
is one of the best, and so free in growth and flowering
that it needs no care; the daffodil-yellow standards are
as bright a yellow as any Iris could produce, while the
falls are netted with crimson and white and so proclaim
it a form of *I. variegata*, but in size and colouring it quite
eclipses its parent, who has to live a little further along
round the bend to avoid being put to shame by her handsome child.  The best orange-yellow one is known as
*aurea*, a regrettable name, as it leads to confusion with
the tall, beardless splendour from Kashmir that bears that
name specifically and by right.  This false fellow, however, whether we call it *germanica aurea* with many lists,
or *variegata aurea*, which is the nearest to correct nomenclature we can achieve, is very handsome and the tallest
of these yellow, bearded flags.  Maori King, a good dwarf

15

# My Garden in Summer

form of *variegata* very rich in velvet-crimson falls with gold braided edges and pure yellow standards, lacks the vigour of the others and wants more looking after than it gets here, and Mrs. Neubronner is quite as shy and retiring; so they make but little show, and three or four older, but less brilliant forms, whose names have floated down the River, are elbowing them out. Innocenza is a charming dwarf white, thought to be a form of *variegata*, but of mysterious origin. It is a warm-looking flower in spite of its whiteness, as the claw of the falls is stained orange and a touch of red netting on either side of the rich orange beard enlivens the colouring. I have a very warm spot in my heart for it, as it is so neat in growth, accords charmingly with yellow and bronze varieties when growing, and is equally delightful as a cut flower either in a vase all to itself or with yellow sisters for companions. Another good white is the amoena variety, Mrs. H. Darwin, but from its purple and violet-marked relations it inherits a cold scheme of colouring, in spite of red-purple nettings on the base of the falls, and I prefer it, both growing and cut, when among purple and lilac forms, so we shall find large clumps of it further along among the *pallidas* and *plicatas*, for it is one of the freest of all to flower, and has such stiff, strong stems it always makes a good solid mass of white, and therefore is well worth planting in repeated clumps among darker forms.

De Bergh and La Prestigieuse with several now nameless forms represent the bronze varieties of this corner, but I am promising myself a newer set when next they are replanted if a spare hole or two can be found. *Jacquiniana*

# The Iris Beds

is one of the best we have for deep sombre colouring, but it has a most pernicious habit here of growing outrageously fast, like Alice in Bill the Lizard's house, if a good soaking of rain reaches it when the flower scape is young ; then it outgrows its strength, splits its stem, or at best curls it in uncouth curves, and sprawls all over its neighbours. So it has been banished to the *I. florentina* bed, and there coming into flower after the rest of the plants have finished it can have the stage to itself. Now we must proceed round the inner curve by the River's bend, and in the next bed I want you to admire a fine piece of Ivy timber. It smothered a Yew many years before I can remember it, and of late years has been a source of much anxiety in every gale, leaning further over after each, and giving awful warnings of what it meant to do by the cracks and raised furrows its strained roots produced in the ground close to the stem. We wired it up to the living Yews from time to time as it was a handsome mass of Ivy, but this Spring we hardened our hearts, and digging round it, and loosening as many roots as we could find, released its wire supports, and let it gently down into the place we wished for it, at the back of the border between two of the Yews, instead of waiting for it to crash down and smash itself and its lesser neighbours. The operation cracked more of the Ivy's roots than was desirable, and in spite of a mound of good soil placed on those we had to lift out of the ground the poor old thing was hungry and thirsty when it came to the time to be thinking of new leaves. The old ones hung down with a very dejected expression for about a week in April, and

# My Garden in Summer

in spite of frequent syringings they all fell off one gusty night, and our invalid looked wretched. The fall of those leaves cheered me, though, for I felt sure had the tree meant to die they would have withered and died hanging on to the twigs.' So we syringed on steadily, and now here you see a convalescent, rather sparsely furnished with leaves, but a handsome great tree of Ivy for all that. It is a capital wind-screen and background for the Regelio-cyclus Irises whose praises I have already sung, and some weird Aroids that I hope will thrive even though over-hung by the Ivy, as they will be so well baked and scorched by the southern sunshine that will reach them there. This bed contains more shrubs than most of these Iris beds, so the space for Irises is not so great, and the narrow band is composed mostly of *amoena* varieties, that is to say those with white or pale lilac standards and wholly purple or purple-veined falls. Several of these live in incognito, thanks to the gulls, but some can be recognised at flowering time as Donna Maria, Duchesse de Nemours, and other lofty folk. Victorine is easily named as it has the deepest purple falls of any and white standards to contrast with them, but the effect is somewhat marred by a splashing of the deep purple on the inner surface of the standards, so that Thorbeck, although it is not quite so deep in the purple, is a better thing on account of the spotless purity of its standards.

We have now reached a point where we can look down a straight path which is planted on both sides with Rhododendrons for most of its length and then passes Tom Tiddler's ground, now very bright with its

# The Iris Beds

gold and silver groupings, and ends where it leads on to the old bowling-green lawn. The end of this walk near the River has been lately replanted, for it was a tangle of elderly and scraggy R. *ponticum*, no doubt the result of shoots from below the graft that had escaped detection when young and had lived to strangle and starve out the scions. So there was an opportunity to plant a few of my favourite varieties, such as Sappho with its white flowers and large purple spots like imitation Bumble-bees, and R. *fastuosum fl. pl.*, which is the nearest approach to a lavender shade reached by any of the *ponticum* type, and a very beautiful variety when well grown, as it flowers rather later than most kinds, lasts long in beauty owing to its double flowers, and is a strong grower. This path makes a pretty picture on a fine June day, and is framed by two of the straightest and most picturesque of the old Yew trunks, one standing on either side of the path and at the back of the Iris beds. A Honeysuckle puzzles people at first sight, for it stands up with a clear stem of dove-coloured satiny bark, and then forms a narrow pillar of growth for some fifteen feet, and appears to stand up stiffly without any support or touching the Yew overhead. The fact is it used to scramble over a spindly, starved Yew that grew in front of the one with the grand stem and hid its beauty, and was being driven out and kept scraggy by the larger tree. So we cut it down, disentangled the Honeysuckle, and, loth to lose it, fastened a wire to its stem and hauled it up towards the Yew, and very pretty its yellow trumpets look hanging in mid air

# My Garden in Summer

backed by the dark Yew leaves and the rich red stem. The bed now on our left is the largest of those devoted to the Bearded Irises, and contains the *pallida* varieties in large groups among other kinds of Iris, and also a central group of Crinums, some sunken half tubs for Japanese Irises, a large square planting of *Iris unguicularis* that, flowering later than those under the walls, is very useful to pick from in February and March. Here, too, grow some clumps of *Scilla peruviana*, that generally manage to give a good show of blossom at the end of May and in the beginning of June, both the blue and white forms, and while the large pyramidal heads have a tight cone of buds in the centre, and not more than three rows of flowers expanded, they are very handsome ; afterwards the many overblown outside flowers make them look shabby. They no more came from Peru than the pretended Charley's Aunt did from Brazil, and they are plentiful as wild plants in Spain. It has been said that a ship named *The Peru* carried some bulbs of the plant, and from it they got their name, but I have not been able to hunt down this tale. Clusius seems to be chiefly responsible for the error as to its native country, for he records that it was brought from Peru and grown and flowered by Everard Munichoven, who made a drawing of it, a copy of which was sent to Clusius in 1592, and Linnaeus appears to have been misled by this statement, and to have saddled it for ever with its lying specific name. But Parkinson knew it came from Spain, and tells how one Guillaume Boel sent him bulbs from Spain in 1607 " after that most violent frosty winter which perished

Rhododendron fastuosum fl. pl.

(See p 19.)

# The Iris Beds

both the roots of this and many other fine plants with us " ; and, writing of the names, he tells us : "This hath been formerly named Eriophorus Peruanus and Hyacinthus Stellatus Peruvanus, being thought to have grown in Peru, a Province of the West Indies : but he that gave that name first unto it, eyther knew not his naturall place, or willingly imposed that name to conceal it or to make it the better esteemed, but I had rather give the name agreeing most fitly unto it, and call it, as it is indeede, Hyacinthus Stellatus Boeticus, the Spanish Starry Iacinth." Well done, old Parkinson ! You have given Clusius and his friends a nice rap over the knuckles.

These and a few other plants needing warm quarters, lest another "most violent frosty winter" should carry them off too, inhabit the front of this border; but the main planting is of Iris. *I. pallida dalmatica* is the most glorious of them ; in fact, I rather think it is the most glorious of all Irises when it does well. It has grown here for a long time, and was one of the very few really good plants I found a large stock of in the garden when I began to sit up and take notice of garden affairs. It has the widest blue leaf of all my Flags, and is wonderfully distinct and effective even when out of bloom ; but how can I fitly describe its blossoms ? It is too well known to need describing, except inasmuch as I must try to make good my assertion as to its exceeding glory. It is one of the largest and tallest of Flag Irises : its near relative, *pallida* Albert Victor, is a trifle larger, but is of a deeper, less satisfying shade of lilac. Dalmatica's shade is a mingling of Rose-madder and Ultramarine blue, as I have learnt from painting it ; and

# My Garden in Summer

one must keep on squeezing one's tube of Rose-madder at a ruinous rate to give the warmth of the shades in hollows and on the sides of the falls. It is that soft rosy lilac to be found in certain Crocuses, notably *C. longiflorus* in Autumn and *C. Imperati* in Spring, and in the paler forms of *Iris unguicularis;* but much purer and cooler than the rosy-mauve I associate with Cattleyas and their nasty heavy balsamic scent and vulgarly rich, purple and gold blotchings. I can admire and enjoy most flowers, but just a few I positively dislike. Collerette Dahlias and those superlatively double African Marigolds that look like india-rubber bath sponges offend me most of all. I dislike the cheap thin texture of Godetias almost as much as I do the sinful magenta streaks and splotches that run in the blood of that family. I loathe Celosias equally with dyed Pampas grass; and Coxcombs, and spotty, marbled, double Balsams I should like to smash up with a coal-hammer; and certain great flaunting mauve and purple Cattleyas cloy my nose and annoy my eye till I conjure up a vision of them expiating their gaudy double-dyed wickedness with heads impaled on stiff wires like those of criminals on pikes, in a sea of *Asparagus Sprengeri,* and forming the bouquet presented to the wife of a provincial Mayor on the occasion of his opening the new sewage works. There! I feel ever so much better for that denunciation. I wish the subjects thereof could all turn white with fear of the public exhibition of their decapitated heads, for I can love an albino Cattleya.

Now scurry we back to *Iris pallida dalmatica's* charms,

# The Iris Beds

another of which is the way the ample standards open out and show the remarkably wide style branches, as if the flower knew how beautiful they are. I think pellucid must be the right adjective for them, only one must free one's mind of visions of the pale, pellucid periwinkle soup of the *Nonsense Book* and think of an opal without any fire. They are a pale bluish-lilac, as pale as a basin of starch, and just transparent enough to show a trace of the orange lower portion of the beard. Aha! now I've got it—they are like a delicious plover's egg just shelled and ready to eat; and that idea recalls to my mind a glorious evening effect I saw from the great Mont Cenis Road, looking down from just above the dip that leads to the lake, when the snow on the Cottians was glowing with golden sunshine, but veiled from us by a thin blue mist that hung over the Susa valley. The artistic one of the party likened it to an amber gown with a blue chiffon scarf over it. My practical, material mind saw it as a plover's egg; and after that long day up on the snow slopes among *Geum reptans* and *Campanula cenisia* how I should have liked to eat it!

A wholly orange-coloured beard would be too gaudy for this perfect Iris, and the lower portion is white, and the orange half lies in the hollow entrance under the crests of the stiles, to guide the hungry bee into the honey, so that his furry back may push pollen into the cunningly planned flap that is the stigma. It must take a large and strong Bumble-bee to manage it effectively, and I hope those metallic blue-winged, purple-velvet-bodied kinds one sees in Italy and warmer countries visit this Iris, as they must look so fine against the soft colour of its flowers. The typical *I. pallida* is a fine, sturdy growing thing, but its smaller blue flowers must take a lower place when *dalmatica* comes out. A variety called Coeleste is worth having, as it possesses a neater and dwarfer habit than any variety of *pallida*, and has very pale lilac flowers that contrast well with the deeper forms. Queen of May is rather a stiff, upright-stemmed lady, proud of her title, perhaps, in spite of its inappropriateness, for she never appears before June, but the rosy-pink of her flowers is so good, with their orange–coloured beards, that she ought to be allowed to queen it in every Iris collection. Also where *I. pallida* is happy room should be found for the variety with variegated leaves, one of the most effective of variegated plants, but rather im-patient of wet feet and chills. The amount of soft primrose and cream colour in well-developed leaves is surprising and charming, with the sea-green and grey elsewhere on its leaves, and as a contrast to the glaucous foliage of other *pallida* varieties. The Iris walk is hard to tear oneself away from when the *pallida* varieties are in festal array in June, whether viewed close at hand to peep into each flower, or taken as a whole from the opposite bank of the River, especially when reflected in it on a still day. I am very glad that I removed the ancient Laurels and Snowberries that once filled the beds almost to the edge of the grass walk on the River bank, and gave over the space to Irises. I cannot leave my favourite *pallida* Irises without mention of their chief botanical character, an unfailing guide to their identity,

# The Iris Beds

that is the curious way in which the spathes that wrap their youthful flower-buds dry up and become papery and withered. Scariose is the botanical term for it, said to be derived from scaria, which was some thorny, leafless plant, and does not seem very sensible; it would be much better if one could only connect it with the scare one gets the first time one sees the precious buds of one's *Iris pallida* apparently drying up and withering. Among these lilac glories I grow a tall dark violet form that I have always called Leonidas, and I think may be a hybrid of *pallida*. It seems to have disappeared of late years from catalogues, at least under that name. It makes a good contrast in colour with the *pallidas*, as the falls are a fine deep violet-purple, and its stems are tall enough to hold their own among that race of giants. The best of all dark forms, Black Prince, said to be a form of *I. neglecta*, unfortunately resembles its protonym here in more than his dusky panoply and has always died young, so my Leonidas has stepped into his shoes.

Somewhat similar in form to Leonidas, but of a reddish purple, is another form that I bought many years ago as *Iris plicata*, and never having found another name for it I keep it so labelled when the gulls permit me to, though it seems that name belongs to a group of garden hybrids among which should stand Mme. Chereau and Bacchus, and certain others with white flowers veined with lilac round their edges and very distinct and useful as a contrast among self-coloured forms; so here they are in good square clumps, in the next bed on the further side of the

# My Garden in Summer

path that starts from the River walk and goes through the Pergola and Rose garden to the bowling-green lawn, running parallel with the Rhododendron walk. The Intermediate Irises raised by Mr. Caparne fill much space in this bed, and are by now going or gone out of flower, and their place is taken by *I. flavescens*, an especial favourite of mine. Its soft sulphur flowers are so clean and fresh in appearance and very freely produced, and make a fine show in a bold mass. I have one group at the corner of this bed, and another forms a broad line at the back of one of the beds. The falls are a little lighter in shade than the standards and faintly veined near the claw with brownish nettings, otherwise it is a nearly self primrose-yellow variety. It is not known as a wild plant, and it is so shy at setting seed that it seems likely it is a hybrid from *I. variegata*, and I should think possibly *variegata aurea* crossed with *florentina* or *pallida* might give us something similar. In the big herbaceous bed here it has sported to a greyish white form, and I have grown the sportive portion on into a good clump, and like it very much, as it distinctly recalls a vision of *florentina*, long after that variety's normal flowering season has passed. *I. albicans* grows here by the River close to *I. flavescens*, and after hot summers flowers pretty freely, but it is a plant of the South and is seen at its best in Greece and Italy, where it is widely cultivated. The compilers of lists have lately taken to calling it Princess of Wales, and selling it at a slightly higher price in consequence, but I can see no difference between my old friend *albicans* and the

# The Iris Beds

new Princess, any more than there is between *pallida dalmatica* and *pallida Princess Beatrice.* Mr. Dykes has recently made the discovery that *albicans* is the albino form of *I. Madonna.* Here are his very words quoted from his sumptuous monograph : " A recent introduction under the name of *I. Madonna* was said to come from Arabia. When I watched the two plants developing in my garden, I could not help thinking that they were only colour varieties of the same species, and this supposition was confirmed by the discovery in the Paris herbarium of specimens of both that were found growing together on a mountain in the Yemen in Arabia as long ago as 1837."

" This discovery, and the fact that *I. albicans* is the common ornament of Mahomedan cemeteries, gave the solution of the puzzle, and we see now that the wide distribution of *I. albicans* is due to the fact that the Mahomedans took it everywhere with them as a sacred plant, or at least as a conventional ornament for graveyards."

A still more beautiful pure-white Iris is that known as *I. kashmiriana*, especially the seedling form raised by Sir Michael Foster and called the Shelford variety. It is larger and more widely branching than *albicans*, but there must aye be a summat, and the summat here is as big a one as that of the Scots maiden. Mother asked, " Why will ye no marry Angus ? Is he no rich ? " " Yes, Mither." " And is he no tall ? " " Yes, Mither." " And he has a fine braw hoose ? " " Yes, Mither, but I canna abide the man." " Ah weel, lassie, there must aye be a summat." *I. kashmiriana* is tall and richly

# My Garden in Summer

scented, but it cannot be induced to live and flower in ordinary gardens. I had a fine spike here this summer, and gazed lovingly on its milk-white glory as day by day it opened its many flowers. From what I had heard of it I daily expected to hear it begin to sing a swan song, but so far—and perhaps if we whisper it gently it will not hear and begin to fail—it has made good growth and looks none the worse for the great flowers it bore.

If you want a puzzle that will last you longer than a jig-saw, buy a few plants from different nurseries of *Iris Kochii* and *I. germanica* var. *atropurpurea* or Purple King, or even var. *nepalensis,* and worry out which is which, and at what time they flower, and how to make them flower regularly every season. It is now said that the last three are all one, and that their flowers show the white netting of the claw by the side of the blade, whereas you must hunt for it, and can only find it hidden away by the style-branches in *Kochii,* which is also a more slender flower. I think I have three things here, and can recognise true *Kochii* by its graceful slimness, but I'm blest if I know which is which of an early and later flowering pair of dark purple ones of the same colouring as *Kochii.* I have at times shaken my fist at a big square of green leaves that has no sign of a bud at flower-giving time, and said, " You must be the shy flowering Purple King, you lazy thing, and you shall go to a throne on the bonfire." After the *auto-da-fé,* I have split up a clump that was a solid block of purple, and planted the dethroned and calcined monarch's place with it, and then perhaps for a

# The Iris Beds

season or two never a bloom do I see on one or other of the clumps, and I begin to wonder whether my stocks are mixed and in replanting I unconsciously single out one form for one patch. Sometimes unseasonable flowers are borne by them, and once, the year after replanting, quite a crop appeared in November, and in the end of that month I cut nearly a dozen good stems to save the great purple blooms from the frost. When I do get a good flowering either in late May or mid-June of one or other kind, I always wish for more and larger clumps, and then a sterile breadth of leaves confronts me for a season or two, and I feed the flames with it. I have an idea that the early flowering one is Purple King, and is a form that requires something unusual in the way of seasons to flower well, but goodness knows what the other form should be called.

Here ends the list of Bearded Flags which contribute to the annual display of the Iris walk in summer, and we can now turn to the beardless section of the family.

# CHAPTER III

## Beardless Irises of Summer

THERE promises to be a great future for the new race of bulbous Irises that have lately emanated from Mynheer C. G. Van Tubergen's nursery under the name of Dutch Irises. They are really Spanish Irises gone one better, being larger, more robust in constitution, and of varied and beautiful colouring. They are the result of an attempted crossing of *Iris Xiphium* with such species as *tingitana* and *Boissieri*. Mr. Dykes, however, sees no trace of any characters save those of *Xiphium* in the new race, and it seems likely that they are descended from a large and early form of the Spanish Iris that he suggests should be known as *I. Xiphium* var. *praecox*. It is an old favourite of mine, and I have grown it for many years, but always under its trade but false name of *I. filifolia*, a name it filched from a little-known, purple-flowered kindred species. It generally begins to flower when the last of the Tulips has vanished, and in the end of May and beginning of June is very useful as a cut flower. Others have found this out, and it has gone up in price lately, I am sorry to say. These Dutch Irises are almost as early as the so-called *filifolia*, and are more beautiful in colour, for while the colour of this latter is invariably blue, the Dutch varieties resemble some of the best-named forms of Spanish Iris, and contain many shades of yellow, lilac, and purple, while some are partly white. They have all been named after Dutch painters, on a very sensible and useful plan. I cut a goodly number this June, and enjoyed their beauty for quite a fortnight, and if I have a favourite among them perhaps it is that named Rembrandt, which reminds me somewhat of the shy flowering but glorious *I. tingitana,* but has no trace of the long perianth tube of that distinct species. It is curious, though, how frequently it has happened that when rather bold crossings have been attempted between somewhat distantly related species, and seed has been obtained, the offspring may not show any character that can be recognised as belonging to the pollen parent, and yet may possess some very distinct break in colour or size ; as though there had been no complete fusion of the nucleus of the pollen with that of the egg cell, and the latter alone had developed to form the embryo, but in so abnormal a condition that its balance has been sufficiently upset to induce it to launch out into unusual colouring or some such vagary. I have been shown some fine races of Polyanthus Primroses that resulted from pollen of *P. sinensis* and *P. Auricula* having been placed on ordinary Polyanthus forms: no botanical character of the pollen parent was discernible, but rich colourings and handsome eyes were very noticeable and an advance on those of the seed parents. So I think it possible that though the pollen of *I. tingitana* and others failed to produce a hybrid with *I. Xiphium* that could show any characters save those of

# My Garden in Summer

*Xiphium* it may have excited and stimulated a change of coloration. Anyway the Dutch Irises with their artists' names are showy and sturdy, early and beautiful, and well worth growing. The first set I purchased I left unlifted for three years in the peach-house bed, and they increased well and flowered each season, which is more than Spanish Irises have ever done under similar treatment.

I grow a good many varieties of Spanish Irises, but chiefly for cutting purposes, and so they are planted in rows in the kitchen garden, and are lifted annually, the best bulbs picked out and planted again, and if they have not lifted well enough to promise a good supply of bloom we purchase reinforcements—not a serious matter, as they are about the cheapest bulbs for their size that one can buy. The variety Chrysolora, a good clear yellow of very elegant shape and slender stem, is one of the best for cutting, and there are many good, white forms that are useful to mix with it. But one of the most effective of all is Thunderbolt, a fine massive flower, bronze and orange shot with purple in a way that justifies its name. Now and then I get a few hundreds of Spanish Irises and plant them wherever I can find a vacant spot among the earlier Bearded Irises by the River, that they may follow them in flower, but they do not approve of the enforced competition with the stronger-growing Flags, and die out in a season or two. Sometimes I vary the effect by using *Gladiolus brenchleyensis* in a like way, and with a similar fatal termination for them. English Irises, *I. xiphioides*, are such lovers of fat and juicy soil that they are none too happy in this dry, bony garden, and a few hundreds in

Iris ochroleuca.

(See p. 33.)

# Beardless Irises of Summer

rows in the kitchen garden provide cut flowers in early July. I always buy those declared to be self-coloured, abjuring all described as flaked, splashed, speckled, veined, feathered, marbled, marked, pencilled, blotched, mottled, spotted, striped, or flamed. I have extracted the first eleven of these, to me, damnatory adjectives from one list of twenty-eight varieties, twenty-six of which are thus stigmatised, and it would appear difficult to find any variety without a stain on its character. Many good selfs exist, though. Mer de Glace and Mont Blanc are good whites ; speciosa, Julius, and Mr. Veen dark blues ; and Ariadne and Psyche pale blues. But one season a hitherto immaculate variety appeared with flowers bearing the mark of the beast all over them. I hoped it was only an attack of floral measles, but have since heard that it is not unknown for a plain variety to become brindled, tabby, flea-bitten, freckled, or dappled all of a sudden. I offer this list of adjectives free of extra charge to all list-compilers who possess a copy of this book. This peculiarity might be worth investigation, as a parallel case to the breaking of Tulips.

Whenever I see *I. ochroleuca* I feel grateful to Mr. Dykes for having made it legitimate for us once again to call this stately member of the *spuria* group by its Linnaean and most descriptive name, for it is *par excellence the* yellow and white Iris. It varies somewhat, but in a really good form with wide and not too much tucked under falls, the rich golden blotch contrasts magnificently with the pure white of the rest of the flower. A form has been selected and named gigantea and is the tallest of all Irises, and when treated as it deserves, which means getting good rich soil in an open position, and plenty of moisture and sunshine in the growing season, it should reach six feet in height, and as a stem will bear buds in three or even four tiers and two or three in each tier, the effect of a well-flowered stem is fine indeed. *I. ochroleuca* is one of those well-known old garden favourites whose origin and history are somewhat mysterious. Miller evidently knew the plant and gives a figure but with the extraordinary addition of a beard, a silly scrubby little beard it must be owned, and growing across the fall more like a moustache; and in the great Dictionary he describes it as bearded three times over, and for this reason Mr. Dykes sets us free from using Miller's name of *orientalis*, for nowadays there is no trace of a beard to be found on it. Miller also says Dr. Pococke, a Bishop of Ossory, brought its seeds to the Chelsea Garden from Carniola, but Scopoli, who wrote the Flora of that country, knew no such plant, and now it is found in Asia Minor and on the coast of Palestine. Then it is recorded that Sir Michael Foster sowed seeds of *ochroleuca* which he believed were not in any way cross-fertilised, and when they flowered there was not one true *ochroleuca* among them, but they were slate-coloured or pale blue forms of *I. spuria!* Even if we must rank it as a sub-species of *spuria* it is a grand garden plant, and grouped with its near relations, as I have it here at the back of two of the Iris beds, it makes a fine picture in late June and early July. Its nearest relative is its hybrid offspring *I. ochraurea*, an even handsomer plant, for the deep yellow

# Beardless Irises of Summer

of *aurea* has given a creamy-yellow tint to the white portions, and the falls are wider and a very rich yellow edged with creamy white. It is a good doer, and flowers more freely than most of the *spuria* group. *I. Monnieri* is a still nearer approach to *I. aurea,* and is a good canary yellow, but like *ochroleuca* in shape. I well remember the first time I saw this beautiful flower. It was standing in a large vase on the hearth in the drawing-room at Bitton Vicarage, some half dozen stems cut full length and arranged with a shoot or two of the variegated form of *Arundo Donax.* It was my first visit to Bitton, and I was astonished at the sight of such things being cut for the house, and when I saw the stately lines of the Iris down the long Iris walk I was still more deeply impressed with the rich treasures of that best of gardens, and superlatively so when I saw the clump of *I. Monnieri* that Canon Ellacombe bade old Miller dig up for me to carry home. *I. Monspur* is one of Sir Michael Foster's many creations, *Monnieri* crossed with *spuria,* and combines the purple and gold of its parents. I like it better than typical *spuria,* and as for *spuria alba,* though I should be sorry to lose it, yet I feel it is best to plant it some distance away from *ochroleuca* to give it a chance of admiration. Our chief group of these giants of the family had to be lifted and replanted lately, which means a wait of two seasons before they regain full flowering vigour ; but yard-high leaves, stiff and solid and of rich warm green, such a pleasant contrast with the blue and grey greens of their neighbouring *pallida* cousins, are already repaying our toil and promise great events in the near future. Even if they flowered less freely they would be worthy of a fair space for the sake of these same stately leaves. *Aurea* alone of this *spuria* group refuses to respond to our efforts to make it happy and bright, and sulks itself into a leanness that robs even its leaves of beauty. Another ingrate here is the white form of *I. orientalis* known as Snow Queen, which although it has had many of the choicest quarters in the garden allotted to it has only rewarded us with first yellow then brown leaves and finally a mass of decay. I admire it so much, and as I can grow its purple form almost any-where, I am trying once more whether seedling plants will be more obliging. The tall white form of *I. sibirica* grows magnificently in the hot, dry bed in front of the peach-house, and provides many a tall wand bearing ivory blossoms for cutting, but when divided the portions that I try elsewhere in the garden, even in similarly sun-baked positions, give me but few flowers and those on diminished stems. If I had never tried it by the peach-house I should have declared it was not worth growing here, which shows how careful you should be to " Do all that you know, and try all that you don't " just as much in choosing a place for a plant as in hunting a snark.

All the other forms of *I. sibirica* I find do best in our nearest approach to moist positions, and one I like more than the rest is called gracilis, and grows very tall, with branching and gracefully-curving stems, supporting rather paler blue flowers than those of most of this group. It resides in the rock garden, in a stiffish bit of soil that holds up the bank by one of the tiny ponds, and would

# Beardless Irises of Summer

very likely be dumpy and hideous in a drier position ;
just the opposite, however, happens in the case of *I. fulva*,
for in it we have a plant from the swamps of the Mis-
sissippi Valley that will grow vigorously in a wet, boggy
position, and will refuse to flower there, but in the
hottest, driest spots in the garden, where it looks half
starved, and on hot July days often rather limp, it will
throw up tall stems that produce, day after day for a long
period, copper-coloured flowers with spreading segments,
much more like some Moraea than an Iris. I suppose, in
a warmer climate, it would flower in the bog garden and
be larger than it is here in a counterfeit Sahara. It is
one of the Irises that proclaims to the world at large its
thirsty disposition by the possession of dark spots in the
leaves, best seen when a leaf is held up against the light.
This useful mark of distinction was discovered by Mr.
Dykes, and in case some of my readers have not yet
purchased the great monograph, I quote his words there-
from : " Nature has provided us with an infallible sign
which will show us whether an Iris is a native of a dry
or a wet soil. This will be seen if leaves of *I. Pseudacorus*
or *I. versicolor* are held up to the light side by side with
a leaf of a *Pogoniris*, for instance, of *I. germanica*. The
latter will appear of a uniform green, but the former will
show a number of minute, blackish spots, which, on micro-
scopical examination, prove to be due to the fact that at
these points the vertical channels in the tissue of the
leaves are blocked by growths of apparently the same
structure as that which surrounds the passages. The
increased thickness of the structure at these points pro-

duces the appearance of the black spots." This curious correlation of a minute structural peculiarity with a natural habit of character is just one of those things I like to know about my plants, and gives them an interest that I enjoy quite as much as the beauty of their colour effect and artistic value in a grouping. A parallel instance may be found in the curiously tessellated appearance of the leaves of certain Bamboos when held up to the light, which, so far as I know, is only found in species that are hardy enough for our climate. It is also found in the only really hardy Palm, *Trachycarpus excelsus*. The leaves of those Cassias that possess the most reliable medicinal qualities for producing Senna, have one leaflet missing from the terminal pair found complete in the useless members of the genus. The twisted leaf generally present in seedling Daffodils with *maximus* blood in them, the bearded and unbearded sepals of Roses derived from *Rosa canina*, occur to me as a few among the many signatures borne by plants which are of real use in contrast with the fancied ones prated of by the upholders of the Doctrine of Signatures.

It is a hard matter to find accommodation for *Iris Kaempferi* here, as the edges of the New River and pond are not suitable. The river has closely-shorn grass banks that are slapped and banged to keep their clay foundations hard and water tight, and so are not available for any sort of planting, and the pond is puddled with clay so that the stony banks are cut off from the water by the clay, and we must either choose plants that can stand drought for them, or build out promontories into the

Double form of Japanese Iris (I. Kaempferi).
(See p. 38.)

# Beardless Irises of Summer

water for thirsty subjects. Japanese Irises will do for a short time planted on a specially prepared promontory, but soon exhaust it, and require a good deal of looking after, so I have not got the long stretches of them that I should like, but only a yard or two that give me great flat white and purple flowers in July when other Irises are becoming scarce. We have made special provision for a few extra choice kinds, such as Morning Mist, with its flush of blue on the sparkling white two-ranked falls, and *I. laevigata*, as it seems we must now call the *I. albopurpurea* that, except for its taller standard, is so much like a single *I. Kaempferi*. This provision takes the form of sinking halves of paraffin barrels in the Iris border, and having put some coarse crocks and stones in them for drainage filling them with rich soil and peat. Japanese Irises thrive wonderfully under such treatment in a hot, dry border if only their tubs are freely watered just as the flowering stems are being produced, but after three or four years the soil must be removed and replaced by fresh soil. Our wild Yellow Flag, *Iris Pseudacorus*, does well in the pond, growing in the shallows into huge masses. Its young foliage is very beautiful in Spring rising out of the water, and the display of flowers lasts a long time, and then when the great fat seedpods begin to weigh the stems down we have to go round the clumps in the punt, and cut off all the pods we can find, to prevent the pond and half the garden being filled with greedy young *Pseudacorus* seedlings. For the seeds float and are not only carried to the edge of the pond and anchored there to germinate, but they are scooped up freely in water-cans, and thereby sown wherever plants are watered, and handsome as this native plant is one can easily have too much of it. There is some confusion as to the names of its varietal forms, the name *Bastardii* being often used for a pale sulphur form which I think very beautiful and which sometimes appears in lists called var. *alba*. I believe *Bastardii* should be a form of the ordinary canary-yellow colour, but in which the central blotch at the base of the fall is no darker than the surrounding yellow, a form I have come across in more than one of my rambles in marshy spots in search of plants and insects. There is a good variegated leaved form, with bold stripes of pale yellow on the young leaves of Spring, which shade gradually into the normally darker green portions, and produce a pleasantly soft-golden effect, making it very suitable for grouping, for sake of contrast, alongside a clump of the ordinary form ; but towards the end of June the lighter yellow portions deepen until there is little of variegation noticeable.

*I. versicolor* comes from the eastern side of North America, and there fills swamps and grows along the sides of streams just as our Yellow Flag does in Britain. The Yankee makes a fine companion for the Britisher, and will grow almost anywhere it is put, but is certainly best with its toes in the muddy edge or even slightly submerged, and looks especially well at the foot of a colony of *I. Pseudacorus*, growing only half the height of the yellow fellow, and having flowers of every imaginable shade of purple and lilac, and in one variety called *kermesina*, almost crimson. Another feature I like is the way the leaves, when half-grown, arch over and make a charming contrast with the stiffer swords of *Pseudacorus.* I have one form that has the good taste to produce brilliantly golden leaves during April and early May, which are wonderfully effective among the various greens of other youthful waterside plants ; but as it is a crimson-flowered form, one is glad that these golden leaves mature to a rich green before the flowers appear.

I had seeds given me of an Iris from Newfoundland that turned out to be a very pretty pale lilac form of *versicolor* of particularly graceful, slender habit, and distinct enough to have found an honourable mention in Mr. Dykes' book.

Two more Irises of the Summer call for notice, and then we must leave the family. These are *I. Milesii* and *I. tectorum,* closely related in structural peculiarities and geographical distribution, for both come from Eastern Asia, Northern India, or China and Japan, and both have a curiously-fringed crest in place of a beard, and there the likeness ceases, for *Milesii* is tall and lanky and free flowering, but the flowers are small, of a rather mawkish claret and water colouring, and always rather disappointing, after the amount of fuss the plant makes in sending up such a tall and freely-branched stem from among such great handsome leaves.

The flowers of *I. tectorum* are almost too large for their length of stem, but very beautiful whether of the typical blue-purple, the lilac, or pure white forms, and always a pleasant surprise, with their large spreading standards and white crests, when one sees them again for

the first time in the season, as their colouring is so charming and the whole effect so orchid-like. But most people,
and just latterly I too, rarely get enough blooms on our
plants, and I want large patches of them thick with
flowers both to look at and tell yarns about. It is so
useful to have plenty of plants with a history. When
one trots a Nature-study class or a local Horticultural
Society round the garden it is enough to point out interesting structures, botanical peculiarities, and relation-
ships, but bodies of non-gardening folk require condensed
novels, weird legends of plants with a past, such as
Mistletoe and Mandrake. Many find a morbid satisfaction in gazing at the Edelweiss, for their one notion of it
is that it only lives on the edges of treacherous precipices
to lure its would-be gatherers to an awful end. This
may be true of the last plant left within the compass of
an afternoon toddle from a fashionable Swiss hotel. Had
it not been protected by its position it would have been
grabbed by Mr. Brown or Mrs. Jones, instead of waiting
for Mr. Robinson's London boots to glissade him over
the edge just as he had it in his hand. But go high
enough among the mountains and you will find the level
pastures so thick with it that you cannot even dig up other
plants without getting its rosettes among their roots. It
would not do, however, to enlarge on that part of the
plant's story to such visitors, for they want you to make
their flesh creep. *I. tectorum* always makes a good text,
but is better when in flower. You can work up the
agony of the awful famine and the wisdom of the Japanese
Government in ordering every scrap of garden ground to

be planted with grain, and the despair of the ladies who depended on the Iris for hair-dye, face powder, or corn-plasters, or anything you think interests your audience— even the love of Beauty which led them to almost worship its flowers, if you have an Art-class before you. The final brilliant idea of planting it on the thatch of the houses, and how it thrives there, &c., and then you had better hurry on to your next penny novelette before too many questions are asked about this pretty but none too authentic story. If only the Burning Bush, *Dictamnus Fraxinella*, would burn when you wanted it to, and New Zealand Flax, *Phormium tenax*, grow as freely here as in Ireland to provide enough leaves for each visitor to scrape and extract the strong fibre to twist into whip thongs, one could do without lying about *I. tectorum*. Some plants never fail to interest even the most unbotanical folk. *Schinus Molle* is one, better known, perhaps, as the Pepper Tree of streets in towns along the Mediterranean. Its pretty, pinnate leaves smell deliciously of freshly-ground pepper-corns when broken, but of course have nothing to do with the plant that fills our pepper-pots, and which is *Piper nigrum*, a climbing plant. These leaves are so highly charged with a volatile oil that, when the leaflets are broken in half and thrown on to water, the broken cells absorb water, and the result is a sudden discharge of the resinous oil, a momentary iridescent patch on the surface, and a sudden shooting along of the portion of leaf, due to the recoil of the explosion. On a hot day these expulsions of oil will recur at short intervals, and the leaves, looking as though they were possessed of voluntary motion, will shoot about in all directions like green water-beetles. The tree is not hardy here, so lives in a large pot, and when it emerges from its winter home in the peach-house, is plunged in one of the beds of the terrace by the river, where it is handy for aquatic displays and foliar regattas.

Another never-failing attraction is hunting for four-leaved Shamrock on the dark-leaved form of *Trifolium repens* known as *quinquefolium*, which mostly produces five leaflets on each stalk, but also a goodly number of the lucky four-leaved ones, so that they require a little looking for, and when found carry the luck with them, let us hope, that is supposed to follow the finding of a four-leaved Shamrock. The hardy, rubber-producing plant, *Eucommia ulmoides*, is planted near the gate, and is useful to speed a parting guest on occasions when speed is desirable. You say, "But have you seen the hardy Rubber plant? No? Then come along," and you move briskly to the place and pluck a leaf and roll it, and then pull it asunder and the latex forms gummy strings that harden in the air, and can, by twisting the separate portions of leaf, be made into a stoutish rubber string. It will stretch out a little, but will not contract, so I fear will not be of any commercial value, nor shall we make our own rubber tyres of it. When interest flags a little you ask, "Wouldn't you like a few leaves to take home with you?" and the departure of the most lingering visitor generally follows soon afterwards.

But we have wandered a long way from *Iris tectorum*, and I want to tell you of my disappointment over it—for

# Beardless Irises of Summer

in this garden it is at present one of the has-beens. Do you know the tale of the old maids who quarrelled, and Pussy Cat said with a sniff, " You needn't talk, you are one of the has-beens," and Catty Puss retorted, " Better than you, anyway, for you are one of the never-wases," and *Iris Milesii* I consider one of the never-wases, but *tectorum* I hope will turn again like Dick Whittington. It never did much in the rock garden ledges I thought it might take for roofs, and then a friend said it did well with him in partial shade, and I tried it under a lop-sided Sycamore, and it throve marvellously until I cut down the Sycamore. Now I am about to move the weakly remnants to the shelter of the Yews to try if they will revive there. Every other neighbouring plant rejoices in the departure of that Sycamore, but *I. tectorum* has pined away grieving for it ever since its fall.

# CHAPTER IV

## Roses

THE postal address of this garden calls up a vision of a rose-growing country with a soil of fat, clayey loam, and the honoured names of eminent Rose specialists for near neighbours. The reality is another thing. I can drive within an hour into regions where thousands of Roses scent the air, and the finest and newest are to be seen grown to perfection by my neighbours—the Pauls on one side, and by Stuart Low on the other—but if you plunge a garden fork into the lawns here you will soon learn that this slightly raised ground that contains the garden is too bony, on account of the deposits of gravel left here by some vast primeval continental river's mouth, to produce show blooms of Roses without Herculean efforts in the way of excavating and a corresponding filling up that would better suit the purse of Fortunatus or the pockets of Croesus, Midas, Plutus & Co. than mine. So the Rose garden here covers square yards instead of acres, and is just pretty to look at and useful to cut from but nothing to boast of or write about at any length. It consists of a central group of four formal beds for Roses and four for Carnations, surrounding the old Enfield Market Cross in an enclosed garden. This is a parallelogram, with a

46

Hybrid Tea Rose, Madame Ravary.
(See p. 48.)

# Roses

pergola for western boundary, several of my favourites among climbing Roses occupying its posts on the rose garden side. The southern side is the most open, and only divided from the Iris beds along the River by a wide bed for standard dwarf roses, with a row of, at present, promising young Eucalyptus trees among them. The eastern side is flanked by a continuation of this bed, backed by the Rhododendrons that line one side of the Rhododendron walk and a Magnolia or two rising above them. The Northern side is another portion of this surrounding bed, but it is divided in its midst by a narrow paved walk of old York stone paving from London streets, now passing their old age quietly and peacefully in the country. This leads into the little formal garden where my best Daffodils grow and up to the new wall and its central garden house, which together cut off the cruel winds and make this paved garden so cosy and sheltered that a list of the bold ventures in planting it must be made before long, but first I must review and dismiss the Rose beds. One of the four round ones is devoted to Frau Karl Druschki, and produces pure white, scentless flowers for an astonishingly lengthy period. They are very lovely to look at and cut for the house, where their lasting qualities are dear to my lazy soul, that likes not daily renewal of cut flowers, but would be driven to action by an off-colour second day Rose, such as one finds in most red and pink varieties. La France for pink and Rayon d'or for yellow are next best to Frau Karl for lasting in beauty when cut. So I value Frau Karl in spite of its scentlessness and its somewhat monumental marble appearance—the sort of Rose, in fact, that you might expect to see in the dress or bonnet of a member of one of those marvellous groups of sorrowing relations surrounding a deathbed, whose lace and buttons and even tears are so faithfully represented in white marble in the famous Campo Santo at Genoa. Caroline Testout fills another bed—I am not quite sure yet whether sufficiently worthily to retain possession—and a third bed pleases me mightily with its never-failing Summer and Autumn supply of single Tea-roses, for the Irish Singles and the real old single China, Miss Lowe's variety, are its generous occupants. The fourth contains yellow and orange-coloured Roses in a mixture until I can make up my mind and my accounts in favour of filling it with Rayon d'or, which so far has proved the best of its inhabitants. It is always good to look at, with its glossy, healthy leaves that seem to be immune from the attacks of fungus pests and grassy-pillars and cat-terhoppers innumerable, according to the nervous curate's rendering of that entomological verse of the Psalms.

The two beds that intervene between the Rose and paved gardens I planned most carefully, with all my notes at shows and all the catalogues of the year to help me, so as to begin at one end with yellows, oranges and lemons both, and those indescribable shades that have sufficient affinity with a yellow to be flattered in catalogues as cop-pery-salmon, apricot, chamois, nankeen, or straw colour. A selection of these easily filled up the right-hand bed, the only difficulty being which to leave out. The Lyons Rose and Mme. Ravary are there, and dwarf forms such as the two La Mesch roses with Canarien Vogel, Sulphurea, and Perle

Rose, Frau Karl Druschki.
(See p. 47.)

# Roses

d'or were used to edge the front and the side by the stone path, and have grown into one of the most effective and productive of my Rose plantings. The opposite bed is edged with white and pink dwarfs, Mrs. Cutbush, Mignonette, Anna Maria de Montravel, for examples, but never a trace of the militant Mme. Levavasseur, whose tint of red, flattered in lists as crimson, is as violently combative with any decent quiet red as Crimson Rambler its horrible self. The main colouring of this bed is pink shading to real crimson, but warm salmon-pink, such as that of Mme. Abel Chatenay, Pharisäer, and Prince de Bulgarie, is admitted besides the rose-pink of La France before we reach Richmond, Liberty and, at last, Cramoisie Supérieure, which is the deepest note in crimson I care to admit in this harmony, just far enough from Richmond to correspond with the inevitable drop from the dominant to the keynote in the bass of two final chords. A-men—Sol-Do.

That sums up the poverty of the garden as far as new or show Roses are concerned, but I will not allow that altogether it is poor in Roses, for to me the various species and their forms and hybrids are the real Roses, and I have managed to find nooks and corners for a goodly company of them. Many of them are easily pleased, and will flourish among shrubs and trees in places not easy to fill otherwise with good effect. I have a very real affection for single Roses, and feel rather annoyed when I hear them called Briers—which, although it is not quite such a term of reproach nowadays as formerly, still is not exactly flattering. " Brere " in early and mediaeval English was any thorny bush, an equivalent of " bramble " and a near

# My Garden in Summer

relative of the word "thorn." Then in sixteenth century English it became "bryer," "brier," and "briar," just as "frere" grew into "friar," and was used of wild roses chiefly, and more of the thorny bush than the flowers. So in the brawl in the Temple Gardens in *Henry VI*, Shakespeare makes Plantagenet say, "From off this brier pluck a white rose with me," and Somerset's rejoinder varies it with "Pluck a red rose from off this thorn with me," and Emilia's figure of the Rose and the North Wind in *Two Noble Kinsmen*, which ends :

> "She locks her beauties in her bud again
> And leaves him to base Briers,"

shows clearly "brier" is not a fitting name for my beloved single Roses.

Let me give you some reasons why they appeal so strongly to me. First, I do so enjoy the beauty of form in the flowers : the central mass or ring of stamens and the simple outlines of the five equal petals in their endless variations of relative positions are always worth drawing, and have an expression, a symmetry, that I can only compare with the charm of a beautiful and familar face. Who wants to see the human object of their devotion improved by a multiplicity of noses of varying sizes, the innermost being little more than slices of nose so as to pack into the centre ? Then why should a Rose need doubling ? Secondly, their habit of growth can be allowed as a rule to assert itself, and so they grow into natural and graceful specimens needing little pruning and no cutting back to stumps like those of ancient Osiers.

# Roses

Thirdly, they are so healthy and satisfactory on rather poor soil where florists' Roses would starve and, therefore, they are better suited to this garden. Fourthly, so many of them have beautiful fruits that carry on their charm into the Winter, and lastly they are so full of character and individuality that there is a never-ending interest to be found in studying and comparing their peculiarities.

Prickles alone would furnish a subject for a lifelong study, if not only the classification of forms were to be fully dealt with, but the use, purpose, and evolution of the different varieties. Just call to mind the strongly-hooked, down-curved sickles of the Dog-rose, splendidly designed implements for allowing a young shoot to pass through tangled growths, and so well adapted for preventing its being withdrawn and to steady it until it gets out in the free air above its neighbours. Compare them with the needles that clothe our Burnet Rose, a plant of open sand dunes and downs. In other Roses the prickles are heteromorphic, varying in shape and direction among themselves. *R. reversa* has gained its name from the universally downward-pointing, needle-shaped spines clothing its stems. There are two distinct forms of *R. nitida :* one has almost smooth stems, while in the other the young shoots, like those of *R. Fedtschenkoana,* are so entirely covered with crimson spines that they look like long hairy caterpillars, and even in their old age are precious prickly to touch. Again, that polymorphic eccentric *R. sericea* can appear with almost any sort of prickle one's fancy can fashion. In its less inventive mood it is contented with two sorts,

# My Garden in Summer

stout hooked ones in pairs close to the leaves, and wickedly sharp needles scattered about between them. In some Chinese forms the young shoots are gloriously beautiful in their armature of prickles, which have wings rising out of the stems an inch long, with transparent crimson skins that glow out when lit up by the setting sun like stained glass in old windows. This Rose of the winged prickles, whence its varietal name *pteracantha*, is worth growing for these ruby gleams alone, and if cut down close to the ground each Spring, though the small and early flowers are sacrificed, the summer display of glowing thorns is so much enhanced thereby that this hard pruning is justified. *R. sericea's* vagaries lead it to appear in yet another guise as var. *denudata*, without prickles of any sort and as bald as a poached egg, thus going one better than the so-called Rose without a thorn, *R. alpina* and its many varieties and hybrid offspring the Boursaults, which have a few prickles lurking here and there ready for a soft finger, as well as plenty of bristly spines at the base of new shoots. I know I ought to call this Rose *pendulina* nowadays to be in accord with the sumptuous monograph Miss Willmott and her coadjutors have launched, but I have hopes that the long-delayed final number [1] and its index will reinstate some of the better-known names, as a period of six months is quite long enough for the discovery of a bristle or suspicion of a gland or something on Linnaeus' type specimen that might allow us to believe it was after all the hybrid he

[1] It has appeared at last, but the name *pendulina* remains in possession of the field.

# Roses

described as *pendulina.* So for the present I shall call it *R. alpina,* which better recalls the joy its crimson flowers have given me in subalpine regions, especially in the woodlands round Airolo or leaning out across the Mt. Cenis Road as one passes those picturesque and impregnable-looking forts on the ridge that dominates the narrow gorge through which river and road have found their way.

After much study has answered the how and when and where of these questions, there will still remain the biggest query of all, Why? So big that years of travelling to see forms in their native homes, hours of patient watching to find out what unwelcome insect guest is out-manoeuvred, or what mechanical advantage is gained, by a downward curved or straight prickle, would be but the beginning of its solution. Still it is good to realise that there is plenty of work for the naturalists of the future, and that even the Roses still provide interesting points for study.

Milton states the rose was without thorn in Eden, and the familiar proverb that this has been changed, but the botanist carries us back to Paradise, for to the botanists no Rose possesses a thorn, which in their parlance is an aborted branch such as one finds on Hawthorn and Sloe, and the weapons of the Roses are only prickles, that is to say, merely outgrowths of the skin or bark, and without a woody core as in a Sloe's thorn or spine.

The sepals are as full of variations and interest as the prickles, and are often good guides to follow in searching out the relationship of a Rose. The best

# My Garden in Summer

example I can cite is to be found in our commonest wild Rose, *R. canina*, which in its own person and also in all its near relations and descendants, even unto the third and fourth generation, bears three patterns of sepals, two being bearded or ciliated, two smooth edged, and the fifth with one edge of either pattern. Many a botanist of older days has found delight in this arrangement, and it has been recorded in various ways, even in Latin verse. Here are two examples:

> "Quinque sumus fratres, unus barbatus et alter,
> Imberbesque duo, sum semiberbis ego."

And the other:

> "Quinque sumus fratres, et eodem tempore nati
> Sunt duo barbati, duo sunt sine barba creati.
> Unus et e quinque non est barbatus utrinque,"

which has been pleasantly Englished thus:

> "Of us five brothers at the same time born,
> Two from our birthday ever beards have worn.
> On other two none ever have appeared,
> While our fifth brother wears but half a beard."

Sir Thomas Browne has partly given the clue to this division of beards, and writes:

"Nothing is more admired than the five brethren of the Rose, and the strange disposure of the appendices or beards on the calycular leaves thereof. . For those two which are smooth and of no beard are contrived to be undermost, as without prominent parts, and fit to be smoothly covered, the other two which are beset with beards on either side stand outwards and uncovered, but

54

# Roses

the fifth or half-bearded leaf is covered on the one side, but on the open side stands free and bearded like the other."

Thus indeed it is, and the edges of each sepal that are on the outside in the closed state of the bud are furnished with beards, and so the bud is protected from some enemy, possibly roving caterpillars like those of certain noctuae and geometrae that emerge at night for a feast, and hide by day, but do not live in a burrow in the heart of a flower. These could find a nicely-prepared meal in the many free edges of these beards, and these would perhaps be enough for one sitting without boring into the flower and so destroying its reproductive organs. But that is only a guess of my own, based more on my experience of the ways of caterpillars than a needful examination of the flowers of a large number of Roses to observe how many have had their beards gnawed away ; and it is better to turn to hard facts, which will at least explain how it is that five edges of the sepals are beardless if they will not tell us why the remaining five need appendages. Aestivation and phyllotaxy are the terms botanists apply to the solutions of the whole matter, and as the Dog Rose makes a very good illustration of their working, I cannot resist the temptation to enlarge on this fascinating study. Those who dislike a lesson in elementary botany, or know all about it already, will please skip a page or two while I take aestivation as my text and turn to those among my readers who, like myself, prefer to have a thing thoroughly explained.

# My Garden in Summer

Linnaeus invented the term "aestivation" to denote the folding up of the parts of a flower in the bud stage, corresponding with the word "vernation," which he used for leaves only ; and the various methods Nature employs in this neat packing make most fascinating objects for study. Here we have to deal with a flower whose calyx and corolla consist of five pieces each, five sepals and five petals ; and you can see at once that there cannot be many different ways of folding five pieces to wrap round one another. The simplest, perhaps, would be to arrange that one edge of each piece should be overlapped by the segment next to it ; thus each would have one edge inside and one free. This plan is found commonly in flowers of five petals, and is characteristic of whole families such as *Apocynaceae,* of which the Periwinkle is an example ; *Onagraceae,* where it is plainly seen in the petals of Evening Primroses and Fuchsias, and also in *Malvaceae, Gentianaceae, Polemoniaceae,* and is known as convolute aestivation. If but one inner edge of this arrangement should become deranged and develop outside instead of inside, one of the segments will be altogether outside of the others, with both edges free, and the segment next to it on the side of its deranged edge will necessarily be altogether overlapped and have both edges inside. This is a second possible arrangement, but is rare, and has been called cochlear, spoonlike, but goodness knows why. Then should one more petal allow the edge that should be inside to escape to the outside (I hope no one is confused, and fancies they are dancing the Grand Chain figure of the Lancers), we should find two

# Aestivation

petals with both edges free on the outside, two with both edges overlapped, and one petal with one edge free and the other overlapped. This third possible arrangement is a very common one, and is called a quincuncial aestivation, and is the form always found in a normally developed single Rose in which the petals overlap at all, and also in a Primrose. Looking into the open face of such a flower we see that two inner petals that are not next each other stand up with all their edges free, and these would be wrapped innermost in the bud; two others, also not next each other, show no free edge and so would lie outermost in the bud, and the last petal, of course, must have one edge free but the other overlapped.

It is rather fascinating to look out for this arrangement in living flowers and drawings of them, and you will find that artists frequently play tricks with the aestivation of their subjects.

This brings us back to Sir Thomas Browne's description of the calyx of the Dog Rose, and we can easily see that the slight overlapping of the edges of the sepals accounts for the absence of beard on five edges out of ten, to wit those that lie overlapped, and so must be unbearded to be packed away inside, and that it is their quincuncial arrangement which determines which of them shall have beards on both sides, or half a beard or none. You can easily make a paper model to demonstrate the variations in aestivation. I will give you a recipe for it instead of the cookery one that most writers on gardens nowadays provide. Take a sheet of paper, your own as you will

# My Garden in Summer

spoil it, and then a half-crown, someone else's if you can get it, place it on the paper, and use it to draw a circle by running a pencil round its edge in the usual manner, then draw by your eye another concentric circle at the distance of half an inch from the former, and trace five half-crown circles at equal distances round the outside, their inner edges just touching the outer edge of the larger circle. Cut the design out and remove the central half-crown-sized circle, and you have five petals separated somewhat from each other on a ring. Then double a fold in the ring of paper between each mock petal so as to bring them as close as you can get them, and their edges will overlap ; you can then arrange them quincuncially, convolutely, or in the intermediate stage that is so meaninglessly termed cochlear, and you will find there are two variants of this, the one I have already mentioned with one petal with both edges outside next to one with both inside, which is formed by pulling out one inner edge of a petal in a convolute arrangement, which has sometimes been called sub-convolute, whereas the other variant is most easily made from a quincuncial arrangement by tucking in one edge of one of the petals that normally has both edges outside. This is called a sub-imbricate arrangement, and has one petal with both edges outside, and one petal with both inside, but in this case they are not next to each other as in a sub-convolute arrangement, and in fact this is the arrangement we find in a Pansy blossom.

If you are fond of mental arithmetic of a mild and easy grade we will go on together to find out how the

# Aestivation

quincuncial arrangement of petals is brought about and is so common in plants whose leaves are arranged *alternately,* that is standing separately at regular distances up the stem, and the opposite of the *whorled* arrangement in which two leaves (then called *opposite* leaves) or more than two occur all at one height on the stem.

If you take a well-grown, straight shoot of an alternate leaved plant, tie a thread to the lowest leaf and twist the thread round the footstalk of the leaf next above it on the stem, and so on to the others, each in their order of nearness, you will find your thread is mounting the stem in a spiral, and in the greater number of alternate-leaved plants, the Rose and Apple among them, it will make two complete turns of the spiral before it reaches the stalk of a leaf exactly in a line above the first one it was tied to, and that this will be the sixth leaf met with. That means each leaf in this spiral has an angular divergence of two-fifths of the circumference, and it takes five leaves and two turns to complete one spiral. Phyllotaxy is the term used to express the mode of insertion of leaves on the stem with regard to its axis—so here we have a five-ranked phyllotaxy, also called pentastichous and occasionally quincuncial, so we are now getting burning hot, as children say when playing at Hide and Seek.

This will be more apparent if you will cut out another paper model. Draw a line half an inch from, and parallel with, the longer edge of a half sheet of notepaper, and at regular intervals along it draw six leaves standing out at right angles from the line; cut the drawing out in one piece, and you have six leaves standing out on one side of a half-inch wide stem. Take a round ruler or penholder, or some other long and cylindrical body that is handy, and twine the paper stem round it, and bend your leaves to stand away at right angles from it. You will find that you can make the paper take two turns to complete a spiral in which the sixth leaf shall come exactly overhead the first and lowest, and you will have the $\frac{2}{5}$ or five-ranked phyllotaxy demonstrated under your very nose. Suppose you could shut up the ruler like a telescope, or better still, carefully slide the spirally twisted paper down to the lower end, keeping it twisted in its spiral and the leaves in their relative places, you, as it were, suppress the internodes between the leaves, and bring all six into a whorl. One, the sixth and uppermost, had better be torn off as it now lies on the top of number one the lowest, and if you have drawn fat round leaves their edges should overlap, and as they settle down they will arrange themselves quincuncially, and you learn that that arrangement of petals, or sepals, is the natural outcome of a $\frac{2}{5}$ phyllotaxy with the axis suppressed.

This mathematical relation between the arrangement of the petals and that of the leaves is also seen by noticing that the lowest petal, which is of course that with both edges outside, is placed at an angle of divergence of two-fifths of the circumference from the next lowest, that is the only other one that can have both its edges outside ; that means, measuring round the nearest way between the two with both edges outside, or in the case of Dog Rose sepals, both edges bearded, you have one between them which must perforce have both its edges overlapped

# Aestivation

by one edge of either of its neighbours, and if we number them as we go, these two outer ones are number one and number two. Number three will be another two-fifths along, and can only have one edge outside, namely, the first edge we arrive at in measuring round the nearest way, making the last of the possible five outside edges, and therefore its other edge will be overlapped and inside, and the first of the five inner ones. Number four will lie between numbers one and two, and, as we have already seen, has its edges overlapped, and number five must lie between numbers two and three. That is, we make a double turn in completing our cycle, and we have each segment arranged just as the alternate leaves were, one at every two-fifths of the circumference.

# CHAPTER V

## Single Roses

NOW it is time that we turned to the single Roses themselves, and we will begin with *R. sericea* as it is generally the first in flower each season, giving a blossom or two early in May, though it continues for a long period, and has not altogether ceased flowering in mid-June. It is remarkable for, and easily recognised by, its four-petalled blossoms, which have the appearance of a Maltese Cross. I have seen five-petalled flowers, but very rarely ; and so far as I know, this Rose and *Potentilla Tormentilla* are the only two members of the great order Rosaceae, of which it is a family tradition to have the flowers with their parts arranged in fives, or some multiple of five, which have but four petals, like some member of the Poppy family. A fine old bush of *R. sericea* crowns one of the mounds on the riverside edge of the oldest portion of the rock garden, and in late Summer bears a crop of bright scarlet hips, which proclaim by their colour that my plant is one of the forms from the Himalayan region, as those of later introduction from further eastward bear fruits that get no further than orange in ripening, and not infrequently remain a deep yellow even at their best. My form makes a very picturesque bush if left alone, for,

# Single Roses

unlike the variety *pteracantha*, which we cut almost to the ground annually for the sake of getting strong growths and the large crimson thorns they produce, it is better to leave the stems of the type many seasons, that they may become furnished with long, arching side-shoots, which bear masses of pure white flowers year after year. I have a young plant supposed to be a yellow-flowered form, but it has not yet flowered and produced its promised gold.

Not many days after *R. sericea* has made her début comes *R. altaica* and totally eclipses her in beauty, for of all the single white Roses of medium height there is none with larger flowers or that is more generous in producing them during its flowering period. It may be allowed to grow into an aged specimen bush of some five feet in height by removing the wandering suckers, and cutting out some of the older wood now and then after flowering, or else may be used as a spreading undergrowth by topping extra lanky shoots, and cutting away two-year-old stems and allowing the suckers to wander as they please ; in both ways it will always produce a charming effect, both when covered with its creamy-white flowers, and again when full of deep purple-black hips, like large Black-currants. It is but a glorified form of our wild Burnet Rose, *R. spino-sissima*, but the finest of that family. Almost as fine is *R. hispida*, its near relative, but it is never so free with its flowers here, perhaps because I have only got budded specimens of it, more suitable, perhaps, for the rock garden, where errant Rose suckers are not pleasant to see or handle in the less wild portions ; but I should like a bed in the turf filled with strong, year-old shoots from suckers of *R. hispida,* as I feel sure the wealth of pale yellow flowers they would produce would be worth looking at. On first opening they are sulphur in colour, but soon fade to a creamy white, except towards the centre, and half their charm lies in the fleeting nature of their yellowness, insomuch that one feels a satisfaction in catching them at the right moment to see their primrose colouring. They are nearly as large as those of *R. altaica,* and none other of the Burnet Roses approaches them in this respect, but I have a great affection for most of them, from the dwarf native form, with its small, cream-coloured flowers, to the double, garden-raised forms known as Scotch Briers. They are all best grown on their own roots, and are then easy to make use of almost anywhere in the garden, but perhaps are never better than in broad drifts in the front of beds of taller-growing Roses, where they may be left alone for the life of the garden with nothing more than an occasional mulch of manure, and a certain amount of judicious clearing out of the older wood. Even the wild form is worth finding room for, though it loses its dwarf habit after a year or two in garden ground, and will reach a height of four feet if permitted to grow into a specimen bush. I could almost believe that *Rosa spinosissima* represents the first attempts of the gods in fashioning the Rose, for its dwarf, wild form is a centre from which branch off so many different types. Its creamy colour may once have been the orthodox yellow of most primitive forms, and, as seen in *R. hispida,* fades easily to white, following the line of colour development. Grant Allen pointed out in his fascinating book, *The Colours of Flowers*, that this was well shown forth by the way in which yellow flowers fade to white, white often die off pink, and blue flowers so often begin life as pink buds. I think the minute *Myosotis versicolor* is the only flower that begins yellow and fades gradually through pink to a dull blue, and thus shows in itself its whole line of colour descent. I always bring it home to the rock garden when I meet it in sandy cornfields; it sows itself sparingly there, and though so small, never fails to interest some during the Summer who have not before noticed its changeable hues. Orange, leading on to scarlet, I imagine is another line of descent from yellow, omitting the white stage, which seems to lead on to rosy reds, then purple, and finally blue.

Many ancient myths declare Roses to have been originally white, until dyed by the blood of Venus or Adonis, or by a bowl of nectar that careless Cupid upset when leading a dance in Olympus, according to the fancy of the teller of tales. But even though we may not believe any of this, it is a fact that *Rosa spinosissima* varies to red, and I have found among the typical white ones growing on the Penally Burrows near Tenby striped, pink, and deep red forms. I failed to make the scraps I grubbed up grow, but I have here a very deep crimson form that in all but colour is a regular Burnet Rose. *R. Albertii* is said to be a form from Turkestan, and has small, deep-yellow flowers, very charming when you get them, but with me they are very sparingly produced, and I much prefer the variety *ochroleuca*, which is one of the best dwarf yellow roses, as it is so generous with flowers. It is rather difficult to procure on its own roots, however, and I daresay would not live long budded, and of course so treated could not spread by suckers to form the delightful colonies natural to the *spinosissima* group. I owe my own-root plants to the generosity of Kew, where there is a fine bed in the grass filled with this Rose. Something like it, but having more glaucous leaves, and an additional three feet of stature, is R. *xanthina*, a very satisfactory yellow Rose, as may be seen by the accompanying illustration of one of my bushes backed by the old Yew hedge by the river. I pondered long before deciding upon this Rose to fill the important space between the stone baluster from Old London Bridge and the Yew hedge at the head of one of the flights of steps in the terrace garden, but have been thankful I chose it, for its blue-green leaves are beautiful for many months, and throughout June it is a delightful mass of clear, soft-yellow flowers. This fine species comes from the Altai Mountains and Northern China, and in spite of a reputation for tenderness, has behaved well here in two very draughty parts of the garden. I wish I could say the same of its much rarer Afghan form, R. *Ecae*, which has had cosy nooks apportioned to it for some five years, and in none of them has ever shown a ghost of a flower-bud on the wiry little growths that look so promising. I long for the flowers, for they are about the size of Buttercups, and of almost as deep a yellow. I have seen it flowering freely at Warley, and that is not so far off but that I may hope to see it do as well here

Rosa xanthina. (See ). 66.)

# Single Roses

some day; and I shall live in hope and expect a due reward, unless there is truth in the definition of the cardinal virtues given by the cynical little beast of a schoolboy that " Faith is belief in what can't happen, Hope is belief in what won't happen, and Charity is belief in what people say has happened." May my practice of Hope soon turn to a chance of the practice of Charity among those who listen to my tales of *R. Ecae.*

Another good yellow Rose lately arrived in our gardens is *R. Hugonis* from Western China—a fine, free-growing bushy species, with small and numerous leaflets and flowers a shade paler than those of *R. xanthina;* but best of all single yellow Roses, so far as depth and brilliancy of colour goes, is that many times misnamed species, the Austrian Brier. From the Crimea to Thibet you may meet with it wild, and it is plentiful in Syria, but never will you see it adorning the banks of Austrian roadsides. It seems now that the law of priority decrees that it must be known scientifically under the unpleasant, though only too appropriate, name of *Rosa foetida,* for it must be owned that under no name, in spite of any amount of poetic licence, would it smell sweet and lose its peculiar odour, so much like that of many of the hemipterous insects, and especially those known, on account of another unfortunate change of name, as Norfolk Howards. I have often wondered what became of that luckless Joshua who made so ill-planned a change; did he revert to his first name of Bug, or has he lost his notoriety among the Smiths or Joneses, or is he still Mr. Norfolk Howard, in spite of the undesired universal change of name for the insect pest as well as for him? The confusion over the name of this Rose seems to be due to Linnaeus, who cannot have been much of a specialist in Roses, for he has mixed up old synonyms and herbarium specimens to such an extent that one feels the whole lot should be put into Chancery, with a final appeal to the House of Lords, as the only chance of getting their legal status fixed. Linnaeus mixed up the Sweet-brier and the Austrian Brier, and described the yellow one under the name of *R. Eglanteria,* in the *Species Plantarum.* In his annotated copy, preserved in the library of the Linnaean Society, he erased the synonyms he cites, which are all those of the Sweet-brier, and wrote " *R. lutea. Bauh. Pinax.* p. 483," showing he then realised his mistake, and wished to connect it with the name cited by Bauhin in his *Pinax* as used by Lobel, Caesalpinus, Camerarius, Tabernaemontanus, Gerard, and other reverend fathers in Botany; but unfortunately this correction must have been later than the publication of the *Mantissa* in 1771, in which it is still connected with *Eglanteria,* so that Herrmann's description of it, published in 1762 under the name *foetida,* is the first correct one after the date at which all botanical nomenclature commences for Phanerogams, namely 1753, the date of the publication of the first edition of Linnaeus' *Species Plantarum.*

I hope those who translate Latin names to make English ones for plants will leave this one alone. Under its present misleading popular name its nationality is misrepresented, but that is better than having the truth loudly proclaimed by such a title as the " Stinking Rose."

# Single Roses

Its leaves, on the other hand, have a pleasant scent that would make such a name the more unjust. True they need pinching before they reveal the slight Sweet-brier nature of their scent, but it is there if wanted. They are of a peculiar yellow-green, which is generally sufficiently marked even in youthful suckers to prevent their destruction by anyone who has an eye and brain that work together to guide his hoe. Also each leaflet is hollowed like a spoon on its upper surface, and the marked contrast of the curiously deep chocolate brown of the bark with the straight, light-coloured prickles ought to be enough to save them, for they are precious possessions, this Rose not being very lavish with suckers. Perhaps this fact accounts for the difficulty of procuring it on its own roots, and the common practice of budding it on Brier stocks, when the plants mostly grow into lanky, thinly-furnished specimens and are not long-lived, but on its own roots the old wood being removed makes room for tall, straight, basal shoots, that for a year or two should produce a shower of gold, and then in their turn be carried to the bonfire. I got my best plant of it in a curiously roundabout way. A nurse, in the intervals of calling to her youthful charge to mind the edge of the river and other dangers, told me of an orange-coloured Rose that grew like a weed in front of her mother's cottage, sending up shoots even in the path. This was good news indeed, and I begged for a sucker, and as I expected, when three beauties arrived, they were the copper-coloured form of the Austrian Brier. That was many years ago, but every season since I have blessed

# My Garden in Summer

her and that country cottage garden when I see the fiery orange of her Rose bushes. One I planted in the rock garden, and it rewarded me for giving it such an important position by reverting suddenly to the yellow form, and the suckers that travel to the eastward are all pure gold, while the westward colony is of copper. When both are in full flower the effect is delightful, and all the more so to me for having come as a surprise.

I am very fond of its double-flowered seedling, said to be of American origin, and produced in a garden of course, named *R. Harrisonii,* and from that richly-stored Irish garden, Riverston, I have at last got what, I believe, to be its very self on its own roots—but I must in justice own that *Harrisonii* makes a very effective standard when budded, at least for a certain period. Quite half of my most precious Roses have come from Bitton, that sanctuary for rare species, where, grown on their own roots, the suckers are respected, and allowed to grow to just the right size for a lucky visitor to carry away with him. My latest treasure from thence is a well-rooted layer of the wonderful old Double Yellow Cabbage Rose, the pride of so many of the early English gardeners, and the despair of so many later ones ; for the various instructions for its successful cultivation, written by the great ones of the past three centuries, are found upon examination to totally contradict each the other—a sure sign that there is no royal road to certainty of flowering with this wayward beauty. Even if buds should be formed, unless halcyon days of full sunshine prevail at the time of their appearance they will refuse to open. We have given it the south-eastern wall of the orchid house, and anxiously await results.

But I have favourites among single Roses that are neither yellow nor cream coloured, and a red one has won much of my affection ; it is *R. Moyesii*, comparatively new to our gardens, and one of the best results of Wilson's wonderful haul of new plants in China. It wants plenty of space, and I had to move mine after its first two seasons or it would have snatched my hat off or scratched my face every time I went by the path it aspired to block up. Shoots eight feet high with arching side growths a yard in length are what you must allow for, then you can enjoy its characteristic, deep-green leaves with numerous leaflets, and at flower time its wonderfully glowing blossoms, the nearest approach in colour to a carbuncle of any flower I know, especially when the evening sunlight assists their brightness. Its ample petals are very substantial and fleshy, more so than those of any other Rose, and of a peculiar leathery texture, and look as though their characters would be valuable to the hybridist who wishes to create a Rose that will last for a month. It is a near relation of *R. macrophylla*, and like it produces the most sensational hips of the family—pendant cone-shaped wonders two or more inches long, of brightest sealing-wax red, almost as lovely as the flowers. *R. macrophylla* itself is handsomest when in fruit, for the pale pink flowers are rather lacking in distinction. *R. Malyi*, a near relative of *R. alpina*, is a very beautiful, rich-red rose, neat in habit, with dainty foliage of small leaflets, and profusely lavish with its annual offering of ruby buds and crimson flowers. *Alpina* itself has never rewarded my hard work on mountain sides when trying to extract a sucker with some fibrous roots attached from a jumble of stones and tree roots, and nothing to do it with but my fingers and a fern-trowel. Now and then an especially richly-coloured form has tempted me to this labour, but Rose suckers are nasty things to remove at Midsummer, even with a good spade and nearer home. Its dwarf variety *pyrenaica* is very happy here, running about freely and flowering and fruiting as though it felt it could never do enough to please me.

On the slopes above the Lake of Mont Cenis there is a little thicket of dwarf Roses among which grows *Anemone Halleri*, and these two plants apparently are nowhere else in that neighbourhood. The Rose looks as though it went through hard times with browsing goats or cows, and is no more than a foot high, so I fetched it home with me, hoping for some particularly interesting dwarf form of *alpina*. After a couple of years of convalescence here it made a fresh start in life, sent up the prickliest of imaginable new shoots, and last year flowered ; it is our native *spinosissima*, and might have been brought from Beachy Head, instead of 6000 feet up in the Graian Alps. *R. rubrifolia* is another very beautiful species from alpine regions, with its curious glaucous leaves shot with purple and red shades. It seeds itself about here, and, if room is allowed it, a youngster soon makes a good specimen, but my form has rather small flowers. I saw some really fine forms, a few evidently hybrids, in the woods just over the river outside Modane this June. We had to spend some hours there between portions of a somewhat

# Single Roses

roundabout journey, and wandered up to this spot hoping to see a particularly fine specimen of *Atragene alpina* I had admired there some years ago ; but though there was only a week's difference in the dates of my two visits, this early season had replaced the blue and white flowers with silky seed-heads, and the Roses were in full pride of beauty. It seemed to me no two were quite alike, and save for *rubrifolia* I could not put a name to any. Canina-like beauties of purest white and deepest salmon graded off into something like glorified Sweet-briers on the one hand and to purple-leaved *rubrifolias* on the other. I wish some enterprising rosarian would go there in Autumn and take samples of them all. The salmon-red ones came very near a beautiful form of *canina* known as var. *Andersonii*, which I think is one of the most lovely shades of pink to be found, so soft and warm, not a trace of blue coldness about it. The hybrid called Lady Curzon comes near it, but is not so warm in tint, and of a coarser make and habit. A fine *canina* form for a bold effect isolated in turf is *R. scabrata*. Its arching, free habit shows off the multitude of large flowers, which are *canina* right enough, but twice as large and twice as pink as in the type, and if it is not too much pruned after flowering, the autumn crop of hips is very effective. There is no lack of good single Roses suitable for most positions, from those that grow into small trees like the last named, to dwarfs like *gallica pumila*, whose height is to be reckoned in inches, and *Wichuraiana* forms that can be used as climbers or for carpeting banks ; an irregular grouping of such Roses can be made wonderfully effective by using some of the

73

most contrasting forms. I planted a rough belt by the side of the carriage drive in this way, covering about a dozen high poles with climbing forms to give height, and filling in below them with bush and dwarf varieties. White and cream-coloured forms were to be massed at one end, and the two whitest of all Roses, the double-flowered forms of *R. rugosa*, make the start ; these are the well-known Mme. Georges Bruant and Blanche Double de Courbet, which, with care, can be grown into good, rounded bushes. That rampant *Wichuraiana* hybrid Gardenia has a pole, and performs marvellous gymnastic feats of climbing and tumbling all over it, and if old wood is thinned out annually and juicy young shoots, as red as a Lenten Hellebore and yards in length, are tied in, one is sure of a summer cascade of orange-coloured buds and white flowers next season. Other poles are covered by a climbing H.P., Paul's Single White, Miss Jekyll's climbing *arvensis*, a vigorous growing form of the pretty white Rose so common in hedges and woodlands of this district, and the Himalayan Musk Rose, *R. Brunonii*, which we must now call *R. moschata* var. *nepalensis* if we remember to do so.

Anyway, whether we honour good Robert Brown in this queer latinisation of his name, or recall the native country of the Rose in treating it correctly as a variety of *moschata*, it will still be the most ambitious of really hardy Roses, and always at the top of the tree so long as it can get food for its hungry roots and a tree to clamber upon. Once it has fought its way up, and can fling out long growths to hang downwards, it begins to show its true

# Single Roses

use and beauty, and the showers of pure white blossoms among the grey-green leaves make one of the best annual treats the Roses provide for their owners. It varies in the greyness of the foliage, and I much prefer the greyest form. I have one, beautifully silvery in leaf, that has fought its way up an old Yew in the Iris beds, and at all seasons the contrast of sombre Yew shoots and grey-blue Rose sprays is delightful. The form on the pole in the Rose tangle by the drive, however, is a very ordinary sort of green as to leaf, which does not matter much there, as *R. Fedtschenkoana* rambles all round its long legs and shoots up six feet high with prickly red stems and elegant grey leaves.

After this group of sky-scrapers, the Giraffes of the Rose world, the bed holds lowlier cattle, and among them *altaica, sericea,* and all the forms of Scotch Roses that I could get hold of at the time the bed was planted, that were either white or yellow. They have been left to run into one another pretty much as they like, and have made a dwarf thicket, out of which *R. xanthina* towers at one end and Lady Penzance Sweet-brier at the other. I want the Copper Austrian to do so too beside Lady Penzance, but have not been able to induce it to as yet. Then, as we reach the upper end of the bed, the yellow colouring is replaced by pink, and at the back corner shades to crimson, where Carmine Pillar covers a tall pole and Maharajah a low one, surrounded by bushes of *rubrifolia,* the shining-leaved *lucida,* the glaucous *hibernica,* the free-flowering hybrid of *humilis* and *rugosa,* and the neat growing *nitida,* to bring the level down to some dwarf

75

*gallica* forms, out of which rise two of the Irish Singles, Irish Glory and Irish Beauty, this last and a fine pillar of *Wichuraiana* Jersey Beauty being the only white-flowered forms at this end of the bed. It has always been a very satisfactory and attractive bed since its first year of planting, now a dozen or more ago, and is the one that I have mentioned in the Spring volume as gradually laying down its own blue carpet of Scilla and Chionodoxa. Now it is striking out another line for itself in starting all unasked a colony of the Welsh Poppy, and I can't make up my mind yet as to whether I will scratch my face next Spring and root them out, or, if I let them go further, they will interfere with the health and happiness of the Scillas. A good undertone of yellow and orange Meconopsis would look charming under white Roses, but Fate has unkindly decreed that the colony should start nearest the end given to pink ones. I must look at them critically another season, and if they are too yellow I will don a fencing mask, and so try to avoid scratches while I evict them.

I have no great affection for Rambler Roses, perhaps because I see so many over arches and rustic poles as I journey up to London by the Great Eastern Railway. Until the nearness to town turns the back garden into a mere yard, each one has a Crimson Rambler, pink or white Dorothy Perkins, a Hiawatha or Lady Gay, or the whole set if near this end of the line, and it is a relief to see now and then a practical-minded householder's garden given over to the utilitarian cultivation of Scarlet Runners on strings, their pure scarlet blossoms a joy to the eye

# Single Roses

surfeited with colours that have had such a narrow squeak to just avoid being classed as magenta.

I make an exception for Blush Rambler, though, whose colour is charmingly soft, and the single flowers have such a wise way of shedding their petals the moment they feel themselves growing old and ugly, so that the large bunches of flowers look fresh and clean from first to last.

The rose-covered posts in my so-called pergola support some very old Roses instead of the newest. I write *so-called*, as my double row of posts for climbers cannot really claim to be a pergola, and only a few of the climbers are allowed to reach overhead from one cross-piece to its *vis-à-vis*, as in this flat garden, short of climbing a tree or having a captive balloon ready for short ascents, one would never get a chance of seeing the outside of its roof where the flowers would be, and I do not see the fun of planning floral displays for dicky birds or angels, and our proximity to Enfield Lock and Waltham and their Government works for warlike goods, places us in a prohibited area for aeroplanes.

The rose-coloured *Wistaria multijuga* before mentioned I am encouraging to roof in the walk, for its yard-long racemes of flowers show well hanging overhead, and in an old Rose called Adelaide d'Orléans that I got from a Norfolk garden I have another plant suitable for the same purpose. It is one of a set of seedlings raised by M. Jacques when head gardener at Château Neuilly to the Duc d'Orléans, who afterwards became King Louis Philippe. *R. sempervirens* was the species he used as seed parent, and the best known of his creations is Félicité

# My Garden in Summer

Perpétue, which covers the post opposite the Wistaria, and is a wonderful sight when in flower, but too well known to need any description here ; however, its elder sister, Adelaide d'Orléans, who first saw the light in 1826, two years earlier than Félicité, seems to be very little known. It makes enormous growths when well established, and they are so pleasantly slender that they can be bent or trained any way or anywhere ; the bunches of flowers appear in the latter part of June on long, slender stalks, so that they hang down most gracefully, and if the shoots of last Summer are tied in so as to form a roof over the pergola you can look up into the faces of the flesh-pink flowers, and they almost seem to smile back at you, as a bevy of cherubs might if they liked you. By shortening a few growths so that they wave free for a yard or two on the outer side of the supporting post quite a different effect is obtained, and there you will have a fine mass of flower-heads almost hiding the leaves. Adelaide is also very beautiful if allowed to ramble into some small tree ; I have seen her thus in another Norfolk garden, but have not yet imitated that effect, as I have the hanging fringe on the pergola of the first garden in which I met her and fell in love with her at first sight.

One occasionally sees some delightful old pink climbing Roses in gardens in Devonshire and Ireland, that bear great trusses of flowers, and no sooner has one crop shed its petals than a mass of green buds will push up to take its turn. They appear to be garden hybrids, and closely related to *Rosa Pissartii* (often spelt *Pissardii* but named after Pissart, gardener to one of the Shahs of

78

# Single Roses

Persia), and which in Miss Willmott's monograph becomes a variety of *moschata* with the name *nasturana*. These pink forms are semi-double, very sweetly scented, and quite charming for clothing a pillar or post. The true *R. moschata* var. *nasturana* is only touched with pink in bud and opens pure white, and is another very useful and beautiful Rose. I have tried a few of the newer pillar-roses, and I think Trier and Fairy will long possess the posts I have allotted them. Their dainty white flowers are delightful, and Fairy is as perpetual as any white Rose I have seen. When newly opened the effect of its golden ring of stamens against the pure white petals makes it look like a miniature copy of *R. bracteata*, which, if only it were a shade hardier and began to flower earlier in the season, would be the finest of white Roses. As it is, however, I love it dearly, and it grows on one of the four buttresses, or whatever is the right name for the legs of the old Market Cross. It has the warmest one, that which faces most to the south, and yet suffers badly in cold winters, and really needs a south wall and perhaps a blanket during sharp frost. It is sad to see its glorious, shining, should-be evergreen leaves turn black and then fall in bad seasons, but when they struggle through and keep green till Spring, I know there will be a good show of the firm-textured white flowers with their rich golden centres later on. If only one could put such a centre into the new single white tea, Simplicity!

Another new Rose with a pillar-clothing reputation is Ariel. I am delighted with its curious scent, so much like the leaves of Sweet-brier, but I am not so greatly

# My Garden in Summer

enamoured of its shade of pink. Joseph Billiard has as handsome leaves as one could wish, and grows like Jack's Beanstalk, so rapidly do fat, fleshy shoots spring up from the base. You look at a 10-inch-long one on Monday, and say, "Next week I will tie you in to take the place of older wood." On Tuesday you do not pass that way, and on Wednesday as you go by in the dusk that shoot scratches your nose, and you have to tie it back to a neighbour of last year's growth on Thursday. On Friday you go away for the week-end, and when you next see your Rose this shoot has shot through the topmost growth of last year, has made a great arch of itself, and is reaching down to have another snatch at your nose ; when you go to bend it up to a cross-bar it goes snap in the middle, but a few days later it starts into side shoots all the way up. If caught young and trained as they should go these shoots cover a great amount of space very effectively and glossily. When first I saw the flowers I thought them lovely with their sharp contrast of rosy crimson petals and lemon-yellow eye after the style of that of a Lady Penzance Sweet-brier, but now I find you must look at half-opened blossoms only, for their pink turns sour in a few hours and proclaims itself a cousin of magenta, and sets one's eye on edge like rhubarb tart does one's teeth. I want a tame fairy to live in the Joseph Billiard bower during flowering time to pick off every blossom as it turns the corner from warm pink to the hue of weak Condy's Fluid.

Although I am not hospitable towards Ramblers I cherish their original parent, *R. multiflora,* which has been

Summer in the Flower Garden.   By A. Fairfax Muckley.

so well named the Bramble Rose. Our specimen was a come-by-chance, in fact a stock that shot up and smothered out its scion, and as it was not badly placed we have given it a succession of ever-heightening supports until it owns the greater portion of a felled tree, and we feel we must now rest contented. It is a fine sight some seasons, depending mostly, I think, on the attention it has received in the previous Summer and Autumn in the way of the removal of old wood, a judicious thinning and shortening of some new shoots, and tying in others full length. The plant well repays such work when it is covered by the cloud of its wee, bramble-like flowers, each of which might be covered by a sixpence.

Another small-flowered, but for all that mightily effective, Rose is the little-grown *R. Soulieana*—a very close relation of *moschata*, though, unlike most of the *moschata* forms, *Soulieana* is no climber, but a veritable tree on its own account.

I got my plant from Spaeth of Berlin, and in its first season it gave me the impression that I had wasted pelf on its carriage, for it looked a mere ordinary Brier and made no attempt to flower. Next season it shot out the most surprising growth I had ever seen a Rose achieve— as thick as my thumb, armed with prickles large and ferocious-looking enough for the jaws of a shark, and soaring up in such a hurry that it soon reached a height of eight feet, and looked as though it had no relationship with the two feet of older scraggy growth sitting at its base. The following season it clothed itself with side shoots, and they again took up another Summer to ramify and build up a handsome tree ; but all that time never a sign of a flower-bud appeared, and we began to wonder whether this ten feet by six of prickles and grey-green leaves was paying us enough rent for its plot of ground. Then in the fifth year, it was ready to make a return for our patience, and every shoot burst out into great bunches of buds, and for several weeks, covering a much longer period than *moschata nepalensis* can achieve, it was one splendid bouquet of pendant bunches of pure white roses, smaller than those of *nepalensis*, but I feel certain much larger than those of the plate in Miss Wilmott's book. A great number of them turned to hips, and till late in the Winter it was a beautiful and interesting sight, for its hips are of a bright orange colour that is very striking when seen in the sunlight.

The true and rare old Musk Rose exists here, but in a juvenile state at present, for it is not many years since I brought it as cuttings from the splendid old specimen on The Grange at Bitton, and I must not expect its deliciously scented, late-in-the-season flowers before it has scrambled up its wall space.

I must mention other Roses only briefly, or this chapter will rival *R. Soulieana* in monopolising space, so of *R. anemonaeflora* I will only say it scrambles about on the trellised wall with no special care, and its long, narrow leaflets and white flowers, so like double *Anemone nemorosa*, surprise many people who have overlooked its charms when planting their Roses. A white-flowered form of *R. Seraphinii* has the neatest white thorns of any Rose I possess. A hybrid of *rugosa* and *foliolosa* bears large, soft, pink flowers with a wonderfully beautiful white eye that gives a delightful finish to their good looks, but they are shy about opening out flat and showing it to full advantage except in hours of full sunlight. *R. foliolosa* itself is a pretty, light-habited, lowly plant with cheerful, pink flowers, useful to let run about as it will in spaces between large shrubs, and a good thing to use in the same way is the Ash-leaved Rose *R. fraxinifolia*, now reckoned a variety of *R. blanda.*

*R. myriacantha*, almost a *spinosissima*, is distinct enough to be worth a place for its pretty, white flowers, and as its name implies, singularly well-armed stems. Of *R. Webbiana* I have only got the variegated form, a dainty little creature, whose young shoots have more of white and pink in them than of green, but it is none too hardy here, and does best in a sheltered corner of the rock garden. It has long been a puzzle what Rose this was a variegated form of, and it has been assigned to both *Wichuraiana* and *Beggeriana*, widely differing species. The latter is a rough-growing bush with rather small flowers. I won't go so far as to destroy my specimen now it is well established, but should it die I should not replace it with another *R. Beggeriana*. Other bush-forming species that I cherish more fondly are *R. nutkana*, a good, late-flowering, pink one ; *Woodsii*, a graceful grower with small pink flowers ; *Dupontii*, which is the newly author-ised name for the *moschata* and *gallica* hybrid we have so long known as *nivea*, a sweetly-scented, free-growing Rose with large, flat, white flowers, generally slightly edged and flushed with pink ; the single white *rugosa*, and its very beautiful weeping seedling variety. I have this last budded as a half standard; it stands on a sloping bank edging a lawn, and has made a wonderful tangle of long, intertwined growths, that would sweep half way across the lawn if we did not cut off their tips or turn them back into the general entanglement. Its flowers are of a singularly pleasing, starry form, and cover the whole plant for a few weeks, but they never turn to hips here. I believe because it has some Wichuraiana blood in it, and the plant is a sterile hybrid. If I had a cliff face that could be spared for it, I should like to drape a good stretch of it with a hanging curtain of this fine Rose.

*R. microphylla* rarely flowers here, but I have only got the double form. When flowers do appear I like their curiously prickly calyx; but of course I never get the still more interesting hips that look more like Sweet Chestnuts than Rose hips. Carmine Pillar is too well known to need description here, but I seldom see it treated as it deserves or allowed enough space to go as far afield as it can. I planted one at the foot of an old leaning Laburnum, and it smothered it from top to toe, and I rather expect helped to bring about its downfall in a gale that treated the garden like a game of ninepins. A tall Yew was another of its victims, so we replaced the Laburnum by the Yew trunk sunk for about two feet and set in concrete, and had a fine scratchy day's work disentangling the Rose from its old consort and wedding it to the new; but in spite of its apparent resistance it has settled down happily, and is a gorgeous sight at the end of May and beginning of June, with its long

84

# Single Roses

arms flung all over the second husband and bearing hundreds of crimson flowers. *R. laevigata Anemone* was much later in flowering this season than is usually the case, not making much of a show until mid-June. It has taken possession of the old displaced Enfield Market Cross, which now spends its old age in the centre of the Rose garden, and now that its long shoots have climbed up among the pinnacles it requires very little attention, just a light thinning of old wood in late Summer and a tying in of a few of the wildest and longest of last year's shoots in early Spring. It must be hardier than was at first believed, for it hangs out through the little arches and behind the crockets on all sides, and the growths on the east and north sides flower just as happily as those on the south, and I do not believe there can be a plant that would look better against the grey stone than this Anemone Rose with its exquisitely shaded soft pink flowers as large as one could wish any Rose to be, to still look real, and not a part of the wings in the transformation scene of a pantomime ; I think if I had another Market Cross to clothe I should arrange for it to wear another *R. laevigata Anemone*. I have given up one of the pillars and bays of the trellis by the terrace to another plant of it, and it is filling its space well, and I hope will soon rival its elder sister on the Market Cross. The real *laevigata*, I fear, will never give a like display of its glorious white flowers here, for it gets the vegetable equivalents of asthma and rheumatics every Winter, and is only convalescent by the end of Summer, just in time to make a growth or two that will be afflicted with similar lung and limb troubles with the advent

85

# My Garden in Summer

of Winter. There is a legend of a much hardier form that comes from Northern Japan, but I have not been able to get hold of that plant to replace my poor invalid.

There still remains one of the most fascinating groups untouched, the class that is composed of families bearing the names of China, Bengal, Monthly, Tea-scented, and Fairy Roses, and includes also even those distinct personalities the Willow-leaved and Green Roses. Their Latin names are more numerous still, and as no two authors seem to agree as to which is which, it is hard to settle upon a chieftain to head the clan. It seems to me that until someone will bring us the living wild plant from the mysterious East, we had better enjoy growing those we have, and leave them without a lord-paramount. As far as I can see, unless the single, crimson-flowered plant known as Miss Lowe's *Rosa indica* is a wild form, we have nothing in cultivation but garden forms, as has so frequently happened with other plants brought from China. The Willmottian monograph declares the correct title for the chieftain will be *Rosa chinensis*. So as it is better to be out of the world than out of the fashion, we must call them the China Roses, anyway until that index volume comes, which may be before these pages are finally corrected in the revised proofs, and I may have to substitute the title *indica* [1] at the last moment. I was taught so early in my gardening career that the single crimson was the wild parent of all the Chinas that I find it hard to renounce this creed. Moreover, I do not feel one bit convinced that the " large climbing shrub armed with brown,

[1] No, it must still be *chinensis*.

86

scattered, hooked prickles," and bearing solitary flowers, of which Dr. Henry collected dried specimens in the glens near Ichang in Central China, has much to do with our cultivated Chinas with such neat habits and large panicles of flowers, although I must own Redouté figures and describes many *indica* forms with solitary flowers.

I have had all the books of authority on Roses that I possess open before me, and have tried to find out which of my growing plants of what I call *indica* forms any two of them have a common name for, but I give it up. It reminds me of the days when I was working for my degree and studying the Psalms. At first I was full of enthusiasm to get at the real inner meaning of certain cryptic words, and would prepare my table like a painter does his palette, but with books for paints : the original Hebrew on my left, above it the Septuagint, followed by the Vulgate, the Authorised and Revised Versions of the Bible, and lastly the Prayer-book. The Hebrew word-root of three letters might be fairly generic in meaning—say, "to move "; the Septuagint's Greek equivalent would be no nearer than a substantive signifying " a bird " (of course I am inventing an instance, but hardly exaggerating), the Latin might be translated as "sheepfold," the Authorised Version would give us " consolation," and the Prayer-book, perhaps, " oblations." Such verses are not frequent, thank goodness ; but they exist, and after struggling with a few I memorised the various words and left the meaning alone—quite reversing the Duchess' moral advice to Alice, " Take care of the sense, and the sounds will take care of themselves." Now I treasure in the garden a very beautiful single Rose, of

# My Garden in Summer

soft cream colouring, flushed at the edges of its large petals with the rosy pink of some sea-shell. I was taught by Canon Ellacombe to regard it as the parent of the Tea-scented Roses, and to call it *R. indica fragrans.* It appears in the great monograph glorified by the possession of a brand-new name, as though it had been raised to the peerage or canonised, as *R. chinensis grandiflora.* Then arises the question, Can we connect this lovely Rose with the two single forms, a yellow and a pink, which when wedded in France produced the Tea-scented Roses of gardens? In comparing authorities and plates in order to get clear evidence, I find myself as much haffled now as erstwhile among the Psalm puzzles, and I do not think the lovely salmon-coloured one figured by Redouté and called *R. indica fragrans flore simplici* is meant for my plant.

The single crimson finds no mention in the great new monograph, in spite of its lovely portrait drawn by Redouté, and I regard this as a slight upon my favourite, which was one of the most precious of the many plant treasures that made up the first armful of plants that kind Dr. Lowe of Wimbledon gave me from his rich store of varieties. Introduced to him by letter, I was rather nervous of my first visit to the man who knew so much, who had made his collection of British Lepidoptera so complete that when over sixty he started to study and to collect Coleoptera, that is to say, Beetles—but not those that the cook called Beadles; and I love that silly story so well, you must please let me tell it in case you like silly stories too. " I can't stop 'ere, mum," said the new cook; " the kitchen's that full of Beadles." And the prim Missis replied, " Anyway, cook, you should spell the word with a T." And the surprised domestic gasped, " Lor, mum, I never 'eard 'em called Teadles before." But Dr. Lowe never collected those, though he soon made many notable captures and discoveries among the true beetles.

In spite of his deep learning, before we had been together in his garden for five minutes I felt I had known him all my life, and he began filling a basket for me with plants that were utter strangers to me. This Rose was one of them, and he told me he had grown it for many years, and it had quite disappeared from other gardens, even on the Continent; and when some account of his plant was published in one of the gardening papers, letters arrived from all quarters asking him for cuttings. I carried away with me two cuttings that April morning; they were rooted in a pot in a vinery, and that Summer they found homes in the garden; the big old bush in the rock garden is one of them, and after twenty years of faithful service, which, sounding too much like an obituary notice, shall be altered to a score of flowering seasons of six months each, is as flourishing as ever. The moral of that is, grow it on its own roots from a cutting, then from May to December one is sure to find flowers and buds on it as rich in colour as pigeon's-blood rubies; yet I see it in very few gardens.

Another old stager is a bush of the Fairy Rose, *R. chinensis* var. *minima*, the double pink form. It too was planted in the rock garden twenty years ago, and still only asks to have an annual Spring cleaning of old wood, if I have omitted to clear it out in the previous August, which is the better season for the job, as it allows the young growths to ripen for next Summer's work. The crimson form grows in the pergola garden among other Roses such as *R. fraxininifolia,* and is rather buried up there, but flowers away with a good heart.

The Green Rose, *R. chinensis viridiflora,* is but little grown, yet it is very interesting as one of the most perfect illustrations of phyllody of petals, for every one of its many rows of them has become as green and firm in texture as its leaves. I greatly like its shapely emerald green buds for cutting to arrange with other Roses whose own are too precious to nip in the bud, and would not be half so elegant and attractive, for the Green Rose manages to make the most of its one charm, and the buds open very slowly, and remain a long while in the first stage of expansion, showing plenty of the green surface of the transformed petals between the sepals. When fully open they turn a dingy olive with dull purple streaks here and there ; they are no longer beautiful, but are eagerly sought after as button-holes by my Sunday-school boys in their Sunday afternoon visits to the garden. A cousin who admires the Green Rose carried off a young plant, and asked her old gardener, " Did you ever see a Green Rose ? " " Noa, miss, nor a blew one neether," was his incredulous reply ; but the baby Green Rose behaved well, and widened his mind later on. Like other Chinas, it seems to wish to flower all the year round, and had many bunches of sound buds at Christmas in 1913.

" The Cinderella of the Roses," Mr. Gumbleton used

to say, waving the umbrella, which in all weathers accompanied his garden rambles, over the head of *R. Watsoniana*. Its flowers would almost justify its being called one of the ugly sisters, for they are crumpled little messes of a bad shade of pink, almost as small and uninteresting as those borne by some of the dreadful new brambles from China. But in its long, slender growths and curiously narrow leaves *R. Watsoniana* possesses a saving grace ; when flinging long shoots of lacy greenery over a boulder in the rock garden it is quite attractive, and if budded as a standard makes a peculiar and interesting feature among more ordinary-looking plants. *R. gymnocarpa* I fear is beyond all hope of transformation by a Fairy Godmother, and doomed to remain the other ugly sister for all time, for it bears dingy-red flowers the size of a threepenny bit that might be considered handsome for a Cotoneaster, but will not pass muster for a Rose. I will not say I have exhausted the list of the Roses of the garden, but I have my patience for recalling their tricks and manners, but not necessarily yours, my reader, for before this happens you can always sleep or close the book, or skip to another chapter.

# CHAPTER VI

## Geraniums

MY interest in Geraniums dates from the day when as a
small boy in a sailor suit I gathered a bunch of the
Pencilled Crane's-bill, *G. striatum*, in a lane near Paignton,
and carried them to be named by my great-aunt, who
was at once the central attraction and cause of our visit
to South Devon, and the representative of all botanical
lore to my young mind.

I owe so much to this delightfully clever and generous
Nature-lover that I cannot resist this opportunity of paying
a tribute of gratitude to her memory. Mrs. Solly, my
great-aunt Cornelia, had spent many years in India, and
could tell tales and show wonderful drawings of plants
and butterflies from " The Jungle " to the eager questioning
child ; but above all I recall happy sunny mornings passed
with her in that wonderful Devonshire garden. I expect
it was very small, but it seemed to me to contain everything worth growing, and I still believe its double Ranun-
culuses and Sparaxis and Ixias were the finest I have
ever seen. Dear kind soul ! how I hope there are sweet
flowers in plenty round your feet in Paradise. She soon
named my treasure, told me of its rarity, and advised my
digging up a plant to take home, and showed me other
Geranium species in her garden, and especially *G. pratense*

# Geraniums

from Gloucestershire meadows, of which two seedlings were marked for me, and at the end of our visit accompanied *G. striatum* and me to my own garden here. Both species still survive from those two stocks, *pratense* almost too plentifully on a wild bank near the rock garden, which it would monopolise were it permitted its own way. The crowd of blue blossoms is delightful in July, and I always enjoy the long line of blue snow that lies on the path under them from late afternoon till next day's hot sun withers the fallen petals, and melts away the snow effect. This particular race has never varied at all, and of all the hundreds of seedlings that have appeared on that bank any one might have been a division from the original plant, but in other parts of the garden there are colonies of *pratense* forms of which it is hard to find any two exactly alike. For I soon learned to love Geraniums and collected them assiduously, which, however, I am afraid is too mild a word for my methods, and such as Miss Prim might substitute, in correcting little Amelia's exercise, for greedily or grabbingly, which come nearer the mark. Anyway I have got hold of a good many, and many good, some only pretty good, but none wholly bad in my eyes. Why do I like them so much? Let me think. Firstly, because of their name. Geranion is the old Greek name used by Dioscorides, and derived from *geranos*, a crane, because of the likeness of the unripe seed-vessels to the head and beak of that bird. Tournefort, and after him Linnaeus, used it to include the plants afterwards placed in two separate genera by L'heritier, who seems to have invented the name of Erodium, from *erodios*, a

# My Garden in Summer

heron, for the one, while for the other he adopted the name Pelargonium, from *pelargos,* a stork, first proposed by Dillenius in the *Hortus Elthamensis* in 1732, because as he says Geraniums were called Stork-schnabel in Germany.

Knuth in *Das Pflanzenreich* states that Burman gave the genus this name, but a reference to the passage reveals the fact that in the *Plantarum Africanarum,* published in 1738, Burman quoted from Dillenius.

But Gerard tells us of the names *Rostrum Gruis* and *Rostrum Ciconiae* being used for some kinds, and also gives Stork's-bill and Heron's-bill, as well as Crane's-bill, and Pincke-needle as English names in use in 1597. It is a pity, though, that L'heritier's lead has not been followed by ordinary gardeners as well as by botanists, and that Pelargoniums or Stork's-bills are still spoken of as Geraniums, for with many folk the mention of a blue Geranium only causes them to class you with Ananias. Secondly, there are so many old books in which the Geranium family has been beautifully portrayed, and these have stirred me up to try and grow the living originals of the portraits. L'heritier's old folio, with its magnificent copper-plates, is chiefly devoted to Erodiums and Pelargoniums, and only finds space for five true Geraniums, but Sweet's *Geraniaceae* is rich in lovely figures of them, and is one of the most beautifully illustrated of the fine books of that period, so rich in the production of exquisitely drawn and coloured flower portraits. *The Botanical Magazine* and Andrews' *Geraniaceae* also served to inflame my zeal for this family. Thirdly, I found they were

94

# Geraniums

favourites with those who first guided my gardening instincts, and gave me what, for want of a better word, I can only express by the term un-nurserymen's plants; and, lastly, they took to me and my gardening as much as I did to them, and I find many of them invaluable for filling half-shaded positions with at least ten, if not the full twelve, months of beauty and interest. The leaves of many are good throughout the Winter, whether last season's turning russet and even scarlet at times, or next season's newly appeared. I reckon the gems of the family are the alpine forms that must live in the rock garden, and *G. argenteum* deserves the first place, for the sake of its silvery leaves that add such value to its general effect, and set off the delicate pink flowers, with their fine tracery of crimson veins. To assure success with this plant, I find it must be treated as Dr. Johnson declared necessary with a Scotchman, and be caught young. If raised from seed and planted out in a rocky crevice, or even the granite chip moraine, they prove as obliging as I could wish, but middle-aged plants are bad to meddle with, and even if they do eventually recover from the fits of sulks and tantrums induced by an up-heaval, it is slow work. *G. cinereum* and its variety *sub-caulescens* I find more obliging, and knobby portions of elderly stems may be torn off in Spring and planted as though they were youngsters, and will root and behave most decorously. I have lost a reputed hybrid called *G. intermedium*, but I know why, and must get it again and treat it better this time and not allow it to become overgrown by *Arenaria balearica* and *Moltkea petraea* as

95

# My Garden in Summer

I did the original poor sufferer. The pure white form of *cinereum* is a very lovely thing, and is getting about the gardening world fairly rapidly now, but I very seldom see or hear of *G. Webbianum*, and it finds no mention in Knuth's new monograph. With the habit of *argenteum*, but not quite so silvery in the leaf, it bears white blossoms, charmingly veined with a purple that is almost black. I am afraid it is not so hardy as the others, as it has too often perished here in Winter, but a seed or two can generally be gathered from a healthy plant to provide successors.

Next precious for the rock garden and choice positions comes the dwarf and soft rose-coloured *G. sanguineum* var. *lancastriense*, so curiously restricted in its range as a wild plant, and only found on Walney Island. I think Knuth is a little unkind to it in sinking it as a synonym of *sanguineum* var. *prostratum*, which I have always imagined to be the close-growing form I have found wild on cliffs between Filey and Flamborough Head, and again in Devonshire all about Prawle Point, and is the form generally cultivated in English gardens. It is quite different in habit from the lanky, leggy fellow I have seen in the Alps, and which settled a doubt that had till then lingered in my mind as to the legitimacy of the title *sanguineum album* for the beautiful white form that is grown in gardens. The slender stem, with a weak habit, inducing it to take advantage of a neighbouring plant for support, that I noticed was typical of the Bloody Crane's-bill of Austrian hillsides, reminded me at once of the scrambling white-flowered tangle of my rock garden, and

# Geraniums

I feel fairly certain it must have been among such spidery-legged members of the family that the albino first appeared. But *lancastriense* is so distinct, not only in possessing a dwarfer, closer habit than even var. *prostratum*, but in the deliciously soft salmon rose of its flowers, that it well deserves a varietal title at least, even if its habit of coming perfectly true from seed taken with its isolated habitat would not permit the rank of a sub-species.

One hot July day, when I was staying with Mr. Robinson at Gravetye, I watched the seeds of *G. lancastriense* being shot out, catapult fashion, by the drying and recurving slings formed by the beaks of the carpels, and as they were easy to collect from the grey flag-stones on to which they were falling, I gathered a little pinch to pocket and carry off home to imitate the charming effect my host had achieved by using it as an edging to one of his beds, the rosy flowers looking especially lovely against the grey stones, and its tufty habit being just right for the position. Every seed germinated, and now I have a Geranium edging here in the enclosed garden that looks very well by the side of one of my paved paths ; but our sparrows or mice have found out that the nearly ripe seeds are worth pilfering, and at times clear off the whole crop. I have a very strong-growing, large form of *G. sanguineum*, that came to me with the utterly ridiculous name of *G. nepalense*, which belongs to a species so small flowered, even when portrayed by Sweet, that even my catholic love for Geraniums has never led me to try to obtain it.

This large *sanguineum* is a handsome plant, especially if grown in partial shade, when its flowers come larger and

# My Garden in Summer

of a slightly less vicious type of crimson than when grown in the open. It must be confessed the family inherits a pernicious habit of flaunting that awful form of floral original sin, magenta, and rejoicing in its iniquity. The magnificent black eye of *G. armenum*, which Knuth declares we must call *G. psilostemon*, saves it from being one of the worst astringents of the vision in the whole garden, but such a colour reacts on my retina much as alum does on my tongue. *G. sylvaticum* in some forms comes perilously near a similar shade, but almost any alpine meadow where this Geranium occurs will provide a choice of shades, and the richer purples with large, white eyes are well worth uprooting to bring home ; I have thus acquired some really spectable forms, to air a good old English adjective too long laid on the shelf. That is the worst of writing so much on one subject, suitable adjectives fail to answer to one's desire for variety—so henceforth expect a few strange-sounding ones till Charming, Pleasant and Co. have had a rest cure. There is no need to grow ugly forms of our native Wood Crane's-bill, for there is a per- fectly alabastrine (poor brain-fagged " snowy " is in a Wim- pole Street Nursing Home ; no letters or visitors permitted) form that flowers in late June and July as well as the flesh- pink form I cracked up so highly for the Spring garden. Knuth wants us to believe that *G. angulatum*, so well figured in the *Bot. Mag.* in 1793, is only *G. sylvaticum*. You have noticed by this time I am a little peevish over Knuth and his goings on in this new volume, and I resent the slight to my well-loved *angulatum*, and its four-shilling- piece sized flowers, in his not even allowing it varietal rank, as he has done for the rubescent ("rosy" is laid up now) pink form which is variety *Wanneri*. *G. angulatum* is a garden treasure, though, and one of those plants that will sit amiably in the same place for a dozen years. *G. palustre* is very rare in cultivation, and does not vary in colour so far as I know, so that I am proud of possessing it at all in spite of its spiteful hue. It came to me under an alias that I have forgotten long ago, but is unmistakable if one has ever seen Sweet's plate, and I have been delighted at being able to return the true plant to most of our Botanic Gardens for the various other species they had at times given me under its name, but it is a sprawling-habited creature, and not to be desired by the ordinary gardener.

When Crane's-bills turn their efforts towards blue flowers they are hard to beat, and here at the head of the line I rank *G. grandiflorum* of gardens, whatever it really is botanically, for it is almost ultramarine blue in colour, and only not quite so, on account of the crimson veins that run into the blue portion, and meet in the centre to form a red-purple eye, and this glorious colouring does not agree with the lilac flowers botanical descriptions assign to the true *grandiflorum* of Edgeworth—which I have never seen.

Max Leichtlin raised this fine blue one from seeds sent from Sikkim, and, like so many other good plants, it made its first appearance in England at Warley. Its dwarf habit, long period of flowering, easy increase both by seed and root division, have brought it into most gardens by now, and it is a good plant for a bold edging to a bed for herbaceous plants.

# My Garden in Summer

Every scrap of root will grow, and I have had some trouble in trying to get rid of it in a portion of the rock garden that I thought would suit Alpine Primulas, whereas any bed would be acceptable to the Geranium.

The next place among dark blues I give to *G. ibericum,* a neat, tufted grower with woolly leaves and bunches of large purple-blue flowers in June, and very effective while in flower, but very punctual and particular about having eleven months and one week in which to get ready for next year's show. It varies much, and some forms are no more than slate-coloured. I used to imagine, following the lead of better men, that a fine purple-flowered Crane's-bill called *G. platypetalum* was a form of *ibericum,* but it has gone up in the world, and is reckoned a species now. Let us drink its health, for it is a beauty, and makes a grand show during its short flowering season, when a good clump will produce a solid central mass of large purple flowers rising above the handsome leaves. It is a wonderfully patient plant, and only asks to be planted and left alone. I gave a large sum, as Geranium prices go, for one of Wilson's Hupeh introductions. Was it not Chinese? And had not all of us then a foolish belief that every flower from the Celestial Empire would be large and lovely? Brambles and Privets have taught us caution now, but a baby *Geranium platyanthum* came here, and was treated with great respect and nursed on till at last it sent up a stout stem of many fat buds, and I longed for the day when the breadth of floral organs promised by its name should be revealed. At last a flower opened, and there I saw my old friend *G. eriostemon* hanging its

# Geraniums

head for shame and afraid to look me in the face, for its colouring could be easily imitated by mixing ink and mud, and I see that Knuth tears the mask of its new name from its face, and proclaims it to be *eriostemon* rightly enough. As the Nemophila-blue flowers of *G. Wallichianum* come so late in Summer, and the plant is never in its best form here till the nights get dewy and cold, I will leave it for another time, and so *G. pratense* is the last I shall mention of my true blue Crane's-bills. I have already told the history of the wild mass, and hinted at variant forms, so here I will trot them out. The deepest blue shades are correlated with crimson central veining, and I have a notion that they represent Himalayan forms. Pale blues of the skim-milk persuasion are numerous, and by a little careful selection the more watery shades go to the woods and the opalescent forms remain in the garden. A good pure white form is as lovely as any, and I also have a strain that is flushed and veined with pink, and in its deeper shades is certainly another spectable form. Even that range of colouring does not exhaust the possibilities of *G. pratense*, for there is an old form known as var. *striatum*, that, like the York and Lancaster Rose, produces some-times white, sometimes striped flowers, and occasionally one sharply divided in half by the two colours, but in the Geranium blue replaces the pink of the Rose. A goodly number of the seedlings of this form come true. Double-white *G. pratense* is not a bad thing, prettier than it sounds, and there are two forms of double blue, one much more purple in shade and later in flowering than the other, and both often masquerade in the lists as *G. sylvaticum* fl. pl.

# My Garden in Summer

These doubles are valuable for the length of their flowering period; the failure to set seed induces them to keep gay long after their single-flowered sisters have shed their seeds, and they form neater, stiffer plants. One portion of the rock garden became rather overrun by seedling forms of *G. pratense*, but among them appeared some interesting double and semi-double forms of lavender and pale blue shades, and I feel afraid of weeding up any unflowered babe on those slopes lest I lose some new marvel, a fresh miracle of metamorphosis wrought by Mahomet, for you must know all Geraniums were once dowdy Mallows, but the Prophet was so pleased with some sheets made out of Mallow fibres that he changed the plants that produced them into the beautiful Geraniums.

Perhaps the most exciting of the pink-flowered Crane's-bills, at least here, is *G. Endressii* from the Pyrenees. In its typical form it is a dwarf, freely spreading, practically evergreen species that will flourish in any spot not too dry to grow a Groundsel, or so wet that it would be wasted on anything short of a bog plant, and besides furnishing green leaves for twelve months of any year with ordinary seasons, it will provide its raspberry-ice coloured flowers from June to December in nine years out of ten. But plant it within range of insects' visits from *G. striatum*, and then the exciting business begins, for in many gardens these two fall in love at first sight, and end in a matrimonial alliance that peoples their near neighbourhood with hybrid offspring. Rosy grounded *striatum* and veined and pencilled *Endressii* fledgings appear in endless varieties of pattern and shade, and I have picked out some

# Geraniums

very pretty things among them, especially an *Endressii* with many more spoonfuls of cream than is usual mixed with its raspberries, a very delicate and unusual shade of colour, and also another that has varied in the other direction, and is a good soft crimson. One seedling is almost ugly, for its petals are reduced to narrow strips like claws, and scarcely fill the interstices between the sepals. It is so curiously unlike a Geranium that I have suffered it to remain but not to spread too much.

New Zealand provides me with two species, both suitable for the rock garden. *G. Traversii* is a fairly dwarf-growing one with rather handsome dark green leaves. I have lost the white form for some years, and now have only the pink one sometimes called var. *elegans*. The other is *G. sessiliflorum*, a quaint little species found in S. America as well as in New Zealand and Tasmania. Young plants form most attractive rosettes of wee palmate leaves, in among the stalks of which bunches of tiny white flowers are packed as closely as possible. After a year or two the plants become a confused mass of leaves, and do not show the flowers off so well, so I am cruel enough to howk up the elderly folk in favour of the younger generation, which, thanks to its free seeding habit, are always well to the fore. It seems to be correct now to call this New Zealand form var. *glabrum*. As a contrast I will present to you *G. anemonaefolium* from Madeira and Teneriffe, which in favourable seasons will grow up with a single stem like that of a small Palm bearing a crown of its beautifully divided leaves. It is none too hardy here, and requires some winter protection, such as a hand-light in severe winters, but when it can be safely wintered it will grow two feet high, and is then a glorious sight when full of branching flower-stems bearing the large crimson flowers. *G. Lowei* is something like it on a smaller scale but without its characteristic stem, and so is more like a gigantic Herb-Robert in appearance. I cannot believe the *Kew Hand-list* is correct in considering it as synonymous with *anemonaefolium.* I obtained my annual or biennial plant from Glasnevin, and I was told it was a Madeiran plant. It seeds freely here, is quite hardy enough to look after itself, and if it finds a clear space in fairly good soil makes a very handsome specimen. It flowers profusely for a long time, and sometimes the leaves turn a magnificent crimson in late Autumn. Our ordinary pink, native Herb-Robert occurs as a weed in parts of the garden, and in some has to be weeded up, but I give a welcome to two forms of it with white flowers. The handsomer has pink anthers and red stems and crimson lines on the sepals, and the leaves turn bronze and crimson in Winter, and I have more than once found this form growing wild. It is a good plant for the wilder portions of the rock garden, sowing itself into all sorts of cracks and crannies that just suit its requirements, and would be hard to furnish otherwise ; and if it appears too freely there is no difficulty about pulling it up, for it has a very slight root system. The other white form is a much smaller plant, grows flat to the ground, and has pale green leaves and stems, and no red anywhere about it—a thorough albino, in fact. I believe all the plants of it I have ever seen in gardens can be traced back to Sir Charles Isham, but I have never been able to find out where he got it from. Both forms come perfectly true from seed, although the common pink form grows rather near them.

I have a curious form of *G. pyrenaicum* that is not quite white, but a faint almost subdued lilac, that reminds me of a red nose smothered in powder. It occasionally produces the typical red-purple form among its seedlings, but they never survive long after I have detected their evil hue. Something like a glorified *pyrenaicum* is *G. albanum,* also known as *cristatum;* to my idea it just escapes being a charming plant, for though I like its long, thin, prostrate, wandering stems, trailing about among other Crane's-bills, I cannot forgive the chilly crude pink of its abundant flowers, and I wish I could get a white form of it. We do not seem to have many of the hosts of American species of Crane's-bill in our gardens, and besides *sessiliflorum* already mentioned, I can only recall *Richardsonii,* both pink and white forms, like a slender and smooth-leaved *pratense,* and *Fremontii,* with large rosy-lilac flowers. *G. polyanthes,* from the Himalaya, is not very exciting, and *yesoense,* from Japan, is not much more than rather pretty, like a weakly pale pink *Wallichianum,* but flowering in early summer.

I like *G. Wlassovianum* in spite of its cumbrous name, and as I grow it, its flowers are paler than those of Sweet's plate and far prettier, as they are nearly white, only flushed with rosy-lilac at the outer edges. *G. nodosum* is interesting, as being found naturalised in parts of Britain, though those I have found have been of a terribly purplish red ; but I have either a good form or a closely

# My Garden in Summer

allied species given me by Captain Pinwill, which came from the Hartz Mountains, that has larger flowers of a passable pink, and I brought one something like it, but paler still, from the Roja Valley this last Summer. *G. bohemicum* is too small flowered to be much more than a weed ; the *G. asphodeloides* I have does not seem to me true, but is a distinct pink-flowered plant for a shady corner. *G. aconitifolium* I brought from Mt. Cenis, and I like its white, black-veined flowers, and rejoice that Knuth gives preference to this sensible and applicable name before the generally received one of *rivulare*—goodness knows there were no flowing brooks on the rugged hillside whence I collected my plants among the rocks. On the contrary, it was from a stream side that I first collected the dusky Crane's-bill, *G. phaeum ;* by the clear stream that flows through the rocky woods behind Cambo, in the Basses Pyrenees, where, among evergreen Box bushes and small Oaks, whose leaves were brown, but hanging on till Spring buds should push them off, as is the way with Oaks of the South, although it was still Winter I could find many plant treasures. The bright green leaves of a Geranium caught my eye, and I soon noticed some plants were marked with conspicuous purple spots, four large and two small ones on each leaf, but in such a curious way that they were placed round the bases of the indentations that divide the sections of the leaves, half of each spot being on neighbouring segments, so that from a little distance it looks as though each indentation ended in a round hole, and gives a leaf the appearance of being more fantastically shaped than it

# Geraniums

really is. When they bloomed next Summer I was delighted with their claret-coloured blossoms, and by keeping
my eye open on gardens and lists I soon added some
colour varieties to my nigger-minstrel form—first a slaty-
blue one from Bitton, then a greyish-mauve, not so pretty,
from Smith of Worcester, and how they have loved me,
and seeded and grown for me, and what a many I do
have to weed up and carry off to the woods! But I
know of no more patient evergreen with fairly showy
flowers with which to fill up bare spaces under even
evergreen shrubs, where drip and drought succeed each
other, and nothing else but Tree Ivies or Butcher's Broom
could grow. I have lately collected a washy pink form
that abounds in the somewhat cow-bitten pastures of the
Brenner Pass in Tyrol, and from gardens some rather
puzzling forms with redder flowers and the petals more
reflexed, until they merge into *G. reflexum*, its nearest
relation, but the blacker they are the more I like the
forms of the Mourning Widow, as *G. phaeum* has been
aptly named. That must suffice for the review of the
Crane's-bill regiment of the garden—others shall not be
called out from the reserves before Autumn calls them
to don their parade kit; and so we pass to a tiny corps
composed of their cousins the Stork's-bills, or Pelargoniums, omitting for the present the tender forms used
for bedding, and I must present to you four sufficiently
hardy to be left to the mercies of our winters.

First we have the only species found in Asia Minor,
*Pelargonium Endlicherianum*, a very remarkable plant,
not only for its home so far away from its relations, but

# My Garden in Summer

also for its appearance. The genus Pelargonium was separated from Geranium on account of its irregular flowers. Even in the most perfectly rounded flowers of the florists' triumphs among Zonal Pelargoniums, persistently called Scarlet Geraniums by the multitude, one can still recognise the two upper larger petals, and trace the little grooves at their bases leading down to a passage in the long tube of the calyx, at the end of which throughout the genus a slight knob or spur shows just where the honey cupboard is hidden. But in this Asiatic species the two upper petals at first sight appear to be all the flower possesses, though a careful search will show that three minute lower ones exist and protect the bases of the filaments. Its pink flowers are very showy, but always have an incomplete appearance owing to the inequality of the petals, and look as though some snail could give an account of the flavour of the other three. A plant has lived out in the rock garden here for many years, and sometimes flowers well after a mild Winter and during a not too grilling Summer, should two such climatic joys come in the right order of precedence. It inhabits a crevice between two large stones facing due south, and enjoys the good drainage in Winter, but suffers from drought in dry, hot weather. I tried another plant in the sand moraine, and in the words of an old song, "Didn't she seem to like it." I thought I had hit off the secret of success when I saw such large, healthy leaves and tall flower-scapes appearing, but a wet Winter caught the plant, not napping, quite the reverse, too wide awake and active, and it rotted off at the collar.

# Geraniums

From far-away Australia and New Zealand come two others, *P. inodorum* and *P. australe.* I believe I have had both, but am not sure they came to me rightly named. The one I prefer and permit to fill choice corners is the smaller of the two, and agrees best with Sweet's figure of *P. inodorum,* but in some winters it has proved more than annual, and so falls foul of Knuth's ideas about it. Anyway it has the smallest flowers you can imagine for a Pelargonium, in wee round heads, yet beautifully formed and white shading to pink with exquisite spots and featherings of crimson on the two upper ones; it would make a delightful flower with which to decorate the dinner-table of a small doll's-house. The seeds are curious and beautiful, as their minute tails are furnished with long, silky hairs, and a bunch of ripe ones looks like some tiny, furry caterpillar nestling among the overblown flowers. The other is a coarser plant, larger in all its parts, but especially in its leaves, which are coarse enough to spoil its appearance. Both of them sow themselves here as a rule, but I save a pinch of seeds in case they do not reappear spontaneously. With the exception of one in Madagascar, three in Northern Africa, and those I have described, I believe all the rest of the family are S. African, and two of the Cape species have lived here for many years on the rock-garden: one I bought as *P triste,* but judging by the long stem it would produce did not each Winter cut it back to ground level, it is more likely the closely-allied *P. apiifolium.* My plant has large compound leaves and bunches of small flowers, each petal of which looks like a piece of buff blotting-paper with a blot of ink in the centre of it. Like so many dingily coloured flowers they have a deliciously sweet scent in the evening, almost as sweet as that of Night-scented Stock. It has lived very happily in a crack between stones on the Cactus bank, and is so quaint in appearance and so sweet that I hope it may continue to thrive. *P. saniculaefolium* is my last outdoor species : it dies down each Winter, and in late Spring sends up rather handsome leaves, with a dark zone on them. The flowers are small compared with the leaves and the fuss it makes over them, sending them up on tall stalks and giving them such long, green calyx tubes; they are white with red spots, but perhaps the best part of the plant is the long, silky beak of the seeds, and the amusing way in which it twists as it dries.

Some of the larger annual species of Erodium provide the best examples in the Geranium family of these hygroscopic corkscrew-twisting seeds, and I like *E. Semenovii* and *gruinum* for that reason. Both have rather pretty, lilac-blue flowers, but they are so fugacious that you must look for them before noon to see them on the plant, for after that the petals will be scattered on the ground. They are followed by huge heron's-bills, two to three inches long ; and if you can catch a seed just ready to break away from the others, it is good fun to take it indoors and watch its behaviour on a roughish table-cloth. As it dries, one side of the beak in the thinnest portion near to the seed contracts more quickly than the other, the long tail is pulled to one side and then begins to revolve, while the thin part is gradually twisted into a spiral. The seed itself has a very sharp point, which is certain to pierce loose earth if it falls on it, and will if dropped from a little height enter the nap of a woollen table-cloth ; the rest of the seed is covered with stiff hairs pointed backwards from this sharp tip, so that every one that enters a hole in earth or cloth prevents the withdrawal of the seed. You will soon notice that the tail is being swept round in a circle by the contracting spiral that is forming below it, and if you stick a pin (a hatpin for choice) into the cloth so that the tail may strike against it as it swings round and its further movement be arrested, then the spiral as it contracts forces the seed itself to revolve, and it is pushed further into the cloth. When all the movement is over and the spiral formed and dried, it is interesting to leave it *in situ* in the cloth and to wet the corkscrew portion with tepid water and watch the unrolling of the spiral ; the tail now moves away from the hatpin in the opposite direction until it is once more stopped by meeting with its other side, and then again the seed has to rotate, and as it cannot work out on account of its hairs it works still further in. Thus in natural conditions, both by drying in the sun or soaking in dew and rain, the seed gets screwed into the ground where it falls, and during June and July I can generally find several tails of seeds sticking out of the ground telling where seeds have been forced in. Several of the Stipa Grasses use the same mechanical apparatus for seed sowing ; it is especially noticeable with *S. formicaria,* an elegant grass with awns some ten or more inches long, that after waving gracefully for some weeks on their long stems fly away and sow seeds so deeply and firmly that

it is quite difficult to pull them out of the ground by
their long tails, which remain like hairs growing out of
the ground all through the Winter until the seeds germinate
in the following Spring.

Erodiums have almost as great a hold on my affections as Geraniums, and I grow or have grown or wish
to grow (in fact for them I conjugate the verb " to grow,"
in the first person singular, in all its tenses—even the
future—with the reservation, so long as I grow anything),
all the Heron's-bills I can get hold of : even the weediest
of our native species have been tried, after seeing neat
dwarf specimens on sea beaches and sand hills, but they
soon become too coarse and leafy to be of value here.
The head of the family, so far as size goes, is *E. Manescavii*, especially a robust form that appears in gardens as
*E. hybridum*, with a reputed pedigree that claims *E. dau-
coides* as father. Now he is a pigmy compared with
*Manescavii*, and this fine child is about half as large again
as its mother, and I cannot help thinking it may be the
variety *luxurians* of Rouy, and that Sundermann's hybrid
has not yet reached me. These giants form handsome
rosettes—two feet or more in diameter—of fern-like
leaves ; and though the flowers are sinfully near " Magenta,
or New Red," as it is named in the Oberthür *Repertoire
des Couleurs*, they are so freely produced in late Summer
and onwards that if kept out of the fighting line, where
they might quarrel with the good old reds, they are useful
and handsome. *E. hymenodes* and *E. pelargoniflorum* are so
much alike they are hard to distinguish, except when in
flower, when the little tails beset with hairs, that grow out

of the tips of each sepal will mark *pelargoniflorum*, as *hymenodes* is without this adornment. Both sow themselves about in dry banks, and it is best to remove the label from a large flowering tuft to a promising youngster in a suitable position, as in most Winters an old plant of *pelargoniflorum* will die, and *hymenodes* is avowedly a biennial. The flowers of both are white, flushed with rose, and handsomely spotted on the two upper petals in Pelargonium fashion; a good specimen is a grand sight when full of flower, which it should be from June till frosts nip it. I had a beautiful white form of *E. pelargoniflorum* for many years. It may not astonish you to learn I got my seed from Bitton. One Winter it died with Canon Ellacombe and with me, and but one seed remained between us, harvested here. I sowed it, it germinated, and I was able to restore it to Bitton, and two years later collected a seed off it which produced my last plant; but ever since then neither garden has produced a seed, and our old plants are no more. I hope it still exists somewhere, and I may yet get a seed. Kind, good reader, if you have it save me a nice, fat, brown one.

*E. romanum*, from the Coliseum's walls, mentioned in the account of the Spring garden, is at its best through the Summer months, and goes on flowering cheerily in the gravel path till nigh on to Christmas, and so does the white *E. amanum*, but golden *chrysanthum* prepares for Winter earlier in Autumn. *E. carvifolium* has the appearance of a small edition of *Manescavii*, and like it is of Spanish origin. I consider it an interesting plant, for not only are the leaves, as its name tells, very suggestive

of an umbelliferous plant, and especially one of the Caroways, but if one were given you to name, and you
happened to call in your nose to help you, as I often do,
you would, I think, in the absence of flowers, decide in
favour of the Caroway, so remarkably carrot-like is the
scent of a bruised leaf. Why on earth should a plant
mimic another so perfectly in scent and appearance? The
Marsh Samphire, *Inula crithmoides*, is a parallel instance
as understudying *Crithmum maritimum* equally well. Most
of the other species I grow are more distinctly saxatile and
form cushions of finely-cut leaves in dry and hot crevices
among the rocks. *E. absinthioides*, with grey leaves and
bright rose-pink blossoms, forms a large tuft in time, and
is a sturdy, good-hearted fellow ; but I prefer those that
have the wonderfully-shaded peacock eyes on the upper
petals, of which *E. macradenum* is one of the best, with
pale rose ground colour, and the eyes have grey-blue
marbled pupils and a rich purple black iris. What to
call a beautiful plant, the counterpart of the last in
all but the white ground colour of its flowers, puzzles
me, for I seldom see it twice with the same name
attached to it. *Guttatum* and *cheilanthifolium* are perhaps
the most frequent, but, whatever is its name, it is one of
the best of all, easy to grow and free-flowering. *E. supracanum* is lovely with its pink flowers and finely cut leaves
with a good imitation of hoar frost running along their
veins, but I cannot give it so good a character as to the
last, for it often dies here in Winter. *E. corsicum* is
fairly new to most gardens and a very distinct gain. It
loves a hot place, slightly overhung by a stone, and

# Geraniums

getting that, should flower all the Summer through and ripen seeds. They are so ridiculously small that I thought the first few I gathered could not be fertile; every one produced a healthy plant all the same, but they varied in colour, one being white with red veins and not so lovely as the rosy-crimson form. I expect it would get a bit flustered by a very severe Winter, especially if wet at the time the frost caught it; and it is lovely enough to merit a glass for the worst weather, even though the flowers are small, for they make up for that in number and brilliancy of colouring. There is yet another species, smaller still, but very beautiful, *E. chamae-dryoides*, often called *E. Reichardii*, one of the closest growing, so neat and tufty that a few inches will be the limits of an old colony, in which it beats *Arenaria balearica*, that will not learn to keep at home where planted and wanted. This might be called the Fairy Heron's-bill, for its white flowers, veined with pink, are small and dainty enough for a wedding bouquet for Queen Mab herself. It grows here among my collection of dwarf and pygmy plants, and is one of the choicest of them.

# CHAPTER VII

## A June Stroll

I FEEL that the last few chapters have been rather botanical, and savour too much of the study and its book-
shelves, so for a change let us take things as we find them
in the garden on this lovely morning in early June.

Before we leave the doorstep please pay a tribute of
admiration to *Crambe cordifolia,* not only for its beauty
but also for its good nature in growing where it does and
has done for nearly twenty years. The front of the house
is a network of foundations and areas with gratings over
them to let light down to underground windows, and it
must indeed be a long-suffering plant that can make itself
happy enough to sojourn there for long. I allow them
all an annual mulch in Spring of Wellson's patent manure
as a reward for their patience in adversity, and because it
is neither unsightly nor too evilly scented to place so near
the house ; and thereby enriched, Crambe gives two crops
of its handsome dark green leaves in each season and one
huge cloud every June, about five feet square (only, like
other clouds, it is round), of myriads of white flowers. It is
earlier than usual this season, for as a rule it makes its best
show about the end of the month. Cut the flowering stem
clean away when the flowers have fallen, and remove any

# A June Stroll

yellowing leaves, for in their senile decay, which generally occurs in July, both will exhale an appalling odour of decayed Cabbage stalks ; and also I advise keeping a sharp look-out on the undersides of the young leaves for eggs and larvæ of our two common Cabbage White Butterflies, which love them, and if let alone soon skeletonise them. The rest of this border is planted with the larger species of Acanthus. *A. mollis*, with its huge shining leaves and tall spikes of prickly blossoms, is handsome all the year except when snow or very severe frost destroys its great leaves. *A. spinosus* is the species of classical renown and architectural fame in the Corinthian capitals, and is one of the best to grow, its leaves adding the beauty of their finely-cut tracery to the colossal size of *mollis*. Its variety *spinosissimus*, from Dalmatia, is more finely cut still and covered with white spines, and though very remarkable in appearance is rather confused in its outline and lacks the beauty of its less spiny brother. *A. longifolius* has leaves longer than broad and something like those of *mollis*, but more deeply cut. It disappears altogether below ground in Autumn, but arises in a wondrous hurry as soon as Spring calls it, and flowers more freely than any kind I know. One I have as *A. Schottii* is very much like it ; though said to possess a branched flower-spike, it has been very stiff, straight, and pokerish so far each time it has flowered. *A. Caroli-Alexandri* ought to be something of unusual magnificence to carry off such a double-barrelled name, but up to the present has looked like a sick and sulky *spinosus*. That is one drawback of the Acanthus family, its members will sometimes sulk for years

# My Garden in Summer

after a removal; but once they forgive you they ramp, and if you try to curb this form of letting off steam peculiar to vigorous plants and heraldic animals by removing large portions to other sites, it is quite possible the large plants removed will begin the hunger-strike method once again and dwindle for a season or two ; while every atom of broken rootlet you have left in the bottom of the two-feet-deep hole you took them out of will sprout up into stronger plants than those removed.

I have a few things to show you in the so-called Damp-bed, so come across the lawn and answer with a word of encouragement the friendly barks of old Flo the Raven as we pass her favourite trees. The Wood Anemones that detained us here so long in April are only green carpets now ; but *Mertensia paniculata* recalls Spring with its many turquoise-blue bells, smaller but scarcely less beautiful than those of *M. pulmonarioides*, which most of us call *virginica*, but must not if we wish to agree with the *Kew Hand-list*, and which has been over for more than a month—I mean the plant, of course, not the book, for that has been out of date many *years*, and it is high time it flowered again and gave us up-to-date names with double *i* terminations ; but as it is still the most authoritative general list of plants it must be followed when no great monograph has superseded it. *Allium Schoenoprasum* var. *sibiricum* grows beside it, and is of a wonderfully pleasing shade of soft purple that always reminds me of old velvet curtains or stained glass. This is but a form of the Chives that are so good in salads and omelettes, but larger and brighter in its flowers; a British rarity and only to be

# A June Stroll

found wild in Cornwall both on the Lizard, whence I collected my original plant, and also near Tintagel, and I think our Cornish form handsomer than any I have found in the Alps. *Oreocome Candollei* has no longer a right to use that sonorous title, it seems, and has become identified with *Selenium tenuifolium;* but it is still the queen of umbellifers, with its almost transparent tender greenness and the marvellously lacy pattern of its large leaves. I think it the most beautiful of all fern-leaved plants, and keep a small colony here. Running wild round its feet is a fine white form of white *Lychnis Flos-cuculi* that I caught sight of one happy day through the gauze of my butterfly net when bug-hunting in the Norfolk Broads. For years I had kept an open eye for a good white form, for I had long possessed a poor one, a regular albino with pale yellowish leaves and stems, and even through the gauze I saw I had at last found what I longed for—large, pure-white flowers and the beautiful crimson stems and calyx of the pink plant. When I had dug up my find I looked further afield, and a few yards away was a soft flesh-pink one almost as charming ; and both of them are with me still, or at least their children are, for though both revert to some extent, the majority of their babes inherit their parents' good looks, and the common pink forms are pulled up as soon as noticed.

Two puzzles for botanists grow side by side in this bed in two Spiraeas that are not only totally unlike each other but mimic other well-known shrubs. One is *S. opulifolia* var. *aurea,* a beautiful golden-leaved thing, and so much

like a Guelder Rose in leaf and growth that anyone
might be pardoned for declaring it to be one. The other
is *S. laevigata,* and has rather glaucous entire leaves
and a clumsy thick habit of growth, and suggests a
Daphne, and most people if asked what it. is will so
name it. Now come across the other lawn and look at
a corner of the large herbaceous bed and some single
Paeonies ; the first was given me by Dr. Lowe, and is still
the finest single white one I know. It is a fine form of
*P. albiflora,* whose chief glories are its immense white
petals and the rich orange ball of stamens in the
centre. These are so conspicuous that a small boy
once asked me if that was orange flower, because he
said he could see the oranges in the centre nearly ripe.
Almost as good is a garden variety I bought as Water Lily,
but it has two ranks of petals, and I think this duplicity
detracts a little from its beauty, but it is very solidly white
and orange. Round the feet of these singles and a few
clumps of double *P. albiflora,* there is now a good show of
*Papaver umbrosum,* self-sown and hoe-spared at tidying-up
times to flame out now with its crimson flowers with deep
black bases. It is far too seldom allowed to sow itself in
gardens, but that is the way to grow it : a seedling can be
left when well placed, or easily moved if too near something too good to be smothered, at the autumnal cleaning
up, and what is a small rosette then will make a fine show
by the following June. I always prized it highly, but have
had an extra affection for it since I saw it growing among
the fallen blocks of marble on the Acropolis. A good form
of *Clematis integrifolia* is also worth looking at ; its large,

# A June Stroll

leathery flowers are such a rich sapphire blue. A few of them have come double each season, but are more curious than beautiful. I always admire the way the edges of each pair of its opposite leaves adhere tightly, and the boat-shaped leaves form a cosy cradle for the next pair, until they are old enough to appear in the world as protectors of a still younger couple or a flower-bud. *Lilium croceum* is a fine colour contrast next to the blue Clematis, but would look well almost anywhere, and being one of the hardiest and most adaptable of Lilies it is strange that one does not more often see broad masses of it planted among herbaceous plants.

It is one of our most reliable Lilies here, though I am sadly muddled in mind as to whether it is the true *L. croceum* of Southern Europe, or some garden form, or whether *croceum* is or is not more than a form of *bulbiferum*. I once worried myself over its literature, and then vowed I would leave the puzzle for someone else to solve or qualify himself for Colney Hatch, and as we have forsworn the study and its books to-day, I will not break vows. I always rejoice to see the Fire Lily in the Alps, whether springing out of rocky ledges as on the St. Gothard, and above Bobbio in the Cottians, or floating over the meadow grass as I saw it above Creto in Austria. I imagine from what books do agree in saying of it that it should be *L. bulbiferum*, but whenever I get close up to it and look for axillary bulbils that would be so easy to gather and to transport home, I never found a trace of them, and have supposed it was *L. croceum* in consequence. In the top of the new moraine bed in the rock garden I have planted side by

# My Garden in Summer

side what I have lately bought from Sündermann as *L. bulbiferum* and *L. croceum*, and one has a plentiful supply of bulbils in the axils of its leaves, and the other nary-a-one, but they are too weakly to flower yet awhile and let me see if there is any feature of their floral faces by which I can distinguish them. Close by the Lily is a fine orange-red glow from *Papaver orientale Silberblick*, a neat-habited variety, whose chief merit, however, lies in its hair having gone grey—at least it reminds me of a young man or woman with grey hair, for the anthers and usually black spot are silvered, and give it an interesting appearance as white locks do to a young face. Double White Rocket is in full blow, and its soft tone of white is a thing of its own. What is it most like ? It is whiter than the grey of an oyster, and greyer than the greenish gleam of Lowestoft china, and I think deserves a new name of its own. It is a bothersome plant to grow, as it wants pulling to bits and replanting so early in the season, just when there are so many far pleasanter operations to be performed among ripening fruits and opening flowers. So it is often neglected too long, and is abused as a difficult and miffy plant, when it is one's own procrastination and shirking of dull toil that have starved the poor thing. *Senecio Doronicum* is a mass of orange flowers, and running about into a wide clump so unlike its refined stay-at-home manners in Alpine pastures ; never in England does it fully wear the iron-grey sheen all over its leaves that is so attractive as a foil to the orange flowers up aloft on its native hills.

I have brought home what I hoped were specially endowed specimens, whose almost silvery sheen would be

# A June Stroll

a matter of family pride, but here they are as green as any boiled Winter Kale. We have skirted the large herbaceous bed all round now while picking out these few plants for notice, and on our return journey the large six-foot-high bush of *Salvia Grahamii* by the door of the conservatory catches our eyes, as it has begun its five months' display of crimson flowers. Twice it has been cut to the ground by frost, but the last few Winters have been kind to it, so please admire its dimensions and woody trunk as well as its brilliant flowers and pleasant odour, for who knows what next Winter may do to it? If you have it not, I advise you to pluck a spray to carry home and put in as cuttings, and by next Summer you will with good luck have a bush half as large as mine. Now you must come along the Eremurus bed to see two more Paeonies. The spikes of early Eremuruses, *Elwesianus* and its relations, are now covered with seedpods like minute Greengages instead of pink and white blossoms, but the yellow foxes' brushes of *E. Bungei* are beginning to light up from below. I like them best, though, just a little later, when the greater part of the spike has opened, and the lowest portion has turned to the rich orange-brown assumed by the overblown flowers, and which shades up so gradually into the pure yellow of newly-opened blooms and buds. The coppery varieties of *E. Warei* will not open for a week or two, but have already shot up tall green spikes. *E. shelfordi*, as it has been named, in defiance of botanical congresses and their many recommendations for the formation of names, is the one that does best here of those late-flowering forms, but *E. Olgae*, the latest of all, has always been a failure, dying of sunstroke, to all appearances, just when its flowers were ready to open. So here, where it once grew, is a really magnificent Paeony, a form of *P. officinalis* called Rivers-lea, in which the petals are wonderfully round and hollowed, and of a most remarkably deep scarlet surrounding a splendid boss of golden stamens. The flowers last longer than those of any other single-flowered Paeony I know, certainly for ten days, and I think even more in favourable seasons. A few steps further along, a particularly good form of *P. lutea* is flowering well, and holds its head up better than does the smaller-flowered, first-introduced plant. The waxy yellow of this flower makes it look like some magnified St. John's Wort of the shrubby kind, such as *Hypericum Hookeri* or the glorious *triflorum*, which, alas ! must live in a pot here, so as to be wintered indoors.

Tom Tiddler's Ground is very rich in gold and silver just now ; Tom must have changed a cheque on the Bank of Summer lately, for I have never seen the golden end more glowing, even though the yellow Tulips have long since gone, and the effect mostly depends on my golden-leaved plants. The Ribes is really golden, *Acer californica aurea* as bright a yellow as any leaf could be, and the cut-leaved Elder almost as brilliant. *Robinia pseudacacia aurea* is not fully out yet, and is a wonderfully delicate creamy yellow, that contrasts and yet blends with its brighter neighbours as well as the perianth does with the trumpet of a bicolor Daffodil.

The grey corner in front is as fresh and gleaming, in spite of the woolly covering to which many of its plants owe their whiteness, as a bag of new silver straight from the mint. *Cerastium tomentosum* adds white flowers to niveous leaves—aha! who said I was hard up for adjectives? *Atriplex Halimus* is as glittering as real silver, and the Artemisias in the front of the bed are just white velvet, while *Salvia argentea* is grey plush. The pink of the Oriental Poppy, Jenny Mawson, in the midst of all this silver looks simply delicious, like a strawberry-ice on a frosted glass plate. I think she is about the best of the salmon-pink ones, being so neat in habit as well as good in colour. What an advance these modern beauties are on the first dingy, faded affair, with straggling stalks and smothering leaves, we thought such a marvellous deal of twenty years or so ago as Salmon Queen. Queen Alexandra, Mrs. Perry, Lady Roscoe, and many others make that poor queen appear overworn, as Gerard and Parkinson would term it, and more like a muddy trout than a salmon. Lady Roscoe is rather wild in habit, but she lives in one of the Iris beds, as her colouring is so pleasing with pale lavender Irises. All of them will stand pretty rough treatment in the shape of cutting down, leaves and all, after flowering; in fact, such treatment generally induces them to send up a fresh supply of neat leaves and a few blossoms in early Autumn. The garden has presented me with a hybrid of its own making, much like the rup-orient one known as Carington-Lee, but mine, I believe, has *pilosum* instead of *rupifragum* for seed parent, and is a fine orange-scarlet, and has neat, thin stems to the large flowers. The same mother-plant mated once with a *P. somniferum* of sorts, and a singularly dainty child was the result, with glaucous, powdered leaves, thin stalks, and pale apricot flowers with a large white satin eye-spot on each petal. Of course, a cross between such widely different parents, the one annual and smooth, the other perennial and hairy as Esau, was not likely to bear fertile seed, and in late Autumn it was puzzled how to keep itself going. It tried the plan of making several juicy side shoots from the collar of its obviously annual tap-root, and the first frost reduced them to the appearance of boiled Spinach.

I am hoping a better fate may befall an exquisite race Mr. Perry brought me flowers of this Summer, I should say of Oriental and *somniferum* parents, for such soft shades of rosy red, such blue leaves, such black spotted centres as they possessed, are too lovely to be lost. *P. pilosum* and *rupifragum*, and its variety *atlanticum*, seed almost too freely here, but where they can be allowed to colonise they are very enjoyable for some six weeks of summer, especially if something can be done now and then to remove some of the hundreds of seedpods and prolong their flowering season. It is not a pleasing operation, as the stalks look ugly if one just cuts off the pods and leaves them of full length, and it is hard to snip among the vast array of buds without cutting as many buds as pods. *P. Heldreichii* and *P. californicum* turned out pretenders, and just forms of one or other of my two old friends *pilosum* and *rupifragum*, but I forget which was which, as it was years ago they imposed on my, credulity, and I removed their labels when disillusioned. The rock garden at this season is full of Poppies. *P. sinense* is a neat, perennial fellow with light orange-coloured flowers borne singly on thin

Poppies and Anthericum.   By Hugh L. Norris.
(See p. 125.)

stalks, and it makes such an attractive tuft of light green leaves under the flowers that it is well suited to grow among rocks. Miss Willmott gave me this uncommon species, and I do not remember seeing it elsewhere than at Warley and now here. Thanks to her kindness also I have the beautiful biennial *P. caucasicum*. Its winter rosettes of blue-grey leaves would alone make it worth growing, and its tall spires of orange-coloured flowers are so uncommon in appearance, rather like some Meconopsis, that it is well worth sowing and leaving to sow itself ever afterwards in either a rough rock bank or the ordinary border, where the hoe will not harass its babes. *P. aculeatum* from S. Africa of all strange homes for a hardy Poppy, also known as *horridum* and *gariepinum*, is something like it, but rougher altogether, not so brilliant in the orange shade, and the rosettes are hairy, Brussels-sprout-green all the Winter, instead of the Seakale-leaf blue colouring of the Caucasian species. *P. pavonium* is only an annual, but I like to see it reappear, with its strangely blotched eye which gives it the name of Peacock Poppy. This eye varies somewhat, but is generally a crimson spot that would go badly with the scarlet ground colour, were it not ringed with a black horseshoe, and sometimes a grey marbling as well. One of the loveliest of all Poppies is *P. arenarium*, which I got seed of many years ago from my dear old friend Mr. Thompson of Ipswich but cannot hear of anywhere nowadays. It used to sow itself so freely in the rock garden that I never troubled to save seeds, but lately it has failed to reappear. It is biennial, a small edition of *P. umbrosum*, but the leaves are more

# My Garden in Summer

beautifully cut, and the flowers the most brilliant scarlet that can be imagined, while each petal has a large, indigo-blue spot at its base, so rich and wonderful in colour that it was a joy to see. I have hopes that if I stir up the bank on which they grew some seeds may germinate that now lie buried, so I am planning an earthquake for that range of miniature mountains, as *P. glaucum* appears self-sown whenever I dig up a bit of ground where it once grew and seeded.

Of course the most delightful of all annual Poppies is that wonderful race Mr. Wilks has patiently and skil-fully brought to such perfection of orange and salmon shades from his original wild find of a white-edged Field Poppy. Thanks to his generosity thousands now enjoy his Shirley Poppies, and I among them annually beg with the rest of the privileged Fellows of the R.H.S., for some seed of the latest crop, and grow them according to his wise instructions and even (though it goes sorely against the grain) obey him literally, and refrain from thanking him until the delight of their lovely shades and silky folded and crumpled petals round their gold-dusted eyes compels me to tell him how I am enjoying them. It took me a long while to learn how to cut them for the house, so that they would not flag and faint within an hour. They never flag now when cut, nor do they fail to last in full beauty for three days if I carry a jug of *hot* water (*hot*, not tepid) down to their bed in the evening, after dinner for preference, and cut the buds that have straightened up their necks ready to open on the morrow or perhaps the day after, and any flowers that have just split the calyx lobes and are showing their colour. I put each one into my jug so that it is almost up to its neck in hot water as soon as I have cut it, and I put jug and all in the bathroom for the night, because I love to see them half open, bursting off the sepals, or even in freshly-escaped glory full of crinkles and folds, the first thing in the morning. Opened thus and transferred to other vases, they will generally last for three days unless stood in a violent draught, or shaken by being moved about, and, moreover, will increase in beauty, for they grow in size daily, until the anthers and petals all descend with a rush and make what the housemaids declare to be a horrid mess, but is often a wonderful display of blended shades dusted over with golden pollen, almost as good to look at as the young flowers themselves. If you cut them regularly and remove the seedpods of the fallen flowers, the patch will continue giving you large, long-stemmed buds for a much longer period than if allowed to bear seed too early. Of course, any plant of an extra lovely orange-salmon shade, or with a more than usually beautiful white eye or lace edging to its mantle, may be allowed to bear one or more seed heads, and in that case I advise your tying a piece of white worsted round their necks, so as to see them easily when removing undesired pods. I suppose everyone grows *P. nudicaule*, one of the most northern in range of known flowering plants, and everyone ought to grow its southern miniature representative, *P. alpinum*, for any gritty mound sprinkled with a pinch of its seed will become a spot of beauty and remain so for years.

# My Garden in Summer

The fringed form var. *laciniatum* has taken possession of part of my rock garden, but I do not like it as much as the lovely, round-flowered, typical form. The Sunday-school boys who review my flowers on Sunday afternoons with me call it the Ragtime Poppy, and it amuses them vastly. I have already praised a group of *Meconopsis heterophylla* in the rock garden in Spring, but those were self-sown plants that had battled through the Winter, and by now are beginning to look shabby and full of seedpods, but those sown in Spring are still in full beauty. It is one of my most favourite plants, its deep orange-red flowers are so unlike anything else in flower at this season, reminding one of one of the best of Orange Tulips, *Tulipa Gesneriana aurantiaca*, but the Meconopsis has an additional charm in a singularly rich brown-madder eye that would ensure a First Class Certificate for the Tulip if it could be transferred to it. The accompanying illustration shows how freely this little American Poppy flowers, but cannot convey any idea of its glorious colouring.

We seem to have run all round the garden after these Poppies, but only mentally, and we are still standing by the grey corner of Tom Tiddler's ground, for I want you, before you move away, to admire a group of a seedling Delphinium that we love very much. It is a tall, strong grower, and has a perfect Bella Donna blue colour and a good white eye, and yet is as robust, hardy, and chop-up-able as any of the fat-growing, easy-going sorts that poison one's eye with baleful mixtures of blue and lilac. We call it Delphinium Dining-room-window, as that describes the position in which it first showed its pure

Meconoysis heteroyhylla.   (See y. 130.)

turquoise colouring, and where the old plant still resides. Here in the middle of the silver variegated plants, and backed by the purple-leaved colony that makes the foil for the gold and silver plants, it shows off its beauty to fullest advantage. *Silene fimbriata* grows at its feet, and is rather a coarse plant, but produces large, pure white flowers, with their petals fringed as finely as the silken tassels that accompany dance programmes, and if some bunches of the seed heads are cut off now and then will continue flowering till frost comes. In front of it a colony of *Verbascum phoeniceum* is trying to reproduce the effect achieved by the lilac and purple Tulips last month, but not quite so richly. This species is not made enough of in most gardens ; the light spikes of bloom vary wonderfully in colour from pure white through rosy-mauve and lavender to deepest purple, and a little selection soon ensures pleasant blendings. It is truly perennial, and if the central flower-stem is cut out when it is becoming lanky and too much devoted in its lower two-thirds to maternal duties, fresh young spikes will spring up in a wonderfully short time. *Funkia undulata variegata* is planted among these Mulleins, and its waved leaves are so beautifully rich in cream, to borrow a phrase from the dairy, that they lighten the general effect very pleasantly, as the Mullein's own leaves are rather sombre.

*Olearia stellulata* is now all white flowers which have snowed under its leaves, and is effective as a high-light, taking the place of the Poet's Daffodils of April days, while *Chrysanthemum maximum* and white Phloxes are planted just behind, to follow on later. I like to cut out

# My Garden in Summer

all I can of the old flowering shoots of this Olearia as soon as their snow has melted, and though it looks like reducing the size of one's bush at the time, it is not so at all, for the young silvery shoots profit enormously by the space and extra share of sap thus allowed them, and build up a very superior bush to reward the hand that wisely wounded it. A group of three well-rooted cuttings planted among herbaceous plants, and treated with kind severity at pruning time, forms a much more lucrative silver mine than the " hole in the ground owned by a liar," as someone so aptly defined the kind of mine that so often yawns for the speculating public.

Some yellow Lilies now stand up well among the ripening leaves of the yellow Tulips. A large zinc label proclaims the tallest and most fully out as *Lilium col-chicum*, but the *Kew Hand-list* insists this should be *L. monadelphum* var. *Szovitzianum*, which is better to remember, and perhaps to shout at one's dog if he is about to curl up for a snooze on some choice seedlings, than to write on a label. Anyway, the form bought under the simpler name is here taller and earlier than those labelled *L. monadelphum*, which you can see have at present got no further than the green bud stage, for here is a large clump of them close beside the earlier form, whose brilliant yellow and peppering of fine black specks is now so attractive, rather outshining its humble and evil-scented neighbour, *Lilium pyrenaicum*, the old, old Yellow Martagon of cottage gardens, and still older Yellow Mountain Lily of Gerard. I am fond of it and its reliable, sturdy ways, but of course it must yield in beauty before *L.*

Lilium monadelphum.

(See p. 132.)

# A June Stroll

*Hansonii* from Japan, which later on makes a fine glow of yellow behind those now flowering, but across the path and among some good forms of Hart's-tongue ferns, of which I must write some day, as they are so very good. Still farther on, but visible from where we stand, a planting of *Primula Bulleyana* in another bay of the fern beds is doing great things, and has expanded its lower tier of orange flowers, and makes a good glow of colour above its cheerful, yellow-green leaves, with their conspicuous red midribs that help the general effect so much. Now I have a feeling that it ought to be luncheon time, and after so much running about we need it, so we will make for the house, and *en route* please notice *Briza maxima*, the Great Quaking Grass, self-sown and left where needed in patches, or isolated plants which of course are the finest, but not so effective as a clump a yard across. Its large pendant heads, wonderfully like Hops, are as lovely as any green thing in the garden at this moment ; their light yellow-green goes so well with their own rich green leaves, and also contrasts with the deeper shade of the edging of *Saxifraga (Megasea) cordi-*
*folia,* behind which this Grass grows just here, in the opposite bed to that given over to Tom Tiddler's gold and silver plants. Later on the heads turn yellow and then buff, and still later the stalks ripen to a rich foxy burnt-sienna red, and especially just before sunset a large patch lights up and looks wonderfully brilliant even among the flaming colours of a July border.

# CHAPTER VIII

## A June Afternoon

Is it too babyish to go on making believe, and so inviting you to take an after-lunch stroll? It is so fashionable to keep young nowadays, when grandmothers take Tango lessons, and octogeraniums, as the aged gardener called himself, dress and behave like the youngest fresh from school. I admire their pluck, even if I do not care for their skimpy skirts, and I hope a bit of pretending on our own part may help to keep us young. Besides, I really did do as I am describing on the day I wandered round to make the notes that are growing into these two chapters.

So come and sit on the semi-circular white seat on the lawn, and we will have our coffee brought out to us there, as it is pleasantly shaded in the afternoon by the Scots Pines and big Beech behind it. As we sit there we see a round bed in the lawn, that I can recall in childhood's days primly bedded out with scarlet and white Zonal Pelargoniums in the centre, and blue Lobelia as an edging. I seized upon this bed one day in Spring when I arrived home from a visit to Dr. Lowe with a bundle of treasures that needed homes. So I threw to the winds its Wallflower tenants, and packed in many of my new friends, and there some of them remain to this day. Here in April we

# A June Afternoon

admired the lovely form of Wood Anemone that Dr. Lowe called in the past, and I in the present still call, Leeds' variety. Its flowers have gone, of course, by now, but the little American yellow Violet, *V. scabriuscula*, still keeps up a show among the Anemone leaves. Just now the glory of the bed is *Stylophorum diphyllum*, a seedling of which came from Dr. Lowe, and has colonised the bed as thickly as I can permit, and has emigrated, not only to other parts of my garden, but to those of my friends. For, easy as it is to grow, and beautiful as are its large yellow Poppy-like flowers and its glaucous leaves, I very seldom meet with it and its relations in gardens, and most of my visitors are glad to add it to their collection. It comes from N. America, so is perfectly hardy ; a good perennial, that will grow into a large but neat clump, and needs no division or fussing with for half a dozen years at least. It flowers from May onward for months, if you remove most of the seedpods before they become too large to weaken the bud supply, and too attractive to be spared ; for they grow into handsome, egg-shaped, hanging pods of a charming grey-blue colour, and very good to look at. It is not well to look at your fingers, though, if you use them unclad, as I generally do in gardening, to remove these seeds, for the plant is closely related to the Greater Celandine, *Chelidonium majus*, and has even shared its generic name at times, and like it and their cousin Bocconia, exudes an orange-coloured juice when broken that stains abominably. That is the worst of my style of gardening, my finger nails are never even respectable, until I have been away from home and visiting friends who do

# My Garden in Summer

not require or permit any help in their garden operations, for at least a week, when I scarcely recognise the pink and white terminations of my fingers as really part of them. Two hours after my return we have changed all that, though, for I cannot garden in gloves. I make a start sometimes, when a lecture from a shocked friend, or the desire to appear fairly clean-fingered at some approaching festive gathering, has aroused ambitions. But sooner or later a bit of earth gets inside a finger of the glove, or I find I am pulling heads off weeds and leaving their tails in to multiply and replenish the earth, and off goes the beastly glove, and my freed fingers do their work so much better without it that it remains off, unless I have to prune such prickly customers as Roses and Brambles, or pull leaves off the greater sword-leaved Eryngiums or the Symphytums, these last two being armed with small bristles of silica as sharp as broken glass.

For a short period I persevered with a most refined and elegant idea I read about somewhere, and carried a cake of soap in a metal soapbox in my garden basket, and scratched it diligently like a cat claws a tree or the leg of one's best Chippendale chairs, until my nails were so well fil'ed with soap there was no room for dirt, and, of course, as some popular song or saying (I forget which) put it, "It all comes out in the wash." But I have long since got used to broken and stumpy nails and a roughened and dyed forefinger any seamstress would shudder at, and I am hoping my friends are getting used to them also. I cannot stand and give orders, and watch them being carried out, for long, without my fingers itching to be in

# A June Afternoon

the pie. If I have gently laid out a root on the soft, newly-dug soil, I feel I have done the best that can be done for it, stretched it just as far as it could and should go without forcing it unnaturally, laid it in the softest bed and so on, but to watch the operation, even though just as skilfully performed, fills one with doubts. Is not the root being strained at its junction with the stem? Would it not be better a little more to the right? The professional gardener is so clever and clean with his tools, too, that he very seldom handles the soil or even messes the handle of his tools. But I cannot acquire his knack; my hands go into the soft thrown-out heap to sprinkle it round the newly-placed roots, to press it down on one side, or make a little hole to push a tributary root into; so on any but the driest days, or when working in the sand of the moraine or Iris patch, I and all the tools I am using are covered with mud in a few minutes. I hope the precious things I plant thus fussily are the better for it all. But let us go back to our Celandine Poppy, take a good look at its handsome two-inch-wide flowers, and note how many of them it bears, and if you have fallen a victim to its charms we will hunt for a yearling babe that will move easily and be thankful for a less crowded home. Round in the pergola garden I can show you another species, *Stylophorum lasiocarpum* from China, with coarser and greener leaves, not nearly so good a plant as the American cousin, but interesting for its remarkable seedpods, about four inches long, and narrow and cylindrical like hairy cucumbers, the right size for a doll's dinner-party. This species is not much

more than biennial, and I rather think will make way for
its betters in this good bed, finding a home somewhere
round the feet of certain shrubs that will look better for
a carpet.    A near relative of this, *Dicranostigma* (formerly
*Cheliodonium*) *Franchetianum*, generally reappears annually
self-sown in the rock garden.   In a few mild Winters
young plants will survive, and come into flower in May,
but it is best treated, or rather allowed to treat itself, as an
annual.   It makes pretty, flat rosettes of grey, many-lobed
leaves, from the centre of which come slender branching
stems that bear numerous bright yellow flowers, and after
them slender pods full of black seeds that one scatters
hopefully for next year's flowering.   *Hylomecon japonica* is
another closely-related plant, and has been reckoned both
a *Chelidonium* and a *Stylophorum* by different authors.   It
is very beautiful, and has richer coloured flowers than its
near relations, but I can never keep it here for long,
and at present am not only out of it, but alas! do not
know where to get it again.

Now let us leave our coffee-cups on the seat and go
into the pergola garden by the path on our right hand.
Please admire the stem of the great Scots Pine at the
corner, as it is the finest in the garden, but can be
matched and perhaps beaten by some up in the wood
at the back of Queen Elizabeth's ponds, in a fine planting
of pines about two hundred years old that form the distant
inky-black outline I see against the western sky all through
the Winter as the background to the rock garden, but lose in
Summer, when the still older Limes of the avenue reclothe
themselves and cut off the distant view.   The old Scots-

# A June Afternoon

man makes this corner rather dry and barren, so as you see I have grouped various Lavenders, that can stand a long time between their drinks, at his feet. One of the best of all is nearly in flower, and even in the bud stage is good to look at, for the calyx is a rich purple long before the corolla expands. It is a very dwarf form, and was given me by a friend who used to come to see the garden when staying in the neighbourhood. She told me she saw it first in a Scotch garden, and found it was more sweetly scented than other Lavenders. I prize it highly, and call it Miss Dunington's Lavender after its donor, and shall do so till I find it has an older name. I have collected all the other dwarf Lavenders I hear of or meet with, and so far none of them exactly matches it, or comes up to it for dwarfness of habit, richness of colour, sweetness of scent, and, above all, earliness of flowering. I picked some the other day for a lady to smell how good it was, and she said, " Why, it's almost as sweet as Lavender-water!" As you stand here by the big Pine you can see that I have planted an edging of this Lavender down either side of the central walk of the pergola for some little distance, and it is now making a good show of purple, but as it is rather overhung and shaded by the climbers here, it is later than in the border at our side and the original old plant in the rock garden, and I fear this edging is not going to do itself justice, as it gets rather drawn in its late summer growth, but for an open situation I think it must be the ideal Lavender for a dwarf hedge.

Two specially delightful souvenirs of good friends greet me on the left in the bed at the north side of the new wall. The first is this singularly glowing, scarlet-orange, double Welsh Poppy which took to itself this extra glory of colour on Mr. Farrer's rock garden at Ingleborough. I never saw any so deep in colour till this race met my amazed eyes on my first visit to him. He kindly offered me a babe from the nursery if I would risk its taking after its parents, or the alternative risk of moving an adult of assured family beauty, and thrust a fork into my hand for me to help myself when I chose the middle-aged specimen, trusting to my luck and skill in moving things, and wanting to see that colour at once in my garden, and so here it sits in the shade of the wall, as glowingly lovely as in Yorkshire. The other is a very dainty, narrow-leaved Veronica, evidently a hybrid child of *V. parviflora*, by a father unbeknown but probably a blue-flowered garden variety. It appeared at Warham Rectory, where it so excited my admiration that it was not long before a nicely-rooted cutting was set aside for me to carry off. It is a very graceful-habited plant, and its long, narrow spikes are like those of its mother in form, but of varying shades of blue according to the ages of the flowers composing them.

The old pillar at the corner of the wall is worth examining, for it is a most beautiful example of old brickwork ; the bricks have been rubbed and are most beautifully laid, and the fine lines of the mortar between them are a great joy to look at. Furthermore, it is of a most curious shape, as it forms a diamond in section, and the angle that is towards the walk is very acute. Also it has a beautifully moulded stone base and capstone of the same diamond shape. I believe it is about two hundred years old, as it came from Gough Park, a neighbouring estate. My father pulled down the house on it, and, as I have already mentioned, many treasures such as scraps of pavement and moulded stones, and the leaden ostriches that guard the river bridge, came from its ruins. This pillar was standing there at the end of a long wall, and when my father planned cutting off a portion of the garden for a newly-built house, he found it would be best to start a length of wall at right angles to the old one from this very corner. I had longed for this lovely pillar to live nearer to me, that I might see it oftener, and so found it easy work to persuade my kind father to let me try to move it. I borrowed his estate masons and talked it over, and it ended in cutting it through half-way up, and so sacrificing one course of bricks. Then by boarding it round and lashing it with strong ropes the two halves were got into a cart and brought up here. I argued that a pillar of such beauty would be wasted without a wall to jut out from as it had always done; and so the wall was eventually planned and built to suit the pillar, and I obtained what I had long desired, a south wall in the garden. The pillar always reminds me of the tale of the Irishman who took a button to a charitable lady and asked her if she would just be so kind as to sew a shirt on to it for him; and so I call my wall the Irishman's shirt. When the pillar was re-erected and its capstone on, we hoisted a round stone ball up on to it, and directly I stood a little way off to see the effect, I was alarmed to see that the top of the capstone sloped downwards away from me so much that the stone looked as if a slight push would set it rolling, and off it would go. But the head mason declared he had levelled it correctly, so I had the spirit-level brought, and I climbed up to investigate for myself, and lo and behold! the bubble centred as perfectly as possible. I went down again and looked—we both looked; the stone ball seemed absolutely dangerous—any puff of wind must surely blow it off. Then we went round and looked at it from the other side, and now could hardly believe our eyes, for the capstone seemed to fall the other way, and the ball would now be rolled off by a breeze from the opposite quarter of the compass; and then it dawned on us that it was the very peculiar slantin-dicular (I don't know the right name for it, so that must do) outline of the pillar and its cap that produced by its too rapidly diminishing perspective an optical illusion of not being level and always sloping downward away from whichever side you viewed it from. See now how unsafe it looks; you wouldn't dare to stand just on the further side of it with a nor'-easter blowing, would you? When I had planted the bed on the south side of the wall full of the tender things I had been reserving for such a sheltered place for several years past, I showed it, with pride in my bold daring, to a friend from Cornwall who knows what severe Winters can do even in that favoured land, and he said, "What fun you will have next Spring filling up the gaps." So many of its doubtfully hardy occupants had already come from his generous hand that I think he was not surprised when I asked him if that was an invitation to visit him next Spring with a hamper.

# A June Afternoon

As I planted at least thrice as many things as there was really room for on that wall and the Winters have been wonderfully kind to them, there have not been very many gaps *so far* (yes, italics for "so far," Mr. Printer, if you please, for you thus help me to touch wood in print). I still expect a day will come, though, when even a south wall will prove insufficient protection for some of my most daring plantings. Let us look at them, and then you can tell me what you think will go the next time our thermometers drop to zero, as they did in 1905; and perhaps you can think of something good you have, a seedling or a cutting, to replace the dead monarch. *Le roi est mort, vive le roi,* is a good motto for a garden. Nothing is allowed to grow up the button pillar, of course ; but we plant up to the very hem of the shirt. *Grevillea rosmarinifolia* is in the border away from the wall, and ought to remain and flourish there. So should *Colletia spinosa,* for it is very happy as near as at Aldenham, which, however, stands on higher ground than we, and escapes our valley frosts. The hybrid Citranges I have already written about, but two fine neighbours of theirs have hitherto had no mention. *Adenocarpus anagyrus* is just now a mass of pure yellow flowers in spikes, each flower as large as those of the Spanish Broom, and exhaling a most delicious scent that I seem to know and cannot classify. It is essentially the smell of indoor plants, I think a mixture of *Cytisus racemosus* and Tuberose or Stephanotis. I wish this lovely thing had been planted against the wall, for I fear it is one of those that a bad Winter will shake up. *A. decorticans* has grown into an

# My Garden in Summer

equally large shrub, but has never yet flowered so freely as *anagyrus;* the buds seem to form too early and then get destroyed by frosts. *A. foliolosa,* which does well out of doors in Ireland, failed here even though planted against the wall. *Boussingaultia baselloides* was planted against the wall and ramped up strings and flung itself over to the other side, seized hold of its neighbours and tried to strangle them, gave us a few inconspicuous but sweetly-scented flowers, and then went to squash and looked as shiny and insipid as a boiled lettuce, with the first frost. Nevertheless, it came up better than ever next year, and I thought just two shoots, and two only, should be allowed up the wall that season, so I guided them to friendly strings and tore up all the others, and shortly after went to gather plants in the Alps.

On my return I found Boussingaultia had behaved as Jack's beanstalkily as ever, so now he has been ejected, and *Passiflora coerulea* Constance Elliott may have some peace and be able to produce her lovely, carved ivory flowers without a cold poultice of Boussingaultia leaves slapped on to their white faces. *Acacia Baileyana* was my wildest bid for a startling achievement in acclimatisation, and my most decisive snub from Fate, for next Spring it was as dead as Queen Anne. So was *Plumbago capensis,* of which I had hoped a breaking up from the base would be possible, and if the wall were not so crowded by now I would try, try again with this plant. *Mutisia Clematis* came up a shattered invalid next season, but never again, and *Manettia bicolor* was not much happier, for though it reappeared it was too late to make much show before

Ctenocarpus amazyrus. (See p. 1.)

# A June Afternoon

frost cut it down again, although in the first season, in spite of being very small when put out, it had flowered well, and kept on after sharp frosts had killed other things. A third season it was still more unhappy, and hadn't the heart to twine up its string, and now it has gone. *Olearia insignis* at the foot of the wall, where the house for shelter during showers is built out and so screens it from the east, is growing leaves that look ridiculously large for its diminutive stature, but as it is still quite a babe has not yet given us one of its Celmisia-like flowers. *Myrtus tarentina*, with its close-set, deep green leaves, looks happy right in the corner, and *Clematis Armandii* has proved a great success up the pillar of the house, and is now half over the roof and right across the front of the house. Its trifoliate leaves are wonderfully handsome, whether the light green, glossy fellows of this year or the duller, deep green, hard-as-leather veterans of last year or the year before. *Solanum jasminoides* is trying to cover up as much of the eastern end of the roof as the Clematis has of the western, and is quite welcome to it. Round its bare stem grows a very handsome form of *Asparagus acutifolius*, named as var. *orientalis* at Kew, and said to be a Palestine variety that is found up to the very top of Mt. Tabor, but my plant originated from a berry a good friend gathered for me in Sicily. It is handsomer than the ordinary *acutifolius*, as the cladodes are thicker and of a richer green. But I am fond of *acutifolius* in its natural form too, and have a grand old specimen in the rock garden, that came to me as a fledgeling from the woods near Hyères. It flowered freely one Autumn some years ago, but too late to ripen

# My Garden in Summer

fruit, and one Winter it was cut to the ground by frost, and again one Spring by me, as it was such a tangle of prickles, that I shrank from the toil of clearing out the dead growths. I see it will have to be shorn down again soon by one of us for the same reason, but I hope Winter will leave it for me to do. The shoots do not grow so high if they have no mass of old growths to pierce through, else I should cut down this rock garden specimen oftener. *Gaya Lyallii*, formerly called Plagianthus, is growing well on the wall, much faster than another planted in the open. When I put it here it still bore its infantile leaves with their crenate edges, and it was not until last year that it shot out flowering growths with the adult leaves, something between those of a Lime and a Mulberry, and this season these shoots have borne the beautiful white flowers, like extra delicately formed Cherry blossoms. *Eucalyptus pulverulenta* has done very well against the wall, and has made quite a stout stem, and branched out into a large head, in spite of our having decapitated it twice already. I think I shall now leave it for winter winds to cut back, as it seems to want to look over the wall so much, and it does look so handsome and astonishingly blue appearing above the red bricks when seen from behind.

Some of the autumn-flowering things I will leave for future mention, so will pass them now and notice that Banksia Roses are running up, and, I hope, will some day scramble about the stone ball on the top of the rather clumsy-looking square pillar, built at the opposite end of the wall to that occupied by the button pillar. The wall is continued at a right angle here, after the big pillar, and is ramped down until it ends in a shorter pillar, and this low portion has been planted with *Diospyros Kaki*, grown from seeds of some extra good Persimmons I bought at the Army and Navy Stores, and having eaten and enjoyed them, I thought I would plant some of their pips. They are slowly growing up the wall, but are far too young to think of flowering yet. A prettily variegated form of the white Jasmine scrambles about on the short pillar, which supports a very fine old lead boar which, like the ostriches, came from Gough Park, and all three are figured in Mr. Weaver's book on English Lead.

As we return along the flagged walk in front of the wall I want you to look at a curious plant spreading on the ground. It has narrow leaves of a coppery-bronze colour, turning to a deep green as they age, about two inches long and a quarter of an inch wide, with charmingly-toothed edges. The stems hug the ground, and it forms a close carpet of these handsome leaves, which rather suggest some Berberis. But it is a Bramble, *Rubus parvus*, and remarkable for being the only Bramble from New Zealand, with unifoliate leaves. Looking among them you will see it has rather pretty white blossoms, somewhat like those of a Wild Strawberry. It is said to bear large, juicy, yellow fruits at home in New Zealand, but I have seen no sign of them here as yet. Twining up a support is a nice young specimen of *Rubus cissoides pauperatus*, sometimes erroneously called *R. australis*, another New Zealander, whose leaf-blades are reduced to a mere scrap at the end of each

of the three long midribs. These midribs are, each
of them, some three inches long, and freely beset with
white prickles. The two side leaflets start away at right
angles from the central one, which looks like a continuation of the petiole, and so forms a cross if a single leaf is
examined, but when looked at from a little distance the
tangle of shoots appears like a confused, leafless mass of
stalks and prickles. It is known in English gardens in
three distinct forms, this one without leaf-blades, and
one with well-developed, dark green leaf-blades, and the
third intermediate and very variable as to the amount of
leaf-blade it possesses. I believe they are called Bush
Lawyers in New Zealand, as it is said that if they do not
get hold of you in one way they will in some other. The
leafless form has a very quaint effect if kept closely tied
in to a central support, looking from a distance like a
pillar of smoke, but it is a nasty scratchy plant to handle.
*Rubus bambusarum* covers one of the pergola poles, and
is attractive when full of young white growths and new
leaves showing their bright silvery undersides. Its flowers
are hideous, with minute petals of an unpleasantly acid
purple-crimson, and the orange-coloured fruits too small and
dull in colour to be attractive except to birds and small boys.
Close by it grows a fine old bush of *Viburnum tomentosum
plicatum*, and now its horizontally spreading boughs are
clad from stem to tip with large white snowballs, and it
is as good a sight as anything in the garden. It is a pity
it is so much shut in here, for it grows just where the
Vine pergola and the main pergola join, and has not sufficient space to sprawl out as far as it might ; but, after all, it

The Vine Pergola and Viburnum tomentosum var. plicatum.   (See p. 148.)

# A June Afternoon

is sheltered, and perhaps flowers better for the occasional trimming we are bound to give it; anyway, it would be hard this season to find a vacant space on its boughs to stick on another half dozen snowballs.

Round its feet I have gathered a collection of varieties of Solomon's Seal, results of the open eye that I keep, when in other gardens and subalpine woods for forms I do not recognise as being already at home here. These range in height from about six inches to eighteen, and vary much in size and form of flower and the date of flowering. Of course they are but foliage plants now in June, but very beautiful still with their arching stems and rich green leaflets, but to keep them so we have to be ever on the watch for a villainous Sawfly, whose ugly grey larvae if unchecked will reduce the leaves to bare ribs, destroying their beauty, and of course weakening the plant. The flies appear in April and early May, and are jet black, wings and all; they fly in the sunshine, and are easy to catch as they are rather poor as aeronauts, but rely on one successful trick for escape; this is not looping the loop, but dropping to earth and trusting to overhead foliage or cracks in the soil for hiding. I try annually what my horny hands can do to destroy the mothers of my future enemies, and I find clapping my hands sharply on a buzzing black lady is a better and quicker plan than using a butterfly net to catch her. They do not feed on anything else but Polygonatum and Convallaria, so far as I know, and so we ought to be able to get rid of them by watching the beds of Lily of the Valley and Solomon's Seal for several succeeding seasons. I do not think you could easily spray the plants sufficiently to kill the larvae, as they feed under the leaves for the most part of their lives, and a waxy powder prevents the under surface of these leaves from being wetted. So we watch in June for signs of the foe, of which the first is a little network of windows on one of the lower leaves of a stem, and if detected early a single application of the human thumb and forefinger is sufficient to reduce a whole family to pulp, as at that early stage they live and feed in a crowd. Two out of our three bushes of *Buddleia globosa* reside close by where we now stand, and are providing free drinks for the bees and a delicious scent of heather-honey for my nose if I apply it to the golden cowslip-balls in miniature, after I have shaken off the bees, which might not behave kindly to my proboscis, mistaking it for a rival to their own in the honey-gathering trade. What a glorious thing this old plant is when in full vigour, and how curious that it is so seldom you see a really fine specimen. In a very severe Winter it is liable to get badly cut back in an exposed situation, but it is very worthy of a sheltered nook and careful treatment, which I take it means the pruning out of old flowering wood and weak shoots as soon as possible after flowering is over. It is altogether wrong to prune at all in Spring, as one can do with the Chinese newcomers the *B. variabilis* forms, as *globosa* flowers on wood ripened in Summer, they on the same year's growths. So *B. variabilis* can be cut back to the bone of the main stem, or even down to ground level, and will throw out all the more vigorous shoots for it, and flower at the end of each of them.

# A June Afternoon

The form known as var. *magnifica* is out and away the best, and we have grubbed up most of the others to make room for more of it, but have left a few seedling forms that we value for flowering rather earlier or later, and so prolonging the season of the banquets for butterflies by day and ball suppers for moths by night. One of the greatest charms of these purple Buddleias is this attractiveness to insects, for if there is a Peacock, Painted Lady, or Admiral Butterfly in the neighbourhood it is certain to spend many of the sunny hours flitting over or sucking at the long purple spikes, and driving off a Large Cabbage White or two from a specially desirable bunch of honeypots; but the Small Tortoiseshells seem capable of holding their own, and so are respected by the larger insects. Then after dark the Buddleia spikes are visited by most of the Noctuae then on the wing, and an acetylene lamp reveals their identity, and the rarities are easy to box from the lower spikes or to tap into a net from those over one's head. These *B. variabilis* forms will grow into regular trees if carefully treated when young and got up into a good strong stem or two; and another way in which we like to grow them here is to tie them in to a tall pole and cut them back hard every Spring, which treatment produces a pillar of silvery shoots, and later on, generally late in July, the shoots hang out gracefully, each one ending in a cluster of flowers.

Do you know the style of beauty of a King Crab? There used to be a tank of them at the Brighton Aquarium in my young, and its palmy, days, and they

# My Garden in Summer

have always been well represented in the Naples Aquarium, which to my idea is one of the best things in that rather squalid city. These King Crabs, you may remember, have a large, hooded shell that covers them completely, as would a dish-cover, when they sit down on the sand floor, and it has a look of leather but is of a beautiful blue-grey colour. Close to my Buddleias is a plant that always reminds me of those large crustaceans, *Funkia Fortunei,* so large and round and blue are its leaves. In fact I can almost fancy one will rise up on spindly toes and scuttle away to sit down in the shade of the big pink double Deutzia in the centre of the bed. *Allium Ostrowskianum* catches one's eye too, as it is of an unusual shade of light crimson, and stands up well here backed by the leaves of some clumps of single Paeonies mostly out of flower, *P. Veitchii* alone bearing a few of its drooping, beautifully formed, but alas! magenta flowers. Its habit and much-divided leaves make it a very attractive plant, though, and until I can get a white variety of it I must forgive its violent colouring. Here comes the rain that has threatened all the afternoon, but only a shower I fear, for this dry soil needs a good soaking just now. So we will make for the little garden house in the wall, and you as a visitor shall sit in the chair and I will perch on the carved oak bench and tell you its history. It was once upon a time the manorial pew in the church at Sandringham, and when the first royal owner of the estate sat upon it he decided to have it altered, and I do not wonder at his decision, for it is narrow, slopes at a most uncomfortable angle even for slim folk, and has a knobby pattern carved

# A June Afternoon

on the back that is not comfy to lean against. So out it went to make way for more suitable sittings. This old bench was presented to the head of the firm entrusted with the work, and he kept it by him for many years, intending to have it made up into some piece of furniture. This he never achieved, and at his death it was sold. An old friend of his and of mine who knew its history bought it at the sale, and when I built this little sheltei offered it to me, so here it is, and as soon as the shower is over I shall be glad to get off it, for in spite of its associations it is not pleasant to sit on for long. How fresh some things look even after so short a shower! The raindrops add a wonderful beauty, for instance, to a fine Lady's Mantle that grows close by, and is happy even in the chinks of the steps at the end of the Vine pergola; I received it from Cambridge Botanic Garden as *Alchemilla grandiflora*, but it is the leaves, not the flowers, that are its notable feature. They are four inches across when vigorous, of a very tender shade of greyish-green, and covered with fine, silky hairs, which help their cup-like shape to hold raindrops which glitter like drops of quicksilver. A few minutes of rain is sufficient to refresh the large leaves of *Petasites japonica gigantea* which grows just across the path and between us and the pond. A really well-developed leaf is nearly a yard across, but to get them in good form they must have both manure and moisture. I do what I can for them; they generally get a Spring mulch, and through the Summer we put the contents of the box of the lawn-mower under the umbrellas of their great leaves to try

to keep some moisture in the soil for their thirsty roots.
But on hot days they get very limp and tired, and sit
down until evening comes, when they again open their
umbrellas, but now after the shower they look as though
they never dreamed of flagging.

This is the plant one sees in japanese prints and
pictured on china vases and fans being used by a peasant
in a straw jacket, huge clogs and no stockings, splashing through the mud and rain and holding one huge leaf
over his head by its stalk just as we would an umbrella.
But *Campanula patula* looked better before the shower, for
when its flowers get wet they hang down, and the frail
segments of the corolla often stick to one another, and the
seamy side only is shown, and they look crumpled. On
dry days its wide-open bells are very cheery, and of such
a warm purple-blue as one does not often see. They
closely resemble the flowers of *C. abietina*, but are more
useful to me here, for I cannot keep that fitful, fretful
beauty for long, and even when it does appear happy,
it makes a mat of rosettes of foliage, and perhaps sends
up only three flower-stems to the square foot, scarcely
paying for the space it occupies. I first saw *C. patula*
growing wild in the hedges of the Wye Valley, where it
is very plentiful and very beautiful, especially along the
road between Tintern and Monmouth, but I brought my
original plants from the woods round Arcachon in the
Landes district. It is only a biennial at most, but sows
itself so freely in cool, half-shaded situations that I always
get more plants than I need, in the rock garden and these
borders behind the Vine pergola.

Dianthus alpinus in Rock Garden.

(See p. 156.)

# A June Afternoon

This season some especially fine white forms appeared that I have saved seed of, hoping I may obtain a white race from them some day. It is rather difficult to purchase the seed of this common plant, which frequently makes a sheet of purple in alpine meadows, as it has been confused by seedsmen with *C. Rapunculus*, which is not nearly so good in colour, and has a much stiffer habit and more crowded bells, in place of the open, sky-gazing cups of *patula*. The wide, round, winter leaves of the large rosettes of *C. Rapunculus* and the fleshy white turnip-like edible root from which it gets its name, easily distinguish *Rapunculus* from *patula*, which has narrow leaves, a thin tap-root, and makes very neat, flat rosettes for its winter form. *C. Loreyi* is well worth growing also, and will sow itself like these other two, but in sunny banks for choice. It has very large flowers for the slender thread-like stalks ; they are like magnified blooms of *patula*, but *C. Loreyi* has an untidy habit, and is best if scrambling among some short sticks or thin dwarf shrubs. Its stems and leaf-stalks are armed with minute, curved hooks that help it to cling to anything it touches. There is a good white form as well as the purple one, and it can be successfully grown as an annual if sown early and thinned out severely, but if an Autumn-germinated seed can be preserved through the Winter to start as a youngster with four or five leaves in Spring, it will make a larger plant by flowering time. Another Campanula that gives the best results here when treated as a biennial is *C. barbata*. It is very happy in the sand moraines, and very lovely when in flower, whether it be the azure-blue form or the pure white. If it is allowed

# My Garden in Summer

to go to seed self-sown babes will spring up in plenty, but far too often where they would smother some delicate neighbour if left to grow into wide rosettes. If the stems are cut away as the blossoms fade, one generally gets a second but less magnificent display of flowers in late Summer.

I wish it could be induced to grow in our hay meadows as I have seen it doing in Tyrol, but of course one of the rarest plants in alpine meadows is grass, the contents of our best herbaceous beds and gayest rock gardens forming the bulk of the hay. *Campanula Allionii* is happiest in the granite-chip moraine, but spreads so far from its central point of planting year by year, that I am afraid it will exhaust the soil and die out eventually. The photograph reproduced opposite p. 158 shows a plant two years after it was transferred to this bed from Mont Cenis.

*Dianthus microlepis* and *D. arvergnensis* promise to spread into compact cushions in the chips faster than in ordinary soil. The former covers itself with its stemless blooms three times in each season. *D. neglectus* and *D. alpinus* (see plate, p. 154) are not happy in moraine, but both species do well in good border soil in flat pockets of the rock garden, and *D. alpinus* generally flowers twice in the Summer, the large rosy flowers hiding its leaves for a week at a time.

# CHAPTER IX

## Aquatics

So many people say, " What splendid opportunities you
must have for Water Lilies and aquatic plants with the New
River running through the garden!"—so many, in fact,
that some day I shall push one of them into it instead of
explaining that, if I did plant a Water Lily in the River,
the Water Board's officials would soon rake it out again,
and, even if they did not, it would catch its death of cold,
as people used to say when I was young, which was before
the days of appendicitis and the general recognition of
bacteria as causes of mortality. The New River water
comes chiefly from chalk wells of great depth, and therefore is hard enough to look blue, and cold enough in
Summer to make you look blue if you were in it for long.
Besides, its banks are made of clay, pommelled and
puddled and slapped and banged with wooden slappers
to a degree of watertightness, solidity, and neat level appearance that admits of nothing but turf margins. So the
River is banned, taboo, *verboden* for planting, but above
all, unsuitable. The pond is almost as bad. It too owes
its watertightness to puddled clay, and most of its water to
the same sources as the River. So it is the more easily
grown aquatics that do best in and around it. Now,

# My Garden in Summer

what is there to make boast of, then, in this heart-shaped pond? In what we may call the left auricle are many wild British plants and but few exotics. The most conspicuous group is a mass of *Scirpus lacustris*, the true Bulrush, the plant from which rush-bottom chairs obtain their name and the soft material for their seats. It is a grand water plant, with its six feet high, gradually tapering, cylindrical, leafless stems, which are a deep blue-green all the Summer, and turn brown in Winter. I brought mine from one of the meres at Wretham in Norfolk, and it reminds me of many happy hours spent in the boats on the Mickle Mere, watching birds or hunting for plants and insects in or round it, and the others of that interesting archipelago reversed, where the sandy flat represents the sea, and is dotted with meres instead of islands. It has grown well here, although there are no Crested Grebes to nest in it, as at Wretham, nor Coots, Tufted Ducks, or Mergansers, and the many other jolly birds I have so often watched scuttering into its thick tufts for hiding. Here, instead, it gives a home to many a brood of baby Moorhens, and when we cut it down in the Spring cleaning we leave a central tuft for the first nest of the season, thereby saving the marginal tufts of *Leucojum aestivum* or *L. Hernandesii* from being seized upon to shelter it. I have heard Moorhens accused of evil deeds among choice flowers in gardens, but have never yet directly traced any damage to their sealing-wax bills, so I encourage them to flirt their white tails and scutter across the water and cry "meeyoop" as much as they please in this garden.

I was very nearly annoyed with them, though, one

season, when a heavy rain lasted for some days, and brooks were flooding the meadows. Instinct taught the Moorhens that the water in the pond ought to rise too, so they added two stories to their nest in a great hurry, and piled it up with the tender green leaves of my japanese Irises. But I thought it so clever and provident of them, and so greatly admired the extraordinary effect of the upper two-thirds of the nest being composed of bright green Iris leaves while the lower third was of the usual dead sticks and Scirpus stems, that I found it easy to forgive them. Water-voles are quite another matter, and are condemned to be shot or trapped as soon as possible when discovered. They chewed down a fine *Phormium tenax* once in Winter, and will chop up good plants into bundles of sham Asparagus. Last year one barked several Willows and other shrubs to get fibre for a Winter nest. Further, they have such an unpleasant habit of running along the margin and beating their path into a muddy bare track, so, in spite of their prettiness, they are not to be admitted in a garden. I once caught a young one, and thought how much I should like to tame it, so I rigged up what I thought a lovely home for it in a large aquarium tank. There was a pool of water occupying half the tank, and a sloping bank nicely turfed, with some stones laid among it, to make a nice dark hole to live in. It looked quite pretty and natural when finished, and I introduced my captive to its home, believing it would feel happy there, as, of course, I had provided plenty of provender. Well, next morning it had reduced the whole arrangement, save the stones, to one puddle of uniform soft mud, and the rat himself was the only clean-looking thing in that tank. So I caught him, and he bit my finger to the bone in his pretty, grateful way, and I took him back to the brook and plopped him in to live and make a mess there.

*Butomus umbellatus* came also from Wretham, and did well here until some common Sedges grew up among it and rather smothered it. Now we have been pulling out the Sedges for several seasons and have nearly got them under, and so I hope the Flowering Rush will become strong again, for it is such a beautiful thing when in flower, and its leaves are so graceful and narrow, considering the size of its heads of soft salmon flowers. Bog Bean, *Menyanthes trifoliata*, from the Norfolk Broads, does almost too well, and I have to curtail its ambitious schemes for filling the pond, and keep it back to a large patch on this side and another smaller one at the other side of the pond. The fringed flowers are wonderfully beautiful, rising up from the water among its large trefoil leaves. I was told in Ireland that in some parts it is claimed as the Shamrock, and a totally different legend from that which is told of the Clover and Wood Sorrel is connected with it: how that St. Patrick and a disciple came to a sheet of water and found no means of crossing; the disciple wished to turn back, but the Saint refused, saying that as St. Peter had walked on the water, so by faith they ought to do. Then the two prayed and set forth and crossed the water on foot, and, as they neared the opposite shore, the disciple said, "We ought to have some token of remembrance of this marvellous day,"

Hollyhocks. By Margaret Waterfield.
(See p. 288.)

and looking down he saw the threefold leaves of the Bog Bean, and gathered some, as they seemed to him a symbol of the Holy Trinity, by whose power they had miraculously walked on the water.

The yellow Buck Bean now appears in the tenth edition of the London Catalogue as *Nymphoides peltatum,* Rendle and Britten, and sounds altogether a new plant from foreign parts, and no relation of *Limnanthemum nymphaeoides* or *Villarsia,* as we have familiarly known it for years past. But as both the British Museum list, where the strange words first appear, and are dubbed *comb. nov.,* and also the London Catalogue agree, I suppose we must now call it as they do. I brought it from the Ouse, between St. Ives and Huntingdon, where it is as plentiful as it also is in the backwaters of the Thames. If only it would give us more of its lovely yellow flowers and fewer of its floating leaves what a gem it would be, even though it still continued to spread itself over a pond as rapidly as it does now. My Water Soldier, *Stratiotes aloides,* dates from a very pleasant cruise in a wherry from Lowestoft to Norwich, with occasional landings to hunt Natterjack Toads at Reedham, Lepidoptera in a fen near Brundall, and plants from a Broad in the same neighbourhood. When we landed at Norwich it looked as though it were going to be difficult to carry the large, wet, pineapple-leaved Water Soldiers any further until my kind host offered his bath towel, the largest ever seen, for the purpose. With its four corners knotted together, it made a glorious receptacle for the muddy collection of plants, but I expect I looked a somewhat strange figure carrying it on my back,

# My Garden in Summer

with black mud oozing out of its lower parts, and with a
breeding-cage full of toads under my arm; of course
we met all our smartest acquaintances at every turn of
the road and every station we had to change at. I don't
care, and here are my Water Soldiers as lively as ever.
They remain at the bottom of the pond eleven months
of the year in a most peaceable manner, but during
August they float up to the surface and protrude their
swords and bayonets and warlike armour, and then their
fleeting white flowers appear to be fertilised, and when
this is accomplished the plant sinks down again. A
Norfolk plant I should have done well to leave behind is
the Ivy-leaved Duckweed, *Lemna trisulca*, for although
a few sprays of its curious growths, always starting off
at right angles to each other, are pretty to look at, yet
a pond full of them is no more lovely than green pea-
soup, and we have to scoop out a barrow-load of it
now and then in Summer. For the greater part of the
year it is innocuous, because it is not a floating species,
and it is only in the height of Summer that it becomes
so prolific and arrives at the surface, but unfortunately
then so many of the elderly portions lose their cheery,
transparent greenness, and fade to unpleasant yellow and
dirty white shades that give a decaying effect to the mass.

It is not so bad as another of my ill-advised importa-
tions, *Azolla caroliniana*, which I came across twenty years
ago, in ponds between Bayonne and Biarritz. In the
February I spent in that neighbourhood there had been
sharp frosts, and this wonderful water-fern had turned to
a brilliant red that showed up from a long distance among

# Aquatics

the grey heathland. So I collected a little boxful, filling one of the glass-bottomed pill-boxes we entomologists use so much, and I sent it home, with instructions that it should be kept in a saucer in a greenhouse. When I got back my red weed was growing and had increased in beauty, for its delicate, velvety, finely-cut fronds were green and crimson, and fascinatingly interesting to play with, to push under water and watch arise out of it as dry as ever, but perhaps carrying a few drops on the fronds, to glitter like diamonds in sunlight. I thought a patch or two would look well on the pond, so in May we turned it loose in a sheltered bay where the Bulrushes and other big plants would keep it in smooth water. It grew and increased and, as I hoped, looked very attractive in irregular-shaped patches of emerald green velvet floating on the water. I believed from only having seen it in greenhouses previously to meeting it at Biarritz that it was tender, so we carefully saved a saucerful to keep in heat when Winter came and it began to turn red. The following Winter was severe, and it was frozen into the ice, and then skated on, and it perished out of doors, so we released our saucerful next Spring, expecting a like pleasant result to the last season's, but then our troubles began. The beastly thing had been lying low till then, and suddenly started to show us what it could do. It filled its bay, it appeared in groups of two or three fronds all round the pond, and before June was over we were removing two or three barrow-loads from time to time in order to see the water at all. " Never mind, Winter will kill it," we said, and we hopefully watched it turn crimson, and did not trouble to save a saucerful this

# My Garden in Summer

time. It froze into the ice as usual, but when the ice melted it looked lovelier than ever, just a more brilliant crimson, and I must own if it would grow no faster in Summer than in Winter, and remain red, it would be well worth the eighteenpence a frond an enterprising nursery-man was at one time asking for it—yea, and selling it too, though many customers lived to regret their purchase. After a shower or heavy dew, when a patch is covered with dewdrops, Streeter's shop window cannot compare with it for iridescent sparkles if the sun is just right to set the show agoing. After two more seasons of raking off and carting away we got rid of it from the pond, but by this time it had got into the rock garden pools, and from thence it refused to be evicted. One day I carried some rushes from those pools to plant on the bank of the cut-off back-water of the New River that divides some of our meadows and woods, and I noticed a decayed-looking scrap or two of Azolla among their roots, and picked out all I could see, but some must have escaped my watchful eye, or else waterfowl carried it there on their feet, for before that Summer was half way through quite a mile of this back-water was solidly green from bank to bank with Azolla. It was so level and turfy in appearance that a small boy who came from London with a cricket eleven that was playing our home team, wandered up the river bank, and thought it looked just right for a run, and was much astonished when he went through the Azolla and had to be helped out and dried in the kitchen before he could teach his fellow-scholars in some London Board-school the Nature-study lesson he had learnt by experience. I believe no-

# Aquatics

thing short of the drying up of the river will dislodge the Azolla now, for it fruits every season, and is in great request for museums and colleges when the backs of the fronds are bearing the large, green spore-cases. Even if we could get it all off the surface some Winter, I fear spores innumerable would arise from the bottom and germinate. So take warning, and if you must grow *Azolla caroliniana*, only put it in a small pool or tub, where it can be kept safely in durance vile without a chance of escape.

One has to run a great risk in planting most water-plants, because, if they grow at all, they often grow too much, for so many of them indulge in runners that bury themselves deeply in the mud, any small portion of which is capable of producing a new plant if left behind, when a raking and scraping has removed the upper portions of the troublesome spreader. The Sagittarias are among the worst offenders, though some of them could be ranked among the most useful of water-plants if only they would form neat clumps, instead of rushing round a pond by means of underground hollow shoots that produce a solid tuber here and there, which, buried in the mud, starts to grow into a plant next Spring, long after the connecting runners have decayed away. Thus you never know where to expect *Sagittaria japonica* or *S. variaeformis* after the first year of planting, whether at the side, in the middle, or half way up the bank. In both species the large white flowers are very beautiful, and look so well above the handsome triangular leaves that give these plants their names, both Latin and English. Our native Arrowhead, *S. sagittifolia*, is more inclined to form a dense colony than to wander, but is not nearly so handsome as the other two of the restless habits, which are both playing the Wandering Jew in the pond, and again in the rock garden pools. The species I want more of is *S. gracilis*, with beautifully slender arrow-heads; but although I have planted it more than once, it never reappears in Spring, so I fear is not hardy enough for me. Water Lilies dislike the pond somehow, and I have dissolved many shillings by investing them in Nymphaeas for its waters to kill and reduce to their constituent chemicals, and I vowed I would buy no more. Then various pink forms were offered me, and I could not resist experimenting with them, and so it came about that this Summer several kinds made a fair show. And as the best of them I reckon James Brydon, whose beautiful soft pink flowers are so chubby and round that they rather take the shine out of a starry *Nymphaea Laydekeri* close by. Of the Marliacea group *albida* is the sole survivor of many, yet they are the strongest growers of all in most waters. The common Reed, *Arundo Phragmites*, was planted at the margin, but soon walked out into deep water, and now has to be prevented from going too far and owning the pond. I find pulling up the young spears where they are not wanted checks its progress pretty effectually, even though the running rhizomes may not always come along with them, for I hope and believe the loss of the green upper portion weakens and kills them if its removal is persisted in. A good colony of this common British plant is worth a place among the best water-plants for the sake of its

# Aquatics

blue-green leaves all pointing one way, according to the direction of the prevailing wind, and its handsome glossy brown flowers during the Summer months, and then its Autumn tints of yellow and orange with the fluff of its seeds above, and finally the Winter effect of bare buff stems. These should be cut down every second year at least, to keep the reed-bed strong and vigorous, as young shoots from the rhizomes grow much stronger and taller and look handsomer than the two or more that will spring from the nodes of an old cane. Along rivers and in reed-beds in the Norfolk Broads it is evident at a glance that the stoutest and strongest reeds are those that are cut annually, and a fine sight some of them are with their seven-foot-high canes bending before a breeze, while their leaves hiss and whisper "King Midas has ass's ears" as plainly and sibilantly now as they are charged with having done in Phrygia so very long ago. There is a good golden variegated form of the Reed, but I have never been successful in establishing it here. I believe it soon runs back green if grown in water, and I cannot spare it a semi-juicy spot, as they are too scarce here for a mere Reed to have one.

I have a plant that does well in deep water and is very handsome, but has so far never shown a sign of flowering here, and I hear of its showing the same obstinate barrenness in other British gardens. This surprises me, as it grows so freely and looks so happy, and it annoys me because without seeing its flowers it seems impossible to clear up the mystery that surrounds its identity.

It came to me as *Zizania canadensis*, Wild Rice, but both

# My Garden in Summer

the *Kew Index* and *Hand-list* ignore this name, so most likely it has never been duly published. The *Hand-list* gives a Z. *latifolia*, native of Siberia and Japan, but the *Index* declares this is only a synonym of Z. *aquatica*, to which plant it permits no further range than North America. Now Z. *aquatica* is an annual, and I have had it here, and don't want it again, whereas I should howl aloud at the loss of my perennial stately plant that provides such a fine effect as a contrast to the stiff blue stems of *Scirpus*, in that its wide, flat leaves arch over most gracefully, and are of a brilliant pea green all through the Summer. I think it may be *Zizaniopsis Miliacea* from Ohio, and if only it would condescend to flower, the figure and description in Britton and Brown's *Flora of the United States* would soon prove whether or no I am right. By occasional reinforcements of old pot plants we have maintained a small group of the White Arum, *Richardia africana*, in the deeper end of the pond, where its roots are always below freezing line, and the white spathes are as effective as anything of their season against a background of *Scirpus maritimus* backed again by a Yew that feathers down to the bank, which is covered by creeping Ivy, with the handsome, pale-green leaves of *Petasites palmata* appearing through the dark carpet, the whole group making a charming picture that has painted itself without any aid from my hand, save respect for its scheme and a studied neglect. *Cyperus longus* is much like this last *Scirpus* in general appearance, but forms a closer tuft. It does very well half on the bank in a bed of soil, but its toes reaching the water ; that is to say, in one of my favourite schemes for outwitting

# Aquatics

puddled clay and stiff, perpendicular banks. I stick some short stakes into the clay bottom of the pond to mark out the new territory we mean to wrest from the water, sometimes laying a few twigs inside them, but generally I find turves sufficient for the purpose of keeping the well-mixed soil I bundle in behind them from slipping away into the water ; and once these beds are full of roots the pegs can be removed from the water front.

The Galingale, *Cyperus longus*, revels in a bed so formed, and is very graceful owing to the long, leafy bracts that hang from the top of the flower-stems just beneath the bunches of flowers. It is useful for tall vases during Summer, and looks like some extra superfine form of the Madagascar Reed, *Cyperus alternifolius*. I am very fond of having a vase on a flower table given over entirely to greenery and stood among other vases with masses of bright-coloured flowers in them. I dislike ferns cut and put in a vase with flowers, but love a vase of one kind of fern placed among the flowers ; sprays of Purple Plum and Purple Almond look well, especially with pink and mauve Sweet Peas or Irises ; and branches of the Silver Maple or Ghost Tree, *Acer Negundo*, have a softening effect among large vases of Delphiniums. White flowers would do a similar work, perhaps, but one does not want too many flowers in a room—sometimes their scent may be too strong—and then these unmixed bunches of foliage are very useful, and Galingale is delightfully light when cut full-length for a tall cut-glass vase.

These water-side beds are very suitable for Globe-flowers, Calthas, *Iris Kaempferi*, and such plants, which

# My Garden in Summer

have already been alluded to as growing in them, and also make the right home for *Typha minima,* which unlike its giant relations prefers to grow on land to being submerged, and is very attractive when doing well, its leaves being so wonderfully slender. But the little Cat's-tails it produces are so short and round they are quite unlike the caudal appendage of any cat I ever saw. A plant I used to call in less enlightened days *Erythrochaete palmatifida* is now *Senecio japonicus,* but looks none the worse for being dumped into a family which includes Groundsel. It is a good plant for the water side; its large leaves are cut up into most fanciful ornamental fingers growing out of a small palm, and its yard-high stems bear rich orange-yellow flowers of a great size. It is especially effective planted among grassy-leaved things, or even in a colony of the Canadian Osmunda, *Onoclea sensibilis.* I find this fern does very well on a pond bank, and will even make a mat of roots running out into the water, and as they become sufficiently interlaced they are followed by the rhyzome and then bear fronds. It has such a tender young oak-leaf green of its own all the Summer, and turns a pleasant foxy-brown in Autumn, so that a yard or two of it is worth having on the water's edge. Its curious, spore-bearing, fertile fronds stand up stiffly from the Summer in which they are formed until the next, when the spores are dusted out if you shake one of them.

The *pièce de resistance* of the pond, however, is a magnificent old *Osmunda regalis* with a history. It was bought many years ago from a tramp in Fleet Street who was carrying it on his back, and it was then only a single

# Aquatics

crown, but history does not relate whence he stole it.
Possibly some marshes not further from Charing Cross
than we are here, may have then contained the Royal
Fern. It is very scarce in the Norfolk Broads now,
but I do not believe its rarity is owing to tramps who
would howk it up first and then hawk it around afterwards ; for I have come across old stools, either dead or
with miserably small leaves on them, in places where I feel
sure no tramp would venture. I expect a greater demand
for chaff fodder made of the mown rushes of the marshes
caused more of the marsh to be mown, and the scythe is
responsible for the disappearance of King Osmund. If it
can grow in Norfolk marshes, it might have once done so
at Hackney or Hammersmith. Anyway, my friend Mr.
John W. Ford bought it in London when a very young
man, and planted it by the pondside in his father's garden
at Enfield Old Park. It grew under their care into the
magnificent clump I have known and admired for many
years, and I can quite believe it was, as Mr. Ford used
to say, the finest specimen between this and Killarney.
When he was leaving Old Park a few years ago, and the
preparations were going on for the sale in which many of
his treasures that he could not take to his new home were
to be sold and scattered, he most kindly wrote and offered
me the great Osmunda if I would move it whole.

Our bailiff and I went and looked at it, and we scratched
our heads over it, and decided that, short of hiring a strong
crane for the purpose, we could not undertake to uproot
it and haul it over the stone wall at its back, and I regret-
fully declined the kind offer. Then came a letter to

# My Garden in Summer

say I might take it in any manner I could accomplish, as
that was better than its being chopped up and distributed
in portions.  So we went with picks and spades, cut the
grand old fern into three pieces, and even then had no easy
job to get it into the cart.  I built one of my pegged-out
promontories for it, filling in the space with the best loam,
peat, and leaf soil we could lay hands on, and by removing
a quantity of dead stem from the centre of the clump we
were able, when fitting the three portions together, to stuff
this central hollow with good feeding soil, and in each of
the last three seasons the fronds have increased in size and
number as though the move had done it good rather than
harm, and we are very proud of its beauty, I can tell you.
I owe a fine specimen of Bog Myrtle, *Myrica Gale*, to the
same kind friend.  He had to wait between trains at
Aberdovey Junction one fine day, and walking along the
platform, which is a sort of pier built over a marsh, or
was in the days when I knew it, he saw the flourishing
Bog Myrtle bushes just below, and longed for one.

" Have you got such a thing as a spade, porter ? "
" No, sir, nothing but the coal-shovel."  " Oh, that will
do ; come along and help me, will you ? " and off the
two went, for my friend never sticks at trifles, and
their joint efforts uprooted a square foot of marsh and
Bog Myrtle.  The resourceful porter produced a bit
of sacking, and the shrub arrived safely at Old Park,
and now that its lovely home there has been dismantled,
it has followed the Osmunda here.  We built it a similar
mound in the pond, and though it had more dead wood
than I cared to see in it a year after its removal, it is

# Aquatics

filling up the spaces I have cleared out in it with strong young growths, and is a very fine specimen, and delightful to pinch so as to bring out its sweet scent. A sniff of this scent always carries me back to happy bug-hunting grounds in the New Forest and the Norfolk Broads, where I have spent many hours tramping through waist-high thickets of Sweet Gale, and have unrolled many of its sewn-up shoots to extract the caterpillars of *Taeniocampa gracilis*, which, in the New Forest, always produce a beautiful red form of this usually dingy moth, when fed on Bog Myrtle.

The pools in the rock garden are on such a small scale that they should hold only choice things, but they have been called upon to provide homes for many plants too coarse and spreading for them, that I must have somewhere. So one pool is dreadfully over-run with the King of Buttercups, *Ranunculus Lingua*, brought from the Norfolk Broads. Still, a good deal can be done by hauling out a barrow-load of shoots in Spring, and those left are all the stronger for the thinning, but never reach the height here they do in the fat, oozy mud of their Norfolk ditches, pools, and swamps. I have walked under their great yellow flowers there often enough, but of course I sank up to my ankles in the mud, and so lost a little in height. The varnished glittering flowers, as large as five-shilling pieces, are glorious to see against the blue sky, especially when the Swallowtail Butterflies, almost as brilliant, are circling among them. So I must keep the great Spearwort here for the sake of the visions it recalls of bird and butterfly of Broadland. *Acorus Calamus* has no business here, but would be hard to uproot now,

and both the wild green form and its strikingly variegated
one are handsome, if kept in check, and the leaves are
interesting to pick for people who do not know the
Scented Rush, and are astonished at its powerful hair-oil
type of scent. They ought never to fail to recognise
it again when once I have shown them its distinguishing
mark of having one side of each leaf beautifully pleated
or frilled—or perhaps goffered is the right way to describe
its waved margin. *Calla palustris* runs about in the mud,
and produces its white flowers like miniature Richardias,
an inch or so above the water, and has occasionally
brought them to the perfection of red berries. *Lastrea
Thelypteris*, the Marsh Fern, brought from Norfolk, does
well here, either on the bank at water level, or as a loose
tangle of black roots, like horse-hair stuffing extracted from
some chair, and just floating loosely in the pool without
any anchorage. *Orontium aquaticum* is a very suitable
plant for its position, though, and has formed a good-
sized tuft ; it is amusing to sprinkle water on to it, for
every drop rolls off the unwettable leaves like pellets of
quicksilver, and, if dropped from a height, will actually
bounce off the leaves. I wish some one would invent a
new kind of waterproof clothes that would be as repellant
to rain. The flowers are more curious than showy, for
they are really the spadix of an aroid plant, and there is
no showy spathe, but the lower portion of each slender
spadix is white, the flowers crowded at its tip are
bright yellow, and they look like some tropical kind of
worm, with a white body and a yellow head, resting
among the leaves. On the bank behind it is a group

of a very pretty Spiraea-like plant, *Astilbe sinensis*, that has spread out for about two feet from a single crown originally planted here. I can remember the days when it was considered the rosiest of the Spiraeas with spiked blossoms, but it looks rather pallid beside some of the newer *S. japonica* forms, such as Peach Blossom and Queen Alexandra, which grow well on the opposite bank of these ponds. A good many Spiraeas that like wet feet have gathered round these pools, some planted by me and others self-sown. *S. venusta* is a great trespasser, and spreads rapidly not only by seed but also by running shoots, and I have rather too much of it, but it is so lovely when in flower I am weak about attacking it. I do not know of any plant the flowers of which are so nearly the colour of a strawberry ice, and later, the seeds turn such a good red as they swell out that I am always tempted to leave them on to enjoy their effect, and then the unwanted seedlings that appear next season make me sorry I left them. *S. camtschatica*, or *gigantea* as we used to call it, grows six feet high by the water, and is a fine thing when at its best, with its large heads of fluffy-white flowers, but stately at all times, from the first appearance of its large leaves in Spring till they turn copper colour in late Autumn, and even the bare stems, which will stand until the new ones are pushing, should be respected at tidying-up time, for, if left standing, they provide an effect of height in the wintry landscape. It hybridises freely with both *venusta* and *palmata*, which latter grows at its very feet here in my rock garden, but I like the tall *venusta* children best, and have one, self-sown, just by the little stone bridge, that is prettier than either parent, as tall as *camtschatica* but of a very soft pink, and greatly enhanced in beauty by brilliantly rose-coloured anthers that give a shaded effect to the open flowers. *Astilbe grandis*, with its solid white spikes, and *A. Davidiana*, with tall rosy-purple ones, are grouped among these others, and follow them in their season of flowering in a very pleasant way. There is a dwarf form of *S. palmata*, known as variety *purpurea*, which is not common, but most people who see it admire and covet it, for it has charming little leaves heavily marked with purple and pretty pink flowers. Its dwarf habit fits it for moist corners of the rock garden, in company with the gem of the family, which changes its name so often I never know what to call it; *digitata* and *lobata* are the two names most often used for it, but very likely both are incorrect. Anyway, it is a treasure, producing palmate leaves only three inches high, and its flower-stems are just one inch higher, and carry large heads of pink flowers almost as temptingly strawberry-ice-like as those of *venusta*. Opposite the group of tall Spiraeas there grows a large tussock of a very beautiful Sedge, with golden-striped leaves, another of my finds in the Norfolk Broads. I noticed two or three shoots of a Sedge with a fine golden band on their leaves, so dropped on my knees and severed them from the main tuft with my pocket-knife, brought them home, and planted them where they have now formed this fine specimen. I believe it is **Carex strictus**, quite a common Sedge in its

Yucca recurvifolia and Spiraea camtschatica.   (See p. 175.)

ordinary green form. A curious thing about it is that, though the scrap I originally collected throve so well under my rough-and-ready treatment, I now find the greatest difficulty in propagating it, and pieces I have taken off for myself and others have invariably died with the exception of two. The late Mr. Amos Perry always rubbed his hands with joy when looking at my plant, and used to say, when he had twenty-five guineas to spare he would offer them to me for this plant. But I have never yet sold a plant, and I hope I never shall, so one day when I was in a good temper I offered him a chunk out of its side, and we got a fork and prized out a good dozen or more of crowns, but like others he had no luck with them, I am sorry to say, for I should greatly like to see this fine variety propagated and distributed far and wide. When the first Spring growths appear it is not very brilliant, being little more than a golden green, but about the end of May, after flowering, it throws up long, arching leaves that have broad stripes of purest golden-yellow, and the colour deepens until August, when it fades gradually back to green. It is an enormous specimen, really too large for its position, so Mr. Perry and I hope to attack it afresh next Spring and to obtain better results this time. Halfway down the most sunken of the paths in the rock garden we came upon a valuable asset in the shape of a slight ooze of water, the result of our almost universal gravel giving out just there and a consequent outflow of some of its surface water where the underlying clay prevents its soaking away. So we hollowed out a small bed for plants that love gravy with their dinner, such as the marsh Orchids, *O. latifolia* and *Habenaria chlorantha*, *Pinguicula grandiflora*, Primulas with thirsty habits, such as *P. rosea* and *P. Poissonii*, and *Mentha Pulegium*, the Penny Royal, which I brought from one of its few remaining wild homes, Slapton Lee, for it has been gathered so vora- ciously for making into Oil of Penny Royal, that it has become very scarce in many of its old haunts. It is rather a rampagious, greedy plant, and needs look- ing after when near choicer neighbours, but its whorls of lavender-blue flowers are worth having. A strange form of *Gunnera scabra* occupies the top of this bed. It appeared among seedlings raised at Newry, and might be a midget or a dwarf—but not a hunchback, for, though growing no higher than a foot, the leaves are well formed and not crumpled, but it never attempts to flower. I used to grow several pygmy Gunneras, mostly species from New Zealand, but they are too tender here for out- doors and not worth the trouble of lifting and keeping in frames, but, as contrasts to the huge species, they are interesting. *G. monoica*, *G. arenaria*, and *G. dentata* are amongst the smallest of carpeting plants ; while *G. chilensis*, more familiarly known as *manicata*, is the largest-leaved of hardy plants. Our large specimen by the pond has been extra fine this Summer, the leaf-stalks being over five feet in height. I believe the great secret for ensuring its reaching gigantic dimensions is to follow the advice originally given for the conversion of a grumbling husband to a happier frame of mind, and to " feed the brute."

# Aquatics

Though Gunneras require a certain amount of moisture, they are, to my idea, not so much thirsty as hungry, and so we plant them farther up the banks than most water-loving plants would stand, and then we heap their plates at feeding-time with the richest food we can afford them. A couple of barrowfuls of well-rotted cow-yard manure is what they like, and, if the flower-spikes are removed early, the strength goes into the leaves, and they do us credit. *G. chilensis* produces the largest leaves and grows the tallest of them all, but its leaves are not so handsomely indented as those of *scabra,* so I am much pleased with a seedling form, another of the Newry children, which has an intermediate habit, tall leaf-stalks, and well-cut leaves, and now that it has spread into a mass, with some dozen or more crowns, it is certainly the most effective of all those I grow. Mr. Elwes has kindly given me the Gunnera he brought home from sub-alpine heights in Chili, which ought to be the hardiest of all. He tells me he saw a man on horseback ride under the leaves, so great things are to be expected of this variety or species ; but so far it has not developed very great dimensions or distinct characteristics in England. The first plant he gave me perished during Winter, but a promising young seedling has lately come from Colesborne (thanks to Mr. Elwes' generosity), and I mean to try and keep it a-going, and "do it proud."

# CHAPTER X

## Succulents

I FORGET the exact date of my acquisition of a taste for succulent plants; but it was in early nursery days, and was started by a gift of two minute specimens in the smallest and reddest of pots imaginable, and so long ago that it is wise to be hazy as to dates. The love of succu- lents seems to be innate in children, and it does not depend altogether on the attractiveness of the wee pots, for I have many times noticed, when I have had classes of school-children for a visit to the garden, that the beds as well as pots of succulents attract them as much as any- thing they meet with that is not edible, and a side shoot of some Cotyledon, or little prickly ball of a babe off some Cereus, is the greatest treasure one can give them to carry away to grow. On the other hand I meet many grown-up people who declare they positively dislike succulents; but these are generally people in the first flush of excitement of their gardening career, and bent on seeing my Romneya to see if it is as good as the one they planted last Spring, which now has *two* buds ; or they only care for pale blue Delphiniums surrounded by salmon-pink Antirrhinums, and ask if I have got a moraine yet, because a friend of theirs has got one and a plant of Edelweiss actually

# Succulents

flowered in it, and so on. If only you can induce them to carry off a shoot of *Kleinia articulata* like a blue candle, or an infant Mammillaria with attractive stars of golden spines topping each of its knobs, you may rest assured the germ has been injected that will produce Succulent Fever, and some day you will receive an appeal for any odd scraps you are throwing away, as they want to enlarge their collection. A love for these prickly, fleshy plants, although it may be a disease that, like Mumps and Measles, is more easily taken by the young, also resembles them in being more deadly in the adult; for although it may be an acquired taste it seems to be ineradicable once it is developed.

It is hard to say why succulents are so fascinating to the young and also to the initiated. Their neatness appeals to children, for as a rule they prefer a small rosette to a large one; but grown-up people soon learn to appreciate a well-grown, old specimen. I think their charm must lie in the contrast they afford to the ordinary native forms of plants, the foreign air they wear, and the suggestion they give of warmer climates. In support of this I may instance the usefulness of a Prickly Pear and an Agave to the mediocre makers of illustrations—I can't call them artists nor their efforts pictures. They often depend on these two plants and a liberal allowance of sharp shadows to furnish an eastern or southern effect. But it amuses me to note how often they appear in illustrations of Bible scenes, for as both of these plants are of American origin neither could have been known in Palestine before the days of Christopher Columbus.

# My Garden in Summer

To any who have travelled, even so far as the Riviera, a group of Agaves and Opuntias recalls pleasant memories of sunshine and heat, if the selective faculty of their memories leads them to omit dust and drought. Drought is of course the *raison d'être* of this thick-skinned race of plants ; they are representatives in living vegetable tissue of the wine and water skins of the East. A few of them, like the Cotyledons that people will still call Echeverias, and the semi-transparent forms of Haworthias, do really live up to the name they are classed under in English, and look succulent as one generally understands it—juicy and tender ; but short of cutting them open and seeing the store of pulpy succulence, one would imagine certain venerable Cacti, covered in tough woody horns and crowded spines or a wrinkled, leathery skin, to be as dry as any old tree trunk.

I rather like the French name, *plantes grasses*, for them, but should not care for it translated into English, and I greatly love the pachydermatous plants themselves. The shadow of a branch of Opuntia on one of the rock garden stones appeals to my love of the South and the sunshine very strongly, and a grouping of pots of old specimen Aloes and Agaves with a minor cluster of Cactuses, with roundabout figures like large sea urchins, at their feet, standing on the stone steps by the pond, is to me the embodiment of summer heat, and plants that enjoy it no less than myself. It is not only the bold, picturesque, seen-from-a-distance effect, though, that delights me, but also the marvellous charm of symmetry to be found in most Cereus and Mammillaria species,

# Succulents

the regularity of the arrangement of their ribs, ridges, or rows of protuberances, decorated with such marvels in the way of prickles, that vary from curved horns to long, straight needles, arranged singly or in beautifully regular, starlike groups; or again as pins stuck into a round pin-cushion, as we find in the Echinopsis section of Cereus, but always with a mathematical precision that is both interesting and beautiful. The beauty of their regular arrangement is that of some art treasure, some old Venetian glass goblet, with raised beads of glass at regular distances, or an engine-turned design of interlacing lines; and the interest lies in the fact that it is all reducible to rule and to be accounted for by the spacing of each spine or protuberance according to the rules of phyllotaxy, for they really represent metamorphosed stipules, leaves, or aborted branches from the axils of leaves that have never been developed, but whose places on the stem have been marked by these representatives of the usual concomitants of leaves. For, with the exception of the genus Pereskia, true leaves are not known in the Cactus family.

The genus Opuntia provides the key to the nature of the prickles on Cactuses, for their young growths are furnished with fleshy, cylindrical outgrowths that are obviously leaves, and in one species with a cylindrical stem, *O. subulata*, these peculiar leaves are several inches in length, and remain on the stem for a year or more, and then drop off, leaving only a few short prickles to mark their site. In the species with cylindrical stems there is no doubt as to which is stem and which leaf, but in the species with flattened, battledore-shaped joints it is a common fallacy to fancy each stem-joint is a leaf. If the young growths are examined they will be seen to bear fleshy outgrowths, similar to, but smaller than, the leaves of *O. subulata*, and that they fall before the joint has reached its full size, leaving in the case of most species a formidable spine or two to mark their places, which may represent stipules, or emergencies, a name invented by botanists for prickles such as those of Roses and Brambles, which are mere outgrowths of the skin only. But whatever they are, as I have said, they mark the places where leaves have been, or should have been, and whether in cylindrical or flattened stems, or even the nearly spherical ones of certain Echinocactus and Cereus species, whether raised on ribs or mammillae, or on the smooth skin itself, the spiral order of these pin-cushions can be fairly easily traced ascending the stem just as the leaves would on an ordinary plant.

It is possible that in species which produce no early-falling, fleshy leaves, one prickle in each cluster may represent a leaf reduced to nothing but a hard midrib. But if there are doubts as to the morphology of these prickles, there can be none about their being of definite use to the plant in protecting it from hungry and thirsty beasts, who otherwise would chew the tough skin to get at its juicy inside. Some of these spines are cruel weapons, and make fearful wounds. It is said that mules will kick some of the large Cacti during seasons of drought in America to get at the soft pulp, and that many die from the poisoning of their heels and hocks by the spines that enter them and break off. Many species have spines that

# Succulents

are cruelly barbed, and so once in cannot be easily withdrawn; and this is especially common with the Opuntias, and makes them very disagreeable for the gardener to handle, but very useful in hot countries for barriers, as a good hedge of some of the larger and more formidable kinds is impassable. On an occasion when a West Indian island was divided between the English and French, the frontier was planted with a triple row of *Opuntia Tuna*. I have suffered much from these little barbed prickles; they are so sharp they run into one's flesh at the slightest touch, and unless pulled out at once they often break, leaving the barbs in to set up inflammation, and presently work their way out along with the matter that forms round them. Therefore, when I wish to replant Opuntias or weed among them, I take out the fire-tongs and a pair of glove-stretchers to catch hold of them, or the weeds that are close to them. It is worse than useless to put on gloves, as the prickles go through them, and then in drawing off the glove you break off the ends by means of which you might have pulled them out.

One day when weeding my Opuntia bank, my foot slipped on a wet rock and I sprawled into the prickles, and it was three weeks before I had got myself altogether cleared of them. So sometimes I wish I had never learnt to love them, especially when my hands are smarting with several hundred punctures. Some of the barbed prickles of the Opuntias are a special invention of their own, for unlike those of other Cactuses they are renewed and increased from year to year on old stem-joints among the longer spines that were formed while the shoot was young; so it would appear that they are something of the nature of abortive stem growths growing out of the axils of the leaves, and a joint that was only armed with two or three long, straight spines from each leaf scar in its first season, when it has become old and woody in the course of four or five years may appear quite hairy from the vast numbers of these loosely-attached, barbed spines; and were it not for the very attractive appearance of Opuntias, I expect no one knowing their wicked ways would ever have anything to do with them.

Our succulents here are divided off for four separate usages, and we rank first and highest the clothing of a bank of the rock garden given over to them, for that was the origin of my collection. I have told in the volume of the Spring garden how two kinds of Opuntia I saw in Veitch's Exeter Nursery won my affection, and how their enjoyment of good health on the rock garden caused me to hunt for others equally amenable to outdoor cultivation. Then came the displacement of all other plants from that particular bank, yard by yard and year by year, until now a stretch some thirty feet long belongs to the succulents, and they are so dear to me that, from November till April, they are covered by a hideous lid of glass —old lights from a dismantled vinery—laid on a framework of wood, that the plants below may be kept comparatively dry during the colder months.

Come and look at them on a blazing July day, and I hope you will think the interest and beauty they provide in Summer compensate us for wounded fingers and the eyesore of the glass cover in Winter. Look at *Cereus*

# Succulents

*paucispinus* with its many cylindrical growths, all produced here in this very spot from a single crown planted some fifteen years ago. Admire its crimson, unopened buds, and the dazzling vermilion of its opened flowers, and notice how marvellously the emerald green star that is the stigma shines out in the centre by its contrast with the red. Surely that is worth a little trouble to grow on the rock garden, for I have counted fifteen flowers open at once in good seasons. Looking at its fierce spines you can hardly believe that slugs will dare to journey up the stems and eat the buds, but I have caught them in the act, and I can answer for it that those I caught never ate any more. When the Opuntias are in full bloom their semi-transparent flowers look as if made of thin Chinese silk. They are mostly of various shades of yellow, from a very pale, greenish-primrose tint to rich orange, but some are of most beautifully soft shades of rosy buff, and crushed strawberry, that are very pleasing, and unlike those of any other flower I know, coming near to some of the hybrid Verbascums of coppery shades, but with more crimson in them than the Mulleins can boast. They all possess a curious power of movement, that is most noticeable on a very hot day, and when the flowers are widely expanded. The stamens are irritable, and a light touch on the anthers will cause them all to close inwards in a curious, spiral wave that takes about half a minute to complete, and then after a few minutes of rest they will reverse the movement and slowly open out again. I do not know of what use it is to the plant, unless it serves to rub more pollen on to

# My Garden in Summer

a visiting insect than it would otherwise collect of itself, and I have not noticed any other Cactus behaving in the same way. A succession of wet Summers and cold Winters greatly reduced a fine grouping of the division of Cereus most frequently called Echinopsis. They form very symmetrical, spherical plants, most of which are strongly ribbed, and have rows of tubercles bearing short prickles set at regular distances on each rib, like rows of buttons. A good colony of them, with the many babes they bud off from the lower part of their stems, looks like a family group of green sea-urchins, and their name, Echinopsis, is of course derived from the scientific name of those animals—*echinos* in Greek doing duty for both the hedgehog and the sea-urchin. Their flowers are very large, and mostly white or pale rose-colour, and appear in July and August from the upper portions of the ribs. They begin life as grey, furry knobs not unlike the Sallow blossoms that constitute Palm Sunday "Palm"—but they soon lengthen out to four inches or more of narrow tube, and then at last the upper portion swells out into a fat, grey bud, and finally opens late one afternoon into a large star-shaped bloom with a hollow throat. The first night the anthers shed their pollen and the flower remains in full beauty next day, but is not quite so widely opened as during the evening hours. The second night the stigma opens, and would in nature be dusted with pollen from a first-night blossom, collected and carried by some large moth, and cross pollination would be thereby effected. About noon on the following day the flower begins to flag, gradually closes, and becomes flabby and dies off,

Cereus paucispinus.   (See ). 187.)

# Succulents

but an old plant will provide four or more flowers in a season. All the Echinopsis forms are slightly tender here, and better suited for growing in pots, to stand out in Summer on walls and steps. Still, I have a good colony of them, but in much less variety than formerly, only the hardiest being left of the old group of which I was so proud before certain bad seasons killed some of the plants, for I have not yet recovered heart to try newer forms.

Many Opuntias are very hardy, and the most reliable of the showy-flowered kinds are the varieties of *O. camanchica*, of which something like a dozen are known, most of which I have tried, and nearly all are flourishing well. The only really hardy one with large growths is *O. cantabrigensis*, of which there is such a fine specimen in the open in the Cambridge Botanic Garden, from which it was described and named by Mr. Lynch, who kindly gave me a piece of it that is now growing into a large specimen here. The handsomest of all is *O. glauca* or *robusta*, with huge, round stem-branches a foot or more in diameter and covered with a bluish powder. I have twice succeeded in getting it to grow into a good specimen here, but alas! each of them fell to bits through the lower joints rotting off in bad Winters, and I am starting again from one of the sound joints. *Cotyledon (Echeveria) Purpusii* is very hardy, and makes a good contrast among the bristly Opuntias, with its smooth grey-green rosettes of leaves and showy red and yellow flowers, and *C. farinosa* is even more attractive on account of its mealy, blue-grey leaves. *Crassula sarcocaulis* is somewhat of a newcomer

# My Garden in Summer

here, a memento of a visit to Glasnevin and its generous Director, but in its three seasons with me has grown into a most picturesque little tree with a smooth, fleshy stem to justify its specific name, and this August it was a mass of crimson and white blossoms. *Agave Parryi,* which sends out suckers a foot away from the parent plant, arranges itself as a picturesque group, the youngest and smallest members farthest away from the patriarchal centre-piece. The position on this hot bank, and the slight help of overhead cover for Winter, agree with its comfort, and I have been able to place several of its babes out in the world with friends I thought worthy of such treasures, my estimate of their virtues being based on the amount of attention I reckoned they would pay to the precious babe's future happiness. Otherwise the colony would have become overcrowded. One old specimen has had to battle with frosts and rains for fifteen years, and has had his ups and downs ; he also assumed patriarchal dignity at one time and placed young cadets in advantageous positions, even on the other side of a good, lumpy rock that forms his south wall. This was rather rough on those youths, amounting to choosing the career of an Arctic explorer for them, and they all perished in their second year when the thermometer dropped to zero. After that the chieftain had a bad time himself ; a soppy, wet Autumn kept him too sappy, even in his well-drained rocky home, and several inner leaves, that were swelling up to outgrow all others before produced, rotted in Winter, and left nasty masses of basal fibre for wet to lodge in that for several seasons injured the central growths. But he has battled

# Succulents

through, and is looking dignified again, and has once more acquired a fine stout heart for himself, but not sufficiently brave an one to start another nursery. My first specimen is not a Goliath by any means, for either *A. Parryi* is a very slow grower in cool climates or else is a pygmy form. I should have believed the latter to be the case if I had not seen flowering specimens at Tresco almost as large as an *A. americana* when it has reached its final effort of flowering. These looked like my plants in the deep green of the thick leaves and the shape of the terminal spine, but goodness knows what will become of their neighbours if my colonies, whose largest members now measure about two and a half feet in diameter, their longest leaves being about a foot long, should suddenly grow up and produce leaves five feet in length.

*A. applanata*, said to be equally hardy, has never survived a bad Winter here, even under the cover of the lights ; but *A. utahensis* preserves the same stolid calm, and only half-alive appearance, Winter and Summer alike. It produces its offsets freely, but thickly clustered under its oldest and dying leaves, and without a morsel of runner or stem to them, so that they are hard to get off uninjured, and still harder to root when removed. I have tried many Beschornerias and Furcraeas on this bank, but a bad Winter interferes with their central crowns, and even if they shoot out again, they lose so much strength and beauty that they look like invalids for several seasons, and are generally incurables. Dasylirions, however, fare better, and even if the central tufts of unexpanded leaves get a bit browned now and then, they generally recover.

# My Garden in Summer

*D. longifolium*, with wide as well as long, bright green leaves, is a good one, but *D. Hookeri* has bluer and handsomer leaves, with an edging of shark's teeth from base to tip; and both have grown into large specimens, their long, grassy leaves providing a good contrast with the rounded outlines of the Cactuses.

I have a mental millstone hanging about my neck, which consists of a recollection of having said a good deal about this Cactus bank in the Spring volume of this garden record, and as both the manuscript and the proofs are in the printer's hands, and I cannot for the life of me remember just how much I did say of the Bromeliads and Cape Bulbs that share this parched spot with the prickly Cacti, I write in fear of repetition; but I should be sorry if I failed to mention some worthy and faithful plant. At least three species of Rhodostachys have met here after their exile from their homes in Chili. *R. pitcairniaefolia* does the best, and makes wide clumps of pineapple-like greenery, but has never yet flowered; not that I much want to see the actual flowers, which are small and a dull greyish blue; but as the inner leaves of a flowering rosette turn a vivid crimson in honour of the occasion, I do want to see that sunset effect. *R. andina* is much greyer, in fact, nearly white on the backs of the leaves, but not quite sure as yet whether it likes this open-air treatment. The other, I believe, is *R. littoralis*, and this poor plant would like to go to the Riviera or the greenhouse for the Winter, for its more exposed leaves turn a sad drab hue after a week of sharp frosts.

# Succulents

So far *Bilbergia nutans,* which comes from Brazil and so could hardly be expected to look happy here, has come through more smilingly than any Bromeliad. All these named figure in the *Kew Hand-list* under the title of Tender Monocotyledons, so are certainly what one might call·risky plantings. I keep duplicates of all of them in pots, and these are growing into handsome specimens, and are useful for standing out in the Summer on the pavements, and on the wall at the back of the terrace; this is our second, and I think largest, use for succulent plants ; the third use is bedding out those that are suitable, to fill some of the terrace beds when the Tulips are garnered ; and the fourth comprises those that, like Phyllocacti and *Cereus grandiflorus,* always live under glass. I have already mentioned the steps by the pond, and that they are the Summer rendezvous of many specimen succulents, a sort of Brighton or Eastbourne for them during their summer outing. Two fairly large spaces, paved with black and white pavement from a hall, were planned on purpose for groupings of these pot plants, and a low balustrade at the back of each accommodates many of the smaller specimens, and some large ones on the tops of the pillars. Four very handsome old stone vases by the edge of the walk hold four large pots, and *Aloe arborescens,* the commonest sort of Aloe grown, and *Sedum dendroideum,* equally common but very seldom encountered with a name attached to it, return yearly to their old lodgings, and a fine old specimen of *Crassula portulacea* and another of *C. arborescens* that is almost as large occupy the two central vases. Both Crassulas have smooth, brown, fleshy stems, like those of some old tree in miniature, that make very picturesque supports for their fat round leaves. I am sorry to see they do not appear in the accompanying illustration of these steps and vases, specimens of the Aloe and Sedum only being in possession of all four vases the season it was taken.

Agaves of many kinds may be seen here, and tender Yuccas, besides Opuntias and Cereus species. It is a great joy to me to arrange this grouping year by year, and I have not yet made up my mind whether I like them best arranged somewhat according to their families or in a thorough mixture of Cacti and leafy subjects, so I can keep on trying first one and then the other to find out. The only drawback to growing these succulents into large specimen plants in pots is their rapid increase in size, which leads to the bursting of pots at too frequent intervals, and the difficulty of packing them all under cover at the end of Autumn. On the terrace wall we can only stand things that will not blow over too easily, so the Rhodo-stachys forms are useful and solid here ; any squat, round Cactus will do, and of course pans of low-growing things are always safe. I am quite certain I like these gathered in their clans on this wall. Even the Haworthias are more effective kept apart from their near relatives the Gasterias. The Haworthias, with their starry rosettes, look as if sprinkled over with pearls or a carefully picked out hand-ful of white hundreds and thousands, which could only have been the work of the little girl who produced a farthing in the sweet-shop, saying, " A farthing's worth of hundreds and thousands, and please pick out all pink ones."

# Succulents

But I do not go so far as to divide the Gasterias into the tongue-shaped forms such as *G. verrucosa* and those which, like *G. disticha,* have their leaves arranged one above another like those of an open book. The wall is punctuated, so to speak, by stone vases which space out divisions for some families, but we have to be careful to make a break in a division now and then—for instance, a small grouping of pots and pans of Haworthias at the foot of the right-hand vase in one space, with two or more large specimen Aloes near the left-hand vase ; or a clustering of Echinopsis forms on either side of a vase, and a space of empty wall to right and left of them, while a neighbouring brace of spaces may be filled entirely, their vases and all, with various Mesembryanthemums. In this way the top of the wall becomes a very attractive feature of the summer garden, that is of great interest to any one who cares for succulent plants. The two last spaces between the vases at the west end of the wall are occupied all the year round by a collection of Sempervivums in pots and pans, that treated thus both grow well and are interesting. The great difficulty in arranging them attractively is to avoid the appearance of a nursery garden produced by so many seed-pans. So I have hunted diligently wherever I went for any sort of pots or pans of different shapes and sizes, and now there are scarcely three alike among the lot. Pigeons' drinking-bowls, pans with ornamental mouldings, and a few ordinary flower-pots of varying sizes, did much to help, and some large pots whose upper portions were broken, when sawn down at varying heights, completed the good work. When I have had

# My Garden in Summer

a game of Chess with them and castled the King, and a fellow too much like his neighbour has made a Knight's move, the general effect is good, much better than is shown in the illustration facing p. 198, the photograph for which was taken when rather too many of the pieces were standing on neighbouring squares, and the effect is too uniform and too much like the commencement of the game viewed from the front.

We give over four of the terrace beds at bedding-out time to succulents, for they are as suitable as any plants could be for this purpose, because, as the Darwin Tulips are their predecessors, we have to wait until nearly mid-June to bed out, that is until the Tulips are sufficiently ripened to be lifted, and nothing produces a much better immediate effect than good specimens of succulents ; the bed shown in the accompanying illustration will give an idea of the effect obtained. Many of the large specimens are sunk in their pots, as they can then be lifted more easily at the approach of frost. I like to group all of one kind together, better than matching them in twos and fours to make more or less of a pattern, as the result is less formal, and they gain in effect by being supported by their own kith and kin. I never had a name for the very tall-stemmed Sempervivum shown in the front of this bed, but with the unbranched stems and single crowns on the top, they remind me so much of the Co-operative Cauliflower of Edward Lear's inimitable story of *The Four Children* that I generally call my plants by that name, and think I must some day plant a couple of tall plants of *Opuntia cylindrica* on either side of one,

# Succulents

to represent the superincumbent confidential Cucumbers that accompanied that very original plant. The large rosettes seen by their side, with the hen-and-chicken-like ring of offsets round each, I believe to be *S. holochrysum*, a very handsome, dark green thing that contrasts well with the mauves, pinks, and greys of the various Cotyledons next to them. The best of all for soft colouring is *C. metallica crispa*, a rather rare form, as it is difficult to increase ; for while many kinds are easily propagated by breaking off and planting a leaf, this beauty resents such liberties and melts into tears, or, in other words, rots off at the slightest insult. The deepest in colour is *C. gibbiflora*, really a rich crimson at the edges of the leaves, with wonderful shadings of blue, grey, and purple. With a little care in blending their shades a very charming effect can be obtained, even without the help of their golden or orange and red flowers. When the Co-operative Cauliflower fellow flowers, he does it so thoroughly that the whole crown becomes a bouquet of branching stems and small, bright-yellow flowers, and then his very last leaf drops off and the flowers turn to seed heads, and that is the end of him ; but he produces a goodly number of offsets with thin stems from his fat central one before he thinks of flowering, so one should always keep a few youngsters as understudies.

*Aloe abyssinica* and *A. Hanburyana* are two fine bold species with long leaves curved upwards at the ends like the horns of Scotch cattle, but green and flat and therefore not a bit like them except in their curve. *A. ferox* has short, almost heart-shaped, leaves with great prickles growing out from their fat round backs and round their edges, and so contrasts well with the other two, but makes a good match for *A. mitraeformis*. *A. saponaria* has a form with leaves beautifully tesselated in two shades of green, but is surpassed in this line by the dwarf *A. variegata*, whose rich green and pure white bands form as remarkable a pattern as one can find in any plant, and have endowed it with the name of the Partridge Breast Aloe. We like to keep one of the smaller beds for extra choice kinds such as this Aloe and the variegated *Sempervivum arboreum*, and a curious plant that looks like a Rhipsalis, but is soon found out to be a Euphorbia by the simple experi-ment of sticking a pin in one of its joints, which in-stantly exudes the milky juice that betrays its identity. Other Euphorbias in bewilderingly different forms stand on the wall; there you will find *E. antiquorum* with horny dark brown edges armed with thorns round its curious five-sided joints, and *E. cereiformis* pretending its best to be a Cereus, while *E. pendula's* cylindrical joints are so many inches in length that they need support. Even the two ends of the stone seat in the centre of the terrace are made to bear a group of choice and small succulents, the large lead vases that stand in the centre of each preventing any large specimen sharing their perch. So here are small Mesembryanthemums such as *M. stellatum* and *M. barbatum*, and Mammillarias such as *M. elongata*, like a pot full of thimbles of all sizes.

These cactacean ' thimbles are beautifully decorated with brilliantly white, or yellow and white, stars, formed of radiating tufts of prickles, and so wonderfully symmetrical

# Succulents

both in their fashioning and in their arrangement round the thimble as to be a joy for ever to look at closely. Their beauty is even greater when a ring of bright red berries ornaments the business end of the thimble, having replaced the rather dingy yellow and brown flowers. *Crassula perfossa* generally has an honoured place here, quite at the edge, so that its growths may hang free of the stone moulding. Its leaves are opposite, and the two in each pair are so thoroughly fused together as to look like one, and as though the woody stem pierced through its centre, much like those sticks of green and red crystallised dainties that are packed along the sides of boxes of mixed preserved fruits ; but as the Crassula's leaves are not so gay they remind me quite as much of sticks of cat's meat, and I fear the plant is generally spoken of as the Cat's Meat Crassula here. A mixed group on the wall contains *Crassula* (once *Rochea*) *falcata* as background ; its great blue-green scimitars of leaves cross each other in a curious manner, and are so solid and blue they alone make it worth growing, but when late in the Summer it bears great heads of scarlet flowers, it is a still finer sight.

Some of the Kleinias contrast well with it, especially those that are fairly closely related to *K. articulata*, the well-known Candle-plant of cottage windows, and of which my first specimen was a gift from a dear old body who lived in the Alms-houses here, and had a taste for succulent plants. Its bluish-white candles are very effective when the leaves have fallen from them. *K. Anteuphorbium*, though its stems are green instead of blue, is an even more remarkable plant, for it will grow four feet

high, and its long candles are striped with dark and light
green, and look like the caterpillars of some giant Elephant
Hawk Moth. It is an interesting plant, too, for several
reasons; thus it is one of the oldest Cape plants in cultivation, and was brought to Europe in 1570—we might have
called it deported, had it happened nowadays — and
Gerard grew it in his garden, and writes of it, "The
whole plant is full of cold and clammie moisture, which
represseth the scorching force of Euphorbium, and it
wholly seemes at the first view to be a branch of greene
corall." Hence its name, being used as an antidote to
the poison of the dried juice of the officinal Euphorbia,
then much used in medicine, as long lists of its virtues
attest. In a similar way *Aconitum Anthora* got its name as
the remedy against the poison of *Ranunculus Thora*. There
are other curious facts connected with this Groundsel (all
Kleinias are but a group of Senecio according to modern
authors), and one is that its wild habitat is now unknown, and another that it has only been known to flower
twice in Europe—in Gloucestershire in 1732, when Dillenius saw and figured it, and again at La Mortola in 1874,
when it was drawn for the *Botanical Magazine*. A glance at
either portrait shows us we do not lose much, the flowers
being very markedly of the Groundsel build and quite ray-
less, and I prefer its coral appearance when naked of both
flower and leaves. The charm of *Kleinia tomentosa*, on the
contrary, is confined to its leaves, for they are covered
with a close, grey felt, that gives them the appearance of
being cut out of a piece of an old grey suède glove.
*Calibanus caespitosus* is a weird thing and a fitting com-

# Succulents

panion for these other freaks : it has a clumsy rounded stem like a piece of tree trunk, and here and there tufts of grassy leaves, much like those of a Dasylirion, spring out and look rather twisted and uncanny, and therefore it is named in honour of the monster Caliban instead of some eminent botanist. A few of the strangest looking succulents are too delicate to be allowed out even in Summer, and we shall find them in the span-roof vinery. Here live the fluffy Mammillarias with silky and feathery fibres among their stars which make them look like decayed grapes covered with mildew in the distance, but are beautiful objects when viewed through a lens, and with them are Mesembryanthemums, which like *M. tigrinum* are armed with two rows of teeth or claws suggesting beasts of prey, or have fat, rounded leaves, and seldom more than two or four of them at a time, which aided by their purple and grey mottlings closely resemble pebbles, and in their native habitats must be well protected by their mimetic colouring. *M. Bolusii* is one of the most extraordinary of these, with pairs of opposite leaves two inches wide, marvellously like rounded stones. As succulents have so many attractions for me, my collection has been constantly added to until it has become quite one of the features of the garden, but many people think it an awful pity we give up so much space in vinery and cool houses to this prickly, weird class of plants, that might be used to produce Tomatoes and other food for the inner man.

# CHAPTER XI

## How July Begins

I GENERALLY arrange to be absent from my garden in mid and late June, for I am one of those badly finished off persons whose mucous membrane never got the last coat of paint, or the right tempering or hardening, or whatever was needful to enable it to resist the irritation of grass pollen that is called Hay-fever. I believe I have tried every remedy that has been put on the market, and though some alleviated my particular forms of sneezing and eye-swellings, none made me feel well enough to be happy. I objected all along to have my nose cauterised, believing it dulls one's power of scent, which means so much to me that I would far rather snuffle and sneeze for one month and be able to smell clearly and keenly the other eleven than be robbed of any olfactory powers; and before the days of anti-toxins and injections I discovered so pleasant a cure that Hay-fever has become quite a valuable asset in my life scheme, for I must, " *absoballylutely must,*" as Grossmith used to say, carry my poor nose away from the flowering grass meadows to Alpine heights where a breeze blows off the snow. Once I reach an altitude of 3000 feet I am cured, and the sight of *Poa alpina* in its viviparous state by the side of a road assures me it is safe to draw in the breeze with expanded nostrils. A sea voyage might take me into a pollenless region ; but I hate the sea as much as I do Hay-fever, and, on the other hand, am glad of so good an excuse to get away to Nature's own rock garden at the very time it is making its bravest show, and looking as if it were doing so on purpose to please me and invite me to help myself to whatever I like. After three weeks of wandering on the everlasting hills just below the snows and in vast treeless spaces, where Roche Melon, the Cimon della Parla, or some other great peak, whether leagues distant or apparently hanging over one's head, is a constant companion of one's walks, till it becomes as familiar a portion of the daily landscape as the Cedar on the lawn, I feel my garden is insufferably crowded for the first few days after my return. I long to push the trees farther apart and to see away beyond the one-mile limit, that is all this flat country affords me, unless I climb to the chimney stacks. But how good it is to smell the Roses that are always in such masses on or about the 30th June, and to find the Strawberries ripe and plentiful after the fruit famine of the high Alps. Of course my own rock garden looks ridiculous until some lovely plant from New Zealand or the Rockies catches my eye, and the plant-love in me causes me to forget the spell of the five-mile stretch of a carpet of *Viola calcarata* or the twelve-acre snowfield whose whiteness is due to *Ranunculus pyrenaeus* and to drop on my knees to peer into the open face of some treasure whose beauty and rarity make a single plant almost as delightful to behold as half a mountain side of some more familiar flower.

# My Garden in Summer

It is a time of poignant pleasure and fresh revelations, though, when after unpacking one's basket and vasculum, and the contents have been watered and can be left to recover the shaking and squeezing of their journey before they are planted, I wander round to see what the garden has to show me, either in the way of a new-comer open for the first time or an old friend surpassing all its previous efforts. This season I find *Lonicera tragophylla* in this last class, for it has taken the two past seasons to fill its pergola post, and now has turned its attention to flowering with a whole heart, and so here we have a full orchestra of golden trumpets that ought to produce a stupendous fanfare ; but those rich yellow flowers only produce a show, and they offer little or nothing for the nose even — rather disgraceful for a Honeysuckle but forgivable in one so daffodilious in hue. *Trollius sinensis* was an out-of-season, solitary-flowered, pot specimen when I first saw its orange glory in a nursery frame, and fell in love with its crown of long-pointed petals rising above the widely-opened, Caltha-like sepals. I vowed then and there I must grow it, and now I find it a tall specimen with branching stems and half a dozen of the rich orange-coloured flowers, a finer plant even than I imagined. *Lilium Washingtonianum* has never flowered here before and may never flower again, so I gaze critically at its waxy flowers with their many lilac shades from lavender to rosy purple. I admire it enough to want to see its tall spike again, but not sufficiently to purchase bulbs every other season to keep it in its place. *Meconopsis Wallichii* is the sensation of the moment, and three tall,

# How July Begins

golden-furred stems bear newly-opened turquoise cups full of gold dust, for I have got hold of a good form at last of real blue colouring, quite different from certain others I nursed along to the flowering age only to find them pinkish or steely grey. But they look so thirsty and flabby after the three weeks' drought that has lasted throughout my absence, that tired as I am after my twenty-four hours of travelling from the plateau of Mont Cenis, I must go and fetch a can or two of water from the river. This errand causes me to pass *Romneya trichocalyx*, and I almost forget the thirsty Poppies, for this relation of theirs is revelling in the heat ; it has opened the first of its great, white flowers, and has many fat, yellowish-green, prickly buds in various stages ready to keep the pot a-boiling. The prickly outside of the calyx, as its name notifies, is the main botanical distinction between this and the better-known species *R. Coulteri*, and if that were the only difference I think even my botanical instincts would be left cold and indifferent towards it ; but as I find it more reliable here in the way of producing early and plentiful flowers I make a fuss of it. Here the year's shoots from the base produce a terminal flower-bud when they have reached about four feet in height, and almost every lateral shoot follows their good example, and a succession of flowers is kept up until frosts spoil the later buds. Both species are generally cut to the ground in our Winters, so this good habit of early flowering on young growths makes *R. trichocalyx* the more valuable form. There is a fine specimen of it at Glasnevin growing in the Orders beds that, aided by the softer Irish climate, sends up wands six feet and more in height, and is a fine sight when in flower. My plant was given me by Mr. Hiatt Baker, in whose delightful garden at Almondsbury it flowered for the first time in England, and is a root-cutting from the original plant ; so I am very proud of it, and I hope grateful to its kind donor. *R. Coulteri* is a variable species, and one can easily recognise two forms · a broad-leaved one that branches out very freely, forming a low, rounded bush, and is a stingy old curmudgeon in its views about providing flowers ; the other sends up straight wands that bear rather narrow leaves, but also a reasonable number of flower-buds, and this form is much more given to sending out suckers at a distance from the parent plant than the other, so should gradually replace the miserly one in gardens.

I wish the Cabbage Moth (*Mamestra brassicae*) could be induced to realise that death and disaster will pursue its brood of caterpillars when asylumed on Romneyas, and therefore Cabbages are safer orphanages for motherless larvae. No one grumbles at a few holes in the outer leaves of Cabbages, and even if these little green pests would eat them up entirely it would save gardeners and cooks from cutting them off ; but surely it is bad policy to bore into the white heart, for though it may be fat living it must often end in disaster under wrathful gardeners' feet, or in boiling and posthumous execration by the would-be consumer of unadulterated Cabbage. Still more rash is it to invade the Romneya of a keen gardener, to fret and filigree its leaves at first when small, and then to bore into fat buds so that they can only open as mere rags, like

Romneya trichocalyx.   (See p. 205.)

# How July Begins

the tattered old flags preserved in cathedrals. If the keen gardener is enough of an entomologist to recognise his enemy's style of work, he will sally forth after dark with an acetylene bicycle lamp and catch Master Cabbage Moth. It is a revelation to go round the garden on mild nights with such a powerful light, for the army of robbers and murderers in the slug and insect line one meets with makes one wonder that any plants are left whole. Caterpillars that are hidden in the ground or under leaves by day lie out at full length after a meal on the upper surfaces of leaves, feeling there is nothing to fear ; or may be seen chewing away at the edge of leaf and bud, and are easily detected, as their colouring is shown up by acetylene light in a wonderful way that renders them conspicuous in spite of the patterns that are useful for hiding them in daylight.

The greatest change that I always notice in the rock garden on my return from the hills is the final two feet of growth and bursting into flower of *Campanula lactiflora*, which has become one of our weeds there, and if it were not ruthlessly evicted wherever it is not required would cover the whole place, including the moraines. It was first planted in the triangular flat portion that is now the Dwarf Almond copse, and is Mr. Farrer's delight and envy. I planted three seedlings, all I had, and if any clairvoyant had been crystal-gazing at the moment and told me I should in a few years be digging them up in hundreds to give away and throw away, I should have dug up those three infants, fearing the ruin of my garden. But as I destroy those which, like the abomination of desolation

# My Garden in Summer

spoken of by the prophet Daniel, stand where they should not, only leaving a row down each side of the path and a few others where they are doing no harm, the rock garden looks exceedingly well during the fortnight of their reign. Nearly all of them at this upper end of the rock garden are either the pure white form, which I think the loveliest of all, or of the skim-milk, bluish-grey tint that provided their specific name, and really blue forms very seldom appear among them. In the lower end, by the *Cotoneaster multiflora*, is another colony, but all of fine blue shades, having sprung from a different ancestor, a fine fellow still alive and hearty, though sent me some dozen or so years ago by Miss Anderson from Barskimming, and is still one of the finest blue forms I have seen. I hope she has many more as good in her lovely Scotch garden, and that she did not send me the best, though I cannot imagine a better form. In some seasons the five to six feet high flower-stems they produce have caused trouble where they grow beside the path by arching over, after a thunderstorm, until they meet in the centre, and the first who ventures to walk through them gets a shower-bath. So now I prepare for such emergencies by nipping off the heads of the stems nearest the path when they are only two or three feet high, which causes them to branch freely, and yet they flower at the same time as their untouched brethren behind, but on shorter stems that do not bend out so far, and have a very pleasing effect in the forefront. I also nip a few here and there just before I leave for Alpine rambles, and these come into flower a week or more later than the main show, and carry the season on a little. It

# How July Begins

is marvellous how soon *C. lactiflora* seems to change from lovely flower-heads eighteen inches high by ten through, into clusters of pepper-pots shaking out thousands of minute flattened buff seeds with every jolt and jar. So as soon as the majority of the flowers of a head look a little jaded it is wise to cut off the whole head, or you must prepare for a year or two's extra weeding of seedlings. If cut off close under the lowest flowers, the stems will branch out and flower again later in the season ; but it is a poor show that is provided by these small heads of lateral shoots compared with the waving masses of early July. In some gardens this Campanula has the reputation of never bearing seed, and I must own I should have put that tale down to over-tidy gardening, both in cutting off fading heads and hoeing the ground, but that I have two distinct forms here that have never so far produced any self-sown seedlings. One of these is a hairy, late flower-ing plant, with extra widely-gaping cups; in fact, they would be better described as small slop-basins, or surplus bowls, as I am told the ultra-refined in Suburbia are wont to name that useful part of the tea service. I saw it shown at one of the R.H.S. meetings, and ordered a plant at once, and though at least six years ago it is still innocent of rearing children. The other is a lilac-blue form, the one often shown and listed as *C. celtidifolia*, a name which it appears is nothing but a synonym. There is a widespread idea that the blue form is *C. celtidifolia* and the white *C. lactiflora*, and I believe it arises from an imperfect examina-tion of the literature of the species, and just shows how careful one must be when working out the identity of a plant. The facts are, I believe, these : Bieberstein first described the plant, and seems only to have met with the lighter forms, and so wrote "corollisque . . . lacteis aut dilutissime coeruleis " Then Boissier met with the blue, and under the name of *C. celtidifolia* described it as " cörollâ azureâ," and he must have had incomplete specimens before him, for he only allows it a stem of two and a half feet. But in his later work, the *Flora Orientalis*, he himself makes his *celtidifolia* to be the same as Bieberstein's *lactiflora*, and writes "corollâ . . . albidâ vel coeruleâ" which quite clears away the myth of a dwarf and blue form which should be called *celtidifolia*. I had spent an hour hunting up references at the Natural History Museum at South Kensington before I discovered this illuminating entry in the *Flora Orientalis*. Several other Campanulas, and their near relations the Wahlenbergias, are now making a show. A good tall one is another of Miss Anderson's kind gifts, namely *C. sibirica*, which has the general appearance of a very much improved *C. rapunculoides*, that horrible pest of most gardens, which runs about faster than the most active gardener can dig, filling one's choice beds with pink roots and leaves like a violet's, only more pointed, and it blossoms so seldom that it is not worthy of having even an untidy corner left to it. *C. sibirica* certainly runs too, but not very swiftly or very far, and it makes up for it by flowering very freely and producing yard-long spikes of beautifully shaped bells. I have had somewhat similar plants under the name *C. Grossekii* and *C. pulcherrima;* but they are great offenders in the running line and flower less handsomely than *sibirica*, so this latter species remains prime favourite. Just when they are at their best it is hard to beat the various forms of *C. latifolia*, such as its variety *macrantha*, both purple and white, and a closely allied plant I have as *C. lamiifolia*, and therefore must be wrongly named, as that seems to be no more than a synonym of *C. alliariaefolia*, while my plant is an even larger flowered form than *macrantha*, and may be a white form of another mysterious stranger, which ever since I knew it has borne the name of *C. tomentosa*, but I think has no right to it.

These are all giants, of course, but there are many dwarf Campanulas in flower in early July, and one of the loveliest is a wee plant I saw for the first time on the Clapham Nursery's table rock-garden at the summer show the R.H.S. held at Olympia, and I thought it the gem of the whole show. It bore the name *C. caespitosa Miranda*, and my admiration of it, and questionings as to its history, brought for reply from Mr. Farrer a healthy youngster in a thumb pot, with no history but an injunction to grow and enjoy it, but not to permit it to go any further until, like the starter of a race, he gave the word "Go." This July it is simply adorable in the fish-hatchery moraine, only two inches high, and its sturdy little grey-green leaves almost smothered with its short, wide-open bells, which are of the most fascinatingly quiet, cool lavender-grey imaginable, lovely enough by themselves, but by accident of both being new treasures, I planted it next to *Lewisia Howellii*, and the two flowered together, and the salmony-orange Lewisia flowers were the very exact bit of colour one's artistic nature would have longed

# My Garden in Summer

for against the cool, grey Campanula. Mr. Farrer has not yet said "Go," but Miranda has started running, though it is not likely to outrun the bounds of this garden for some time, for it is quite possible that, even after she is issuing freely from Clapham at so many florins the square inch, I may still find some chinks between edging stones that want filling with her dainty bells, as I feel sure I can never have too much of her. A somewhat similarly pale-coloured beauty overhangs a stone higher up in the same moraine, but has a slightly warmer tone. It is, I believe, a very nearly white form of *C. linifolia,* but has preserved a slight wash of rosy lilac, which appears chiefly in young blooms. I came across it in a wonderful spot, outside a little village in the hills behind Lago di Garda. At the time I was busily picking up white fragments of lime-stone from a vast stretch of débris at the foot of the hills, picking them up and throwing them over my shoulder as hard as I could do so, in a way that must have looked like an acute attack of lunacy. But there was method in my madness, for these barren-looking stone slides, when viewed at close quarters, were seen to be full of *Cyclamen europeum* in every stage of youth, adolescence, maturity, and old age, from babes with single leaves the size of the King's ear on a penny postage stamp, and a transparent corm no bigger than the eye of a mouse, to those with corms which looked like half a devilled kidney and bore many leaves and crimson flowers, lying on the surface of, or filling the chinks between, the white stones. To gather the roots no trowel was needed, only patience, and the throwing away of the stones until you

# How July Begins

reached the corm sitting on a pinch of soil formed by decayed vegetable matter washed down among the stones. Working up this stone-slide on hands and knees I suddenly came upon a great tuft of the pallid bells of the Campanula, and took away a portion of it to chaperon the Cyclamens in their journey to England.

How the sight of it now carries me back to that hillside behind picturesque Castellar, as Mr. Farrer has renamed the village in his *Among the Hills*, and how I should like a magic carpet to take me there to grub out more Cyclamens, and after gathering enough and a meal under the vine trellis of the Albergo, to go down among the hemp crops at dusk and inhale the sweetness of vine blossoms, and listen to the racket of the tree-frogs. To watch the whole place light up and twinkle with the lucirolli of both kinds, the orange-yellow lighted ones that come out first and turn their light off at regular intervals as they fly, producing two seconds of warm yellow light followed by two of darkness, like some revolving light in a light-house, and then, when the place is twinkling with them, like the lights that dance to one's eyes from a gently rippling sea with the sun in full face of you, the green-lighted fireflies put in their appearance, and fly more steadily and keep their light going all the time. That is the reward for going out to gather one's own plants—first happy hours in quaint and picturesque places, full of good sights, sounds, and scents, to be enjoyed then and remembered afterwards, when the unpleasant ones can be forgotten, and then in after years to have your treasures recall it all again as you look at them. Yes, visions of far away and un-get-at-able Castellar are pleasanter than those of making pencil marks in a nurseryman's catalogue, and adding up pounds, shillings, and pence till they agree somewhat with our spare cash.

*C. cenisia* in the piped moraine carries me up to La Nunda, the fort above the Lac du Mont Cenis, and a curious black shale rather like coal-dust out of which the Campanula's precious white threads must be coaxed. *C. cenisia* does not seem to love granite chips so much as that black mess, and I have been wondering lately whether small coal would not make a very useful moraine. I think I shall try it, for even should it prove a failure it might come in useful next time we suffer from a coal strike, and *C. cenisia's* blue stars would look well against the black surface. I think they are the nearest to blue of any Campanula, for Loddiges' figure of *C. rhomboidalis* in all its azure beauty is just a painted lie. *C. excisa* likes the sand moraine, and has behaved like some common Chickweed might in it this season. I put out a few seedlings last year, as I thought a thin cloud of their hair-like growths would be the very thing to keep *Gentiana verna* shaded and cool during the dog days. But I did not reckon on *excisa's* power of spreading, and it ran like a lamplighter. Why does one say "like a lamplighter," I wonder? Did that useful member of urban life ever run in the days of oil lamps? Perhaps they went wrong so often he had to run round all night putting them right. All the lamplighters I have ever known were very slow-footed folk, and now in these days of automatic bypasses the only one I see goes about on a

# How July Begins

bicycle apparently with nothing to do but to admire the illumination. Anyway, *C. excisa* runs like a lamplighter is supposed to, and it filled the Gentian bed so whole-heartedly that I had to tear out handfuls of its greenery and pale bells to let some light in to the Gentians, but I fancy it will exhaust the chemicals it likes from the soil, and continue to run only outwards in an ever-increasing circle like the ripple caused by a stone in a pond, dying out in the centre. I could give away a hatful of its white underground runners at any time this Summer, and yet perhaps I may be begging a bit back in a year's time, for I like its queer little bells, and the tiny round holes that look for all the world as though they had been bitten out by Bumble-bees to keep their jaws in good form for the days of the Scarlet-runner blossoms that they have learnt to steal honey from in a burglarious fashion.

Two Wahlenbergias from the southern hemisphere have crept into my affections lately, though one is practically an annual here, and the other doubtfully hardy. Both have been lately thrown into the melting-pot by Mr. N. E. Brown as to their naming, and I now feel as much puzzled as to what to call them as Good Queen Bess was in the case of the Bishop's wife. I used to believe the perennial but tender one was *W. saxicola*—but now if I trust Mr. Brown it must be *albomarginata*, for it has not got the "bright light blue" blossoms he declares to be indispensable for the true *saxicola* from Tasmania. It is an awful wrench to my trusting soul to have to imagine that so great, and recent, and on-the-very-spot an authority, as Mr. Cheeseman can possibly be wrong about New Zealand plants. Anyway, though *saxicola* I dare not call it because of its almost but not quite white flowers, it seems to have enjoyed the last mild Winter in the fish-hatchery moraine, and has formed a broad green mat now bearing many slender stems, each with a silvery grey bell or a bud. The other I used to call *W. gracilis*, believing it came from New Zealand and following the *Index Kewensis*—which just lumps everything it can catch under *gracilis*—and Cheeseman, who apparently knows only three species and lives among them. Now I think I must call it *W. vincaeflora*, and try to believe it is a perennial, in spite of not only its annual appearance but also its annual disappearance here.

Whatever it is, it is a beautiful plant, and quite worth the trouble of saving a pinch of its minute seed to start in a pot each Spring, for a baby thing of six leaves put out in the rock garden in April will be a cloud of exquisitely soft lilac-blue from July till sharp frosts spoil the flowers. I cannot see why it should not sow itself, but so far it has not, or else we have failed to recognise its seedlings, and have weeded them out.

*Meconopsis integrifolia* is good in this my latest moraine, in the sandy and peaty portion near the watering drainpipe, and its great, lemon-yellow flowers have long enough stalks for once to satisfy me. Hitherto they have always been short and looked out of proportion to the flowers, and even now I am not greatly in love with it, and think when its nasty biennial ways have carried the last of my plants off I shall not bother about replacing it, and I don't suppose it will sow itself. It always strikes me as looking somewhat artificial, as if made of crinkled paper, and set

# How July Begins

on one of those compressed cotton-wool stalks that support the peculiar class of sham flower designed for the decoration of small tables in provincial hotels, awful plant parodies that make my flesh creep. Quite a contrast to the clumsy build of the Meconopsis is the graceful tangle made by that uncommon little shrub *Atraphaxis Billardieri*, of which I have a good single specimen on the rock garden that is attractive even when out of flower, for it looks something like a Muehlenbeckia with a stiffer habit like that of *Corokia Cotoneaster*, and its fine, wiry stems and small dark leaves contrast well with its neighbours. These are a fine specimen of *Crataegus Oxyacantha inermis*, the Thornless Thorn, the close-packed leaves and thick stems of which are the exact opposites of the Atraphaxis, a round-headed bush of *Ononis fruticosa*, and a spreading mound of a variegated tree Ivy. The Atraphaxis needs a stake or two as it has grown some five feet high, and must be kept from sprawling out too widely into its neighbours, which were planted rather nearer to it than they would have been had I then known the dimensions they would all assume later on. At the end of June *A. Billardieri* covers itself with bunches of small, white blossoms very much like those of *Polygonum baldschuanicum;* they last in flower for a long time, and remain on until the seeds are ripe, which is from about the middle of July into August. As the little triangular seeds turn black, so the parts of the flower begin to flush pink, and finally become a deep rose colour, and are as loth to fall off as I am to lose them, so that well into August the bush glows with rosy tints. As the triangular seeds proclaim, it is a Polygonaceous

# My Garden in Summer

plant and a near relation of the Docks and Sorrels, but I have never yet found a self-sown seedling as the result of the many hundreds of seeds it bears, and how I wish I could say the same of its vulgar, more pushing relations named above. My plant was given me as a yearling by Doctor Müller, and about four years afterwards he saw it here in flower, and asked what that lovely thing was. I was as much surprised at his asking its name as he was to learn it, for his plants of the same age had shown no sign of flowers, and he had no idea they could be so beautiful. I have another species, *A. lanceolata*, from the Cambridge Botanic Garden, but it has a less neat habit and larger leaves, so that in spite of larger flowers it is not so pleasing in general effect. I have tried another twain from Tiflis, of which *A. buxifolia* has lingered on, but it has disclosed no charm as yet, and the other died because it resented being shifted out of a pot the seedlings had occupied for three months.

# CHAPTER XII

## Grasses

ALTHOUGH my sensitive nose suffers so much from Grass and the flowers of Grasses, my eye delights in the beauty of form that the Grass family provides. I give a rather wider meaning to the term Grasses than is strictly and botanically correct, using it for garden purposes to include not only the Bamboos, as is legitimate, but sundry Sedges and Rushes that produce effects in the garden similar to those of the true Grasses. One often sees well-filled gardens where about the only Grasses are those that form the turf of the lawns and a clump of Pampas Grass and possibly a Miscanthus or two, but just as bulbous plants never look so well as when naturalised in grass as, for instance, the Daffodils at Warley, and even the Crocuses in Regent's Park, so I think many of our gorgeous summer flowers look all the better when they have clumps of grassy foliage or feathery flowering heads growing among them to soften their effect.

The alpine meadow is my beau ideal of a large flower bed, and when flowers of every hue are distributed over a waving undergrowth of greenery of all shades from bronze to pea green, and thence to the green of the sea, even the most combative tints are rendered peaceful, and

# My Garden in Summer

their sharp corners rounded off to the sensitive eye, by the wholesome balm of surrounding verdure. I would give anything possible in the shape of toil and thought, even putting up with such evils as dirty nails and worn-out garments, to achieve even a quarter of an acre of such a meadow as those I was rushed past in the autobus on the outskirts of Predazzo in the Dolomites. I passed through those two or three miles of living tapestry three times in one week, and each time I nearly screwed my head off trying to see everything on both sides of the road, longing for the optical opulence of the Beast of the Apocalypse, who was full of eyes behind and before. I never saw such a wealth of *Salvia pratensis* elsewhere, for solid lakes and meres of royal purple were provided by it, whose shores were spangled with a mixture of its own purple mingled with St. Bruno's Lily till the effect reminded me of cream and whortleberries not thoroughly stirred together, and conjured up visions of luncheons at wayside inns and farmhouses on Exmoor. Then *Anemone alpina,* Orchids of almost every species in Europe except those that must have morass or deep woodland shade; crimson Onobrychis, blue Campanulas, yellow Goat's Beard, pink Bistort, and a thousand other delights were inextricably woven into the grassy background. Now the effect of squares and triangles of each of these various plants packed into an ordinary border with large labels to each phalanx and bare soil between them would be a paltry mess without their grass background and the natural and irregular distribution of the clumps or single specimens of each. I want to see a bed full of Delphiniums and orange and white

# Grasses

Lilies, and our best herbaceous plants, but with an undercurrent of tufty grasses. Then, again, on a smaller scale, I long for the close, short turf that makes the natural setting for Gentians and *Primula minima*, *Viola calcarata*, and Douglasia, but so far have failed to find a tiny grass that is content to play second fiddle and will not, like the *Campanula excisa* of the last chapter, insist upon banging the big drum.

*Mibora verna*, a minute annual and a rare native species found in Anglesea, is the best I have found for the grassing of the moraine, but it makes tufts not turf, and dies away in the height of Summer, not appearing again until after the August thunderstorms. It is a dainty little thing, just tufts of pea-green hair like fat paintbrushes filled with Hooker's Green, and then from January onward it bears tiny spikes of purple-black blossoms with conspicuously white anthers and stigmas, that powder their heads so thoroughly they look as white as that of the tallest footman who ever wore powder. So you must not expect to see the miniature alpine turf in the moraine or the waving meadow in the herbaceous bed as yet, for both of these things are still ideals that I am working for but have not achieved, although I believe both are growing nearer to my grasp. I have worked diligently in collecting grasses, and many kinds are under probation, and several only need heaving up and planting among the gayer plants whenever the chance for remodelling a bed may arrive. I make a point of visiting the grass beds in every Botanic Garden I enter, and an open eye and a notebook have already gone far to teach me the range of useful grasses suitable for our climate. I first look for a tufted habit combined with a graceful appearance. It is difficult to harden one's heart to refuse the charms of some species with running habits, but as there is a sufficient wealth of good, tidy stay-at-homes, it is wiser to do so. The grass beds teach one that point, but it is only by trial at home one learns whether or not the grass is too free a seeder. I have only found two that are sufficiently plaguey to cause loss of temper. Of these *Melica altissima* is so handsome with its wide, pale green foliage, and rich purple or pale flesh-coloured flower-heads, that one must have it, and so put up with spending an anxious ten minutes now and then in extracting a tufted seedling from the centre of *Aphyllanthes monspeliensis,* or some other choice plant of grassy appearance in whose sheltering arms it has lain hidden until it has reached a size that makes it hard to extract. The other is *Festuca elatior,* a fine, rough, handsome grass, growing four feet high, but better in a wild garden than in my ideal meadow.

Now for some really good ones ; but please remember that, the sorting out of grasses by botanical descriptions being rather dull work, I have taken the names of those that came to me from Botanic Gardens or reliable sources on trust as readily as a dog does his biscuit, and have snapped up the plants as greedily as my dog does when the magic words " Paid for " close his bargain. Many of the Airas are very useful, and even *A. caespitosa,* though so undesirable in pasture land, where farmers execrate it as

# Grasses

hossacks, is fine for a fairly moist place, and makes a neat rounded tuft ; whilst the tall flowering stems, delightfully light and elegant, appear in July and last until Spring. A very fine form of this plant was brought from New Zealand, called by a new name which I have forgotten, and managed to make a successful début as a new grass until the Kew authorities recognised it as only a large form of our wild grass. I burnt its label but left the plant, and it has made a very handsome tussock in the rock garden, and when in flower is nearly five feet in height from ground to flower top. Another Aira came to me as *A. flexuosa,* but I have misgivings as to its identity, and it may be a dwarf form of *A. caespitosa.* It is very useful to plant among herbaceous things, making low green tufts and a feathery mass of flowery stems, which are attractive from flowering time in July, when the photograph facing p. 224 was taken, until one must tidy them away in Spring. Although it must bear many thousands of seeds, I have never yet noticed a self-sown seedling, and I can only increase it by division.

There is a lovely and interesting form of *A. caespitosa* which I have always called *A. vivipara.* It is a mountain form, and keeps up its habit of increase by young plants produced by the flower-stems in place of flowers just as much in this hot, dry garden as it originally did on cloud-soaked mountain sides, where pollen would have no chance of doing its work of fertilisation ; so from July onwards one gets dense plumes of brilliant green thread-like leaves in place of grey, fluffy flower-heads, their only fault being that when heavy rains soak the thick green plumes they

# My Garden in Summer

fall over to rise no more. As they last green and fresh until late in Autumn it is best to plant it on a bank by a stream side, or in the rock garden where the heads can hang down, and it looks especially well among ferns and tufts of the Gladwin, *Iris foetidissima*, in rather wild places. *Stipa calamagrostis* is a very fine grass ; the long, feathery inflorescences are produced freely, and reach some two feet high, arching out all round the tuft ; they are very soft and feathery when fresh, and as they dry they turn to a pleasing light buff and last on the plant all the Winter. *Stipa formicaria* I have already praised for its long, waving, hygroscopic awns ; but its long, hair-like, deep green leaves deserve a word of praise, too, they are so long and so light, but it sows itself rather too freely for the very unco' neat, perhaps. *S. gigantea* is very well behaved in this line, and does not increase unduly, and the stiff, upright flower-stems bear long awns arching out on either side in a way that gives it an air of its own. *S. pennata*, the long plumes of which look so wonderfully like an extra long piece of ostrich feather blown out of some lady's boa, does not grow too well here, and I want more of it, for it is wonderfully effective in the foreground, and reminds me of Italian alpine slopes. I have made a collection of grasses in a bed near by the pond with just a few showy flowering plants among them, and I am well pleased with the contrasts afforded by the various species. The tallest there is *Miscanthus saccharifer*, whose stems annually reach six feet or more and are very handsome, with ample leaves springing from them. A Millet I have had for a long time under the name *Panicum maximum* comes next for size, and

# Grasses

has grand, arching, deep green leaves, and gets about five or six feet high each season before the first sharp frost cuts it down. It is not over hardy here, and is the better for some ashes placed over the roots in sharp winters; it requires good feeding and the thinning out of its shoots to get the full size of its leaves if it is left in the ground for more than two seasons. A still better plan is to lift and divide the stools in Autumn and start strong pieces in a house in Spring to plant out when frost is over. Even by so doing I have never got it to perfect its flowers here, though in one hot season they began to push out of the top growths. *Panicum virgatum* is hardier, and one of the lightest and most effective of tall flowering grasses, about four feet high and at its best in Autumn. *P. clandestinum*, as its name suggests, is rather unobtrusive about its matrimonial arrangements, and the spikes of flowers scarcely appear out of the large rolled, upper leaves; but it has a neat, close habit and remarkably wide, light-green leaves, the whole plant growing about eighteen inches high. *Oryzopsis miliacea* is a great treasure, as its long flower-stems bend out most gracefully and carry light plumes of great length; it never seems tired of flowering, but throws up fresh stems as green and fair as those of June until well into November, keeping the grass bed waving and summery until hoar frosts transform it into a thicket of corals and crystals fit for a mermaid's garden.

I dug up a very tufted, stiff-leaved grass on Mont Cenis, chiefly because it aroused my interest by looking, in its spring resurrection garb, so exactly like a tuft of Crocus leaves that it often deceived even my Crocus-

# My Garden in Summer

trained eye, and made me believe I had lit upon some extra fine and strong form of *C. vernus,* until I was close enough to look for the tell-tale white, central stripe which reveals most Crocuses. Of course it was never there, and I got a little cross with the Crocus-grass, but brought a tuft home to learn more of its ways. It has taken two years to get settled and pluck up heart enough to flower, and I rather like the close, heavy heads, as they are of a peculiar dark shade of brown, and unlike any other grass I possess. But I thought it better to cut them off young, in case they behaved as they seemed to promise, and sowed themselves everywhere, and made me believe they were Crocuses once more. *Uniola latifolia* is a good perennial grass three feet high, neat and upright in habit, and with pretty flower-heads like those of *Briza maxima,* but as though they had been pressed flat. *Pennisetum macrourum,* from South Africa, gets knocked about here in severe winters, but when kindly treated by Jack Frost produces in July long tails, as its specific name so plainly promises. These are eight inches or more in length and cylindrical, about half an inch in diameter, and look like a hybrid between a Siamese cat's tail and a pipe-cleaner. *Lygeum Spartium* has narrow rush-like leaves, and very curious flowers and seeds that look like one huge oat placed at a right angle with the end of the stem, and wrapped in a silky jacket. It is an interesting plant, because, like the Esparto Grass (Stipa), it has been largely used for paper-making, and I have been told that at one period *The Times* was printed on paper made from it. *Elymus glaucus* is a coarse runner and robber, and many

# Grasses

things that it ought not to be; but it is so blue and so hardy, and so easily rendered happy in a dry corner, that it is a precious possession, not only for its garden effect, but also for cutting for a tall vase, for its foot and a half long, glaucous leaves live well in water. It has made a pleasant picture here near the end of one of the paved walks by walking about among some white-flowered *Thalictrum aquilegifolium* and blue Comfreys, but it would soon strangle them all if I did not occasionally come to their rescue, and loose its cruel fingers from their necks. *E. giganteus* is less violent, and though not so blue, is well worth growing, as it is a tall, handsome grass with large, wheat-like ears.

When a sheltered corner and light soil can be given it *Arundo Donax* is the king of grasses for foliage effect, and will shoot up twelve-feet-high stems, each bearing about forty wide leaves of a fine glaucous green. In warm climates, and here after mild winters, these stems shoot out in their second year from almost every node and make a mass of grey foliage, but then are not so effective as the young shoots of the year, and, of course, if many of the old stems persist the young ones do not grow so tall or so strong; so I prefer to cut them all down in early Spring except two of the very tallest, which I leave to show their habit of shooting out, and also as a gauge to measure the new shoots against. I find it is only hardy enough to be really effective here in a well-drained spot, and my finest clump crowns a mound in the wilder part of the rock garden, a mountain whose main geological feature is a sandiness

# My Garden in Summer

ie to its being composed of road scrapings. The
riegated form of this Giant Reed is one of the most
orious of all variegated plants, but not hardy enough
be more than a chronic invalid out of doors here, and
put out for the Summer the variegation gets scorched,
it has to live in a sanatorium—I mean the conserva-
ry. *A. conspicua*, from New Zealand, is better further
uth or West, as it likes both moisture and warmth, and
: cannot combine the two, so it also struggles along
th occasional illnesses and long convalescences, and it
not every season we get its graceful Pampas-grass-like
umes, that should come two months earlier than those
the Pampas-grass, which latter are too often ruined by
st. With the exception of Bamboos and Miscanthus
ecies, which are at their best in the Autumn, and so
ust be reserved for a later review of the garden, I
ve mentioned most of the larger forms of Grasses I
ve tried, and we must now turn to the smaller fry
ited for the edge, or about a foot from it in the border.

*Melica uniflora* from Surrey lanes is as useful as any,
t easily offended with any sort of treatment ; a graceful,
ir green tuft for most months of the year, and its little
rrow flower-spikes are charming. I have, too, a very
ettily variegated form of it that looks well among its
een kith and kin. *Melica papilionacea* is addicted to ne-
tism, and plants out descendants rather too freely, but
ey are neither deep rooters nor runners, and so are
sily dislodged when not required ; its long flower-spikes
ow delightfully white and silky in old age, and are not
be despised in their proper place. Even in the rock

# Grasses

garden a good tuft growing in a crevice is not always an intruder, and sometimes gives shelter or an effect of contrast one may be glad of. *Bouteloua oligostachya* comes from New Zealand, and is a dainty little species for the rock-garden with very fine leaves and the quaintest make of flower-heads : they stand at right angles to their stalks, and are for all the world like a little brush made on purpose to go with a small doll's dustpan. These little brown brushes last on the plant for a long time, and I like to see a tuft or two of their sombre, soft hues among the bright alpine flowers. A good Cotton Grass I found in Tyrol among the tufts of *Primula minima* has accompanied them home, and waves its snowy-white tassels over their heads to remind them of the Rolle Pass where both were born. *Poa alpina vivipara* also finds an honoured place among Edelweiss and Primulas, and its bright green tassels of budding youngsters stand upright for a good long time, and then fall over and lie on the ground, but do not seem to have the sense to arrange matters well enough for the babes to fall off and get rooted on their own account, and unless I intervene and plant them, they simply lie there attached to the stem until some extra grilling dog-day frizzles them up, or a garden visitor finds a home and use for them. The ordinary form with its dwarf tufts and purplish-grey flower-heads is quite worthy of admission to the rock garden, and is good in tufts here and there among a colony of various Houseleeks. *Briza maxima* I have already praised as a self-sowing annual, but *B. media,* the native Quaking-grass, is perennial, and a pretty effect may be obtained by allowing a tuft or two to grow in the rock garden. It occurs in our meadows, but I never thought of bringing it into the garden until I accidentally introduced it with a Gentian from Mont Cenis. The dwarf Fescues provide some most useful species for forming cushions at the edge of the borders, or velvety mounds among the rocks. *Festuca viridis* is a fine deep green, and *F. glauca* one of the best blue-grey plants in existence. The flowers of these two are not effective enough to add to the attraction of the dense cushions, so I like to pull them out as soon as they appear, which thickens the growth of the tufts. The best dwarf variegated grass is *Molinia coerulea fol. var.*, and in the early Summer many of the tufts have more white than green in them ; it makes the more generally grown variegated Cock's-foot, *Dactylis glomerata*, look grey and dull beside its purer white. *Arrhenatherum bulbosum* has a good silver variegated form, too, but needs frequently replanting in good soil to keep it in its best form. All of these look well if mixed among green forms, but the golden Grasses are better kept away from them. *Phleum pratense* is the best striped golden one, and very brilliant in Spring and early Summer if the flower-heads are pulled out when young, for that helps to keep it both golden and dwarf, so that it is suitable for the front of the border. I have already written of the pure yellow Grass I got without a name from Birmingham Botanic Garden and the pallid gold, like the worn-out gilding in the bowl of an old egg-spoon, of a so-called Golden Cock's-foot, but I must tell of a fine tall one, *Miscanthus japonicus fol. var.*, which came to me from The Holt garden in happy days when its cheery, kindly planner and planter, Andrew Kingsmill, was still among his friends and plants. It is so much like the Common Reed in general appearance that I mistook it for a well-grown patch of the variegated form of this plant when I first saw it at Harrow Weald, and it was after some years of admiration, when I asked how it grew so tall in so comparatively dry a spot, that I was told its true genus, and, of course, instantly asked for a bit. I was handed a basket and fork and bidden to help myself, according to the generous custom at The Holt, and how I toiled to dig down to the running rhizome which I knew must exist somewhere to connect the tall stems, and how they persisted in breaking away with so little of anything that looked of a growing nature, and likely to produce a young plant! I never got down to the runners, but every piece of broken stem I brought away rooted well after it had been potted and petted up for a few months, and now they are beginning to spread in the Bamboo bed here.

Sedges are not Grasses, of course, on account of their more perfectly formed flowers; but for garden effect they can mostly be reckoned among them. Exceptions are *Carex Fraseri*, with dark, broad, leathery leaves suggestive of a small Aspidistra, and wonderful ivory-white flowers among them in Spring; *C. scaposa*, much like it but with pink flowers; and *C. pyrenaica*, with handsome tufts of broad green leaves more like those of a Plantain than a Sedge, and dull brown flowers. These three like moist, shady corners of the rock garden and a good deal of attention; even then they are fussy and fretful, disinclined to be friendly, and will never make themselves cheap. Quite otherwise, *C. baldensis* runs out in all directions, and soon makes a mat of its narrow, bright-green leaves. I have never been up Monte Baldo to see it there, but was pleased to meet with it on the hills on the opposite side of Garda, where also grew a smaller and neater species with white flowers, very attractive as seen there, but which has not yet settled down enough here to display its charms. *C. Vilmorinii* is a tufted species from New Zealand, at least so says the *Kew Hand-list;* but it is not to be found in Cheeseman's *Manual.* I only know it in a variegated form which comes true from seed, and should greatly like to learn more of its history and whether a green form is in cultivation. It makes an interesting-looking tuft of long, hair-like leaves, and the flowering stems are surprisingly long and very untidy as they straggle on the ground, and as it seeds with unpardonable freedom, I cut its hair when it gets too shaggy. *Carex montana,* a rare native, is as neat as the other is untidy, and makes a good wholesome green mat all the Summer, turns a fine fox-red in Autumn, and bears delightful, black paint-brushes for flowers in Spring, which, as they lengthen, hang over and then become dusted with pollen as if dipped in yellow paint. *C. Buchananii* is claimed by Cheeseman for New Zealand, and finds honourable mention in the *Manual.* It must be a curious sight where large districts, as Cheeseman states, are covered with the reddish-purple form of this Sedge. Here, among green plants, it looks as though it were dead, for the upper surface of each leaf is a drab or buff colour and the lower side is a purplish-brown,

# Grasses

even in the youngest leaves, and it looks as though it must feel dry and withered to the touch ; whereas it is actually very cool and smooth, and most likely pleasantly juicy to browse. I have another somewhat similarly coloured Sedge I raised from seed given me by Captain Pinwill, but it is redder and never looks so thoroughly defunct as *C. Buchananii*. *Scirpus Holoschoenus* has tall rush-like leaves and very distinct flower-heads gathered into round balls on short stalks of various lengths growing from the main stalk ; it looks well among other grassy plants, and holds the flower-heads of one year until those of the next are ready to take their place. It is rare in England, and one of the special plants of Braunton Burrows in North Devon.

There are many other grassy plants scattered about the garden, especially in and around the ponds, such as *Cladium mariscus* and *Cyperus longus*, which have already received their meed of praise. *Cyperus vegetus*, on the contrary, will only live here. in very hot and dry places, although in warmer climates it prefers moisture. It is of American origin, but widely naturalised in South-western Europe. Its inflorescences are curiously like green parrot's feathers, as they are made up of closely-packed floral scales in two opposite ranks. Others that like wet feet and catch no colds in their heads from perpetual sloppiness are *Carex Gaudichaudiana*, which came all the way from Japan, but is much like some of our native tussock-forming Sedges; *Schoenus nigricans*, from the Norfolk Broads, which has long, rush-like stems with tufted heads of black flowers on the top of each, and *Juncus acutus*,

233

# My Garden in Summer

quite a youngster as yet, but which makes a handsome clump of stiff, dark-green leaves when mature, very noticeable and distinct among lighter grasses. *Sesleria nivea* looks a rather coarse weed except when covered by its white spikes. *S. coerulea* is neater, but has disappointed me so far in producing precious little blue in its flowers, and it was only because in books it was pictured as blue as a summer sky that I wanted it ; and the same complaint attaches to *Luzula lutea* as regards its golden reputation, for here again the artists have flattered the sitter, and not even at home in the Alps do I ever see it the brilliant creature of their fancy, yet I give it a welcome as it reminds me pleasantly of my first meeting with it at the turn by the Waterfall in the steep ascent to Piora. Several other Luzulas are worth growing, and *L. nivea,* from the Alps, is welcome to sow itself as it likes in the rock garden and to wave its snowy heads from carpets of Aubrietia or cracks in rocks. *L. maxima* from North Devon is a charming lush-green plant for a shady place where it will not dry up, and *L. marginata,* given me by Mr. Chambers, seems easy to please, and looks like a form of *maxima* with the added charm of silver lines edging each leaf. A handsome evergreen grass grows in a bed on the lawn, and provides suitable leaves in Winter for picking to use with *Iris unguicularis,* and sends up tall, thin stems with beautifully light heads, which are good to look at all through the Winter, especially in sunlight or when covered with hoar frost. The sparrows are fond of its seeds, and have found out that they can perch on the heads and so weigh them down till they touch the ground, when they pick out all

# Grasses

the seeds while they hold them down ; then they fly to
another head, grasp it firmly, and fluttering gently bend
it down. I was very angry with them when I first wit-
nessed this performance, making certain they would ruin
the effect of the plant for the Winter ; but I soon noticed
that the grass stems did not break, but as soon as the
sparrow got off them rose up into their places again, so
I now rather enjoy watching the feast. At one time I
grew *Apera arundinacea* very well here, and its wonderfully
long, hanging heads and bronze autumn colouring delighted me both in the rock garden, where it hung over
some big stones, and especially in some fine old stone
vases ; but hard winters killed it, and I have never
been able to get it to grow so strongly again. I shall
keep on trying to do so, as the Pheasant's-tail Grass, as it
is called—goodness knows why, as it is no more like a
pheasant's tail than a pig's—is one of the most beautiful
of all the light Grasses.

I have reviewed some of the material for making a
grass border or an alpine meadow, and even though I
may never achieve it, I should be as proud as a dog
with two tails if some one with greater space and
leisure, and more gardeners and bawbees than I possess,
should be fired by this chapter to bring the idea to
perfection. I can see with my mind's eye how beautiful the soft, waving undergrowth would be if groupings of five to fifteen specimens of the most suitable
Grasses were planted so that Lilies, Asphodels, Eremuri,
and Gladioli might spire up from between them, and
Anchusas, Delphiniums and Monkshoods, Thalictrum and

# My Garden in Summer

*Chrysanthemum maximum,* Heleniums and *Galtonia candicans,*
with Asters to follow, could grow in lines and clumps
between the groups of different kinds of Grasses, while,
nearer the front, Daffodils and Tulips in Spring, and
perhaps Antirrhinums of yellow shades, for Summer or
Autumn, could run in and out of the cushions of Fes-
tucas and light carpets of Briza. If such a scheme
should be adopted and prove a success, I hope I may
be asked to go and see it, and I shall not expect to
find a life-size statue of myself placed in the middle of
the Ideal Meadow, even should this new phase of
gardening become so popular as to supersede moraines,
both in the garden and in horticultural small talk. One
has seen much of the planting of flowers among grass,
where grass already exists in meadows, but I have never
yet met with a flower-bed of herbaceous plants, carpeted
with tufts of Grasses between the flowers—I believe it
could be done, and, what is more, that it would be worth
the doing.

# CHAPTER XIII

## Daisies

THERE comes a time in July when the whole garden suddenly bursts into Daisies. I do not mean on the lawns—they have been old offenders for months already—but in the flower-beds, and where Marguerite would have had to hunt rather diligently for a fortune-telling Composite flower a month ago, she could now pluck a bouquet of all colours, and, if one gave her an undesired answer, another flower could be used of quite a different hue. *Pyrethrum roseum* she might find earlier in most gardens, but here it would not suit her purpose, for it is about the only flower in which I prefer the double to the single form, and a double Pyrethrum would need a deal of picking to bits. I think it is the vulgar, glaring yellow of their discs that makes me dislike the single Pyrethrum. It goes so badly with the crimson or raspberry-ice coloured forms, and I never saw a cream or buff single flower; white ones are scarcely wanted while the fields are full of *Chrysanthemum leucanthemum*, the Dog Daisies of some children, the Stinking Johnny Moons of others. I have a warm affection, though, for some double Pyrethrums, such as Solfaterre, of soft, creamy yellow shades, or pearl white and flushed pinks, but alas so have

the slugs, though their affection is not seated in their eyes
—I am not sure they have any—but in their ever filling,
never full, adaptable stomachs, in which are combined
the functions of progression and digestion. I attribute
the failure of many plants in this garden entirely to slugs,
the damage being done in February and March, when
every bite into a newly-awakened bud cuts through
many closely-packed leaves, and one of the reasons that
newly constructed rock gardens and freshly dug borders
produce such good results is the fact that they are not
yet colonised by those marauding gasteropods. *Aster
alpinus*, in its many lovely forms, loses every bud unless I
visit it nightly with a lamp and hat-pin, or bury its growths
in a sandy top-dressing, and I fear, in most seasons, I have
to forgo the full measure of flowers, lacking time and
patience for either of these operations.

There are daisy-flowered subjects to be found in the
rock garden in June, many Achilleas for instance, such
as *A. Clavennae*, *A. moschata*, and *A. umbellata;* also real
Daisies, varieties of *Bellis perennis* and *B. rotundifolia
coerulescens*, which is flattered in English by being called
the Blue Daisy because it isn't quite white. *Pyrethrum
Tchihatchewii*, with its imitation sneeze of a name, bears
white Daisies freely on its feathery green turf in June,
but if you wish for Composite flowers of the Daisy type,
suitable for large vases before mid-July, you must go to
the hay meadows for Dog Daisies. But when the *Campanula lactiflora* rush is abating, the garden erupts Daisies
everywhere, and a stream of them flows on that will not
run dry until the last of the *Aster Tradescantii* flowers are

# Daisies

overwhelmed by December frosts, and indoor Chrysanthemums have replaced the outdoor vase-fillers. Most daisy-flowered plants are suitable for cutting, and easy to arrange if used freely and naturally, lasting well in water; and I much enjoy the first July day when a whole flower-table is furnished with members of the Compositae. The Erigerons are, as a rule, the first comers, and I can recommend the beautiful seedling raised at Westwick, and now distributed as Quakeress, as one of the best. It is charming in a large group in a border, and equally so when cut, for it is lighter in habit than *E. speciosus*, and of a softer and more rosy-lilac shade. So we now grow a patch in the kitchen garden on purpose for cutting from freely, and I have known a vase of it to last in full beauty for a fortnight, even in hot weather that turned Sweet Peas and Roses into food for dustbins in two days. I imagine it is a seedling with the combined bloods of *E. speciosus* and the nearly white-flowered one known in gardens as *salsuginosus*, but quite wrongly, as is shown by a good plate of the true, stiff-stemmed, blue-flowered plant in an early number of the *Botanical Magazine*. This whitish flowered plant is graceful in habit and has the same hanging buds as Quakeress, but it is not very free in flowering, and produces more blind rosettes than flower-stems, otherwise it would be useful to mix with deeper-coloured forms. Quakeress takes after *speciosus* in throwing up a dense sheaf of flower-stems, so that, even from one's show clumps in the herbaceous beds, many stems can be cut without spoiling the effect. Then comes *Anthemis tinctoria*, of which the pale, cream-coloured form, known as variety

# My Garden in Summer

Kelwayi, is a good companion for the soft canary-yellow one, called **E. C.** Buxton, after that keen and skilful gardener, the owner of that beautiful garden at Bettws-y-coed, in which this fine form first appeared, and whose generous hand soon afterwards uprooted a portion of it to be one of the delights of my garden. Anthemis flowers are inclined to sulk for a few hours after they find themselves removed from the open air and sunshine to a vase in a cool, shady room, putting back their ears behind their round faces in the same way as they do out-of-doors each evening, but the temper fit generally wears off next day, and, like the Doronicums of April and May, when once they put on a smiling expression and look pleasant, as the photographer suggests you should when you are fondly imagining you are looking your best, they keep it up day and night for the rest of their existence.

Pure white Composites are not plentiful before the various forms of *Chrysanthemum maximum* are in full swing, so at the beginning of July, both in the border and for cutting, I prize a good semi-double *Chrysanthemum leucanthemum* that flowers later by some weeks than the wild form of the meadows, and lasts well. I got it from Ware's original Hale Farm nursery at Tottenham, so that alone shows it is no novelty, for the nursery has long since disappeared. It is a plant that requires pulling to bits and replanting every second year, and as boys say, though it is not greedy it certainly likes a lot, and of the best the *chef* of the garden can dish up—a *soufflé* of leaf soil and bone meal for instance. The flowers are to my thinking very pretty, having many ray florets, most of them narrower than in the wild type, and a few of the innermost are nearly as slender as threads, and stand upright in a way that softens the contrast of disc and rays.

Another early white Composite is the fairly new, white form of *Bidens dahlioides*, which has so far proved hardy here. I prefer the white to the pink form, but both are pretty, and look like the flowers of a Cosmos growing singly on long, slender stems above the foliage of an Incarvillea. *Rudbeckia nitida*, Herbstone, is one of Perry's special treasures, and ought to be everybody's. It is a tall, strong-growing plant, seven feet high when well fed; the flowers are very showy and yet refined enough to cut for large vases, and even when so used, with stems of a yard in length they last well in water. The central cone is a good green, like that of a Rose-beetle without the metallic glitter, and it is about two to three inches high, tapering upward like a thimble or a Welshwoman's hat. The ray florets are wide, and hang downwards, and are of a superb rich yellow—I should say that of *Narcissus maximus*, and as the two can never meet it is a fairly safe thing to say. The balance of the flower is good and the leaves are handsome, and its stiff, upright habit is just what I like for plants of the back row that are wanted to tower up above lesser and more diffuse growers, as the towers and spires of a city should rise above its spreading roofs. So it is a fine Rudbeckia all round, and flowers from early to late, especially if the garden scissors claim a few stems once a fortnight. The same treatment is good for the plant and the vases in the case of *Helenium cupreum*, my favourite of its family.

# My Garden in Summer

It begins to bloom with the early Erigerons, and if robbed of some of its stems keeps on replacing them till late in Autumn, whilst it has many other good qualities besides. Thus it is of a wonderfully rich coppery red, unlike that of any other flower of that season, produces crowds of flowers that last long on the plant and also when cut, and is no more than three feet in height. I got my first plant from 'Chenault of Orleans many years ago, so good a tuft that on its arrival I made two plants of it, and goodness knows better than I do how many I have made of it since for my own garden or for distribution to friends. Its rich colouring contrasts admirably with the lilacs of Erigerons, the light yellows of Anthemis, and the Heleniums and Helianthuses, and blends well with orange shades. It is somewhat similar to the brown red forms of *Coreopsis Drummondii*, of which I always like to have a good row somewhere in kitchen garden ground for cutting freely, for the flat flowers are so large and butter-fly-like in poise on the thin stems. But Coreopsis is a fussy thing to cut and arrange, owing to the thin stems and the many one wants and the tangles they get into, for unless you mow down a whole tuft at a time the flower-heads are sure to get interlocked, and almost invariably it is the one belonging to the cut stem that comes off when you pull. Now *Helenium cupreum* makes no bother of this sort, and three or four of its jolly stout stems provide a mass of flowers for a good-sized vase.

*Chrysanthemum maximum* is not very successful as a cut flower ; first it is hard to get long stems when the first flowers open without cutting many buds and making

Coreopsis Drummondii, a free-flowering annual.
(See p. 212.)

# Daisies

sad gaps, then they flag and faint too often to be reliable, but in the border they are very fine. I have grouped most of the varieties I grow at one end of the large herbaceous bed, where, looking across the lawn by the house and under the Deodar, one sees them in a mass with the meadows, the turn of the river, and the distant woods for their background, and with the late afternoon sun catching them they are a great joy to me. My favourite of all the forms is *vomerense*, which came from Herr Sprenger of Naples, and gets its name from his garden at Vomero. Mr. Gumbleton first drew my attention to its charms in his garden at Belgrove, and sent me a division from his plant the following Spring. It is a tall, long-stemmed variety, not so large as to become coarse, and the ray florets have a charming curve, a rise and fall that does away with the stiffness I dislike in some other kinds. Princess Henry came to me from Belgrove too, but though it makes a good solid mass of white from a little distance, when looked into the flowers are rather too round and flat to compare favourably with perfect *vomerense*, and I rather dislike its stems, which are on the fat, lumpy side, reminding one of thick ankles, and are hairy and a boiled cabbage green; so it should be planted a little way in from the edge, and not examined too closely.

The Speaker is fine for the front row, but almost too large to be perfect, though hard to beat for distant effect. Next I rank Edward VII and a variety of it called Edward VII Improved, which I always feel sounds rather disrespectful to a great memory, though not so bad as a description I heard of a diseased potato which

243

ran, " Edward VII badly warted, and the skin showing pink between the black warts." I must digress further to have a grumble at the awful results that sometimes follow on the bestowal of a person's name on a plant. One would think it was harmless enough to allow a new Carnation to be named for one as Americans say, but I found in a Carnation list some years ago descriptions something like these: " Miss Evangeline Tomkins, very free, pale flesh with large crimson spots ; Mrs. Rory O'More, deep red inclining to purple, of full habit, but warranted not to burst"; and I have lately seen with a shock that as a Delphinium I am " over six feet high, but have a large, black eye which is very telling. Stock limited." If the latter refers to Bank Stock I am sorry to say it is but too true, and applies more correctly than the rest of the description.

But to return to the Chrysanthemums. Edward VII Improved is a fine bold grower, and thus carries off what might become coarseness if the flowers grew on a small plant. I find if one has been lazy or busy in Autumn, and these big Daisies go undivided, it is a good plan to pull out many of the stems as they begin to push in Spring, and then vigorous plants with large flowers will follow. I also do this with Phloxes and Asters, and it works well for several years, but of course will not altogether replace lifting, dividing, and replanting in fresh soil. One hardly cares to think of Asters in July, but one of the best of all begins to flower then—I mean *Aster Thompsonii*, and the form of it which Perry now lists as Winchmore Hill variety, which is very much better in colour and shape than a worse form one sees only

# Daisies

too often. I have always grown the better one here, for it was given me by a good friend who I think also gave it to Mr. Perry. It is one of the best lilac-coloured flowers the garden produces, for though it begins flowering in July, it has not finished when Michaelmas brings in the great rush of Asters ; it is rather slow of increase, and a clump takes several years to grow large enough to allow of division, so that it is better to take cuttings in Spring. *A. incisifolius* bears large, white flowers in July, but they have a short period of beauty, and soon turn brown, still it is good-looking enough for an honourable position. The so-called *Aster Mesa grande* is now an *Erigeron speciosus* form, but still just as good, and one of the deepest in colour of them all, but the flowers are smaller and not so numerous as in *grandiflorus* and *multiradiatus*, which are two very useful species much like *E. speciosus*. The second if cut back after its flowering will give a fine second crop that will last until frost comes, and is a good rich violet ; *A. grandiflorus* is paler, but has very round, large flowers and a sturdy habit that needs no tying up. *Buphthalmum salicifolium* is a neat plant, with narrow leaves and a round, bushy habit, so that when covered with its rich yellow flowers it is worth a place in the mixed border or even in rougher parts of the rock garden. I have seen it looking very handsome on the grassy slopes of sub-alpine regions. *Telekia speciosissima* is quite its opposite, though sometimes called *Buphthalmum cordatum*, having immense heart-shaped leaves and large flowers five inches across of a handsome orange ; it is a very fine thing to grow as an isolated group in turf as I have seen

# My Garden in Summer

it in the Botanic Garden in the Park at Bath. But here it is rather squashed up in the herbaceous bed for lack of space in lawns, and archangels to do the mowing, for short of securing the kindly services of such beings I should never induce an ordinary mortal to lift up the leaves gently while the lawn-mower bit off grass, and grass only, and took no lumps or mouthfuls out of the Telekia foliage. *Inula Helenium*, the Elecampane or Cureall of country folk, is another fine stately subject for a hole in the grass, and as its leaves are held up pretty stiffly I have started a group of it in the turf by the head of the steps that lead down to the pond, but keep a reserve clump in the middle of the herbaceous bed, where its immense grey-green leaves and eight feet stems can tower up among promising young Asters.

These bring us along to August, and by then another of the great yellow Composites is commencing to flower—*Senecio Clivorum*, one of the Giant Groundsels from China, so handsome and so gigantic one can scarcely connect it with our Groundsel. It is a very fine plant for a moist place, or failing that the north side of a wall or line of shrubs, where the sun will not scorch it, and cause it to faint. Its great, leathery, heart-shaped leaves are very handsome, and a fine specimen crowned with the large orange-coloured blossoms is a goodly sight from August to October. It is best to cut off the seed-heads, for they sow their seeds almost as lavishly as does the common Groundsel. More of the Heleniums begin to show up in August, and *H. pumilum magnificum* is as good as any of the pure yellow ones. *H. Bolanderi*, with rich brown

246

# Daisies

discs, is an attractive fellow too, both being dwarf forms, two feet high, but *H. autumnale* of a rich yellow, and Riverton Gem, a form of *H. grandicephalum*, almost as rich in colour as *H. cupreum*, are giants, five feet or more high, but these seem to belong to a later period, as they flower on, and join with the hosts of Helianthus and Heliopsis, which with the Michaelmas Daisies form the battalions of Autumn. So at present they are on the reserve in case I am bold enough to carry on the battle with confused synonyms in an autumn campaign. We will leave the herbaceous beds, and go to the rock garden for Daisies. Here we find *Felicia abyssinica*, a fairy Daisy, with finely-cut foliage, that forms cushions of greenery like some extra good Mossy Saxifrage, and bears for months together soft, lilac-blue flowers in great profusion, but not hardy, so that a pot full of cuttings must go into a house every Autumn, to replace their deceased parents next Spring. It roots as it spreads, so there is no difficulty in propagating it, as one can always find Irishman's cuttings, that is newly rooted portions, round the old plants. Of course, if you are taking off a few to give to a visitor from the Emerald Isle, you must be careful to speak of Dutchman's cuttings instead, or take the risk of adding one more insult to the distressful country. *Erigeron mucronatus*, alias *Vittadenia trilobata*, alias the New Holland Daisy although it comes from Mexico, has long possessed one rocky knoll and runs riot there, making a tangle of wiry stems and a curtain of starry blossoms from June to December. Many people complain that it dies out with them, but here if it gets a well-drained, sunny position and the old stems are left on until the worst frosts are over, I generally find it necessary to root out some in Spring to prevent it smothering its neighbours. It seeds about rather too freely, and I fancy some would-be growers may not recognise its juvenile offspring, for they form neat rosettes of trifid or even pectinated leaves for their· first season, and not until flowering shoots are produced do they look at all like their parents. Its flowers are of so many shades, from white to crimson according to their age, that a flowering mass is always pretty. It ought to be a good plant for old walls, for seedlings appear in infinitesimal crevices, and are rather more attractive in the dwarf, starved form produced by their straitened circumstances than the wilder growing, well-fed plants.

Some Composites that are not Daisies deserve a word of praise, so they shall have it here, although they do not fit the heading of this chapter. First there are the Centaureas of Summer, mostly stately giants with handsome leaves and yellow flowers. *C. macrocephala,* well grown and well placed, is worth having, with its bright-green leaves and large, thistle-shaped flowers, but a few more inches of stem would improve it, and prevent its looking a trifle clumsy and heavy-headed. *C. babylonica* has grey leaves that alone pay rent for its site, and there can be no complaint about its shortness of stature, for it will reach six feet in good soil, and the winged stems and small yellow flowers, stuck on at queer angles all up them, are very showy at flowering time and effective all through

# Daisies

the Winter, so long as the wind does not break them, which rarely happens, as they are wondrously tough. *C. ruthenica,* the most graceful of the tall yellow ones, is of a pleasant pale shade, and the leaves are beautifully cut and a rich green ; the plant is very suitable for a choice spot in the middle distance of the border, and as it dies down altogether in Winter, and resurrects itself rather late, will fit in well just behind a clump of Daffodils. I have several times come across white specimens of *Centaurea Scabiosa* among the many evil-coloured, normal members of its household. And what is absolutely " hijjous," as children say, in a Knapweed whose crimson errs on the magenta side, can become a refined and beautiful plant when white, and I have brought some of my wild finds home to the garden, where they make strong clumps and bear a great number of flowers. One specimen in the rock garden is about a yard through when in full flower.

The Globe Thistles have mostly found a welcome here, but some few have overstepped the bounds of polite visitors, made themselves too much at home, seeded by thousands, and so are on the weed list. One that came as *Echinops persicus* heads that black list, for in spite of good, thistly foliage, its round heads are a very poor, starchy-grey blue. *E. horridus* is allowed to place out a half-dozen of its biennial babes, for it towers up some eight to ten feet, and makes a show in the world among shrubs in places where a little life and excitement is to be desired. *E. Ritro* is the gem of the family—compact, a true perennial, very good tempered, and beautifully blue

249

# My Garden in Summer

even before the florets of the head expand, and brighter still when fully open. They are a great joy to Bumble-bees by day and moths by night, though all the members of the family are that; and I have often recommended them for entomologists' gardens, where plants are wished for that can be visited after dark with a lantern, to surprise a supper-party of noctuid moths. I enjoy teasing a drunken (or is it over-eaten?) old Bumble-bee. I rather incline to the latter view, in spite of the similarity of its behaviour to that of an intoxicated old man. The Bee will just wave a leg at you if you touch him, and seems to say : "Jolly goo' nectar, jolly fine evenin', shan't g'ome, stopsh here or ni'. Look out, don't tickle me, if I laugh sure fall off!" And that is just what does happen if you continue to prod him ; up go all the legs on one side, a ghost of a buzz stirs his wings, and flop he goes to the ground.

*E. Tournefortei* is a fine foliage plant, for the leaves are larger and more handsomely divided than in the others, and also wear large white thorns on all their points. It is a most curious-looking object when the young flowering stem is pushing up, as all the cauline leaves have long silky hairs that are caught together, and as the leaves unfold they pull out these threads, till a large ball of cobweb is formed similar to that of *Sempervivum arachnoideum*, but on a much larger scale. It looks as though the caterpillars of some gregarious, nest-spinning moth had taken possession of it, but it is entirely its own invention and manufacture. It is a rare plant in English gardens ; mine came to me—well, I need hardly

# Daisies

tell you, for I expect you can guess — from Bitton.
Canon Ellacombe got the seed many years ago from
Paris, and without a name ; but on writing to the Jardin
des Plantes about it rather lately, he not only learnt its
right name, but found that the plant had been lost there.
So it was not long before the Canon and his wondrous
garden supplied the missing treasure.

# CHAPTER XIV

## Bedding Out

IT is fashionable nowadays to affect a horror of bedding plants. People say they must allow a few to please the gardener, just as they say they eat entrées and savouries to please the cook. The simple life is becoming an affectation in dinners and gardens; the table-cloth goes, but hard labour in polishing tables falls on the footmen, and even if you dine on a Tudor oak table you have a lace mat, and under that another fandangle, some bad conductor of heat for your plate to sit on. Simple? It reminds me of a silly old song that lilted of someone being as "simple as Dahlias on Paddington Green."

So we despise Scarlet Geraniums as we miscall our Zonal Pelargoniums, make a face at Calceolarias, and shudder at the mention of Blue Lobelia. Well, they have been sadly misused, I know, but they are fine plants, for all that, when in their right places. I remember a garden of twenty years ago that was the most bedded out I ever saw. Thousands of bedding plants were prepared for planting out in Summer, but always in straight lines in long, straight borders. It all began at the stable gates, and ran round three sides of the house, and continued in unbroken sequence, like Macbeth's vision of kings, for two sides of

# Bedding Out

a croquet lawn, and then rushed up one side and down the other of a long path starting at right angles from the middle of the lawn, and if you began at the gates with Blue Lobelia, Mrs. Pollock Pelargonium, Perilla, Yellow Calceolaria, and some Scarlet Pelargonium in ranks according to their relative stature, so you continued for yards, poles, perches, furlongs, or whatever it was—I hate measures, and purposely forget them—and so you ended up when the border brought you back again to the lawn. I once suggested, Why not paint the ground in stripes, and have the effect all the year round, even if snow had to be swept off sometimes? I know an instance of a stately, formal garden which was found so expensive to fill with gay flowers that its owner had coloured tiles made to lay in the beds. Well, I do not champion that sort of thing, but I confess to adoring Scarlet Pelargoniums, rejoicing in Blue Lobelia, and revelling in Yellow Calceolaria. But they must be certain varieties, well grown and well placed. An aged Pelargonium, King of Denmark, with a tree-like trunk, numerous branches, and in a pot three sizes too small for it, can be a glorious cloud of warm salmon blossoms ; and Paul Crampel is worth similar ill-treatment. Of course fat sappy cuttings stuck out in rich soil, and that grow leaves fit for cooking and serving with white sauce, are not what we want. I love to seize a few pot-plants in the conservatory or greenhouse, and to take them out for a Summer airing in the garden, sinking their pots among other plants, where they fit in and look as if they had been there all their lives. There is a raised bed near the house bordering the carriage drive that is getting

253

# My Garden in Summer

filled up by degrees with permanent tenants, but among them at present are still a few lodgings to let, and here all sorts of tender plants pass their Summer. Yuccas form a large group at a corner, and next to them some grey-leaved things have gathered together. *Melianthus major* gets cut to the ground annually there, and retires under a heap of cinders we pile on it in November, but hitherto it has reappeared with Spring. *Senecio Greyi, S. compactus,* and *Othonnopis cheirifolia,* the Barbary Ragwort, sprawl down the bank. *Cineraria maritima* and *Centaurea Clementei* join their silvery forces to the others, and so work along till we reach a group of glaucous Kniphofias such as *K. caulescens* and *K. Tysonii.* When Summer approaches it is very good fun to go into the houses and pick out certain things, to add to this mass of subtropical-looking foliage after they have had a week or so of hardening off. Purple-leaved Cannas are simply irresistible to group behind the Yuccas and the great ferny grey-leaves of *Melianthus major. Acacia Baileyana,* as blue as a freshly killed mackerel, can be slipped in among the Kniphofias and will tower above them. Blue Lobelia looks very lovely as a carpet spread among the feet of some of these, and a group of *Salvia patens,* that also has a poultice of ashes for Winter, is thereby kept in countenance and helps to make a patch of blue. Further along the bed we find a good place for sinking some large pots of *Moraea iridioides, M. bicolor* and *M. Huttonii,* as a low Yew hedge makes a good background for the yellow and black flowers of *bicolor,* and the white ones with mauve and orange trimmings of *iridioides.* This is a very curious Irid, and the only one I

254

# Bedding Out

know of in which the flowering stem lives on for several years, branching out at intervals into green spathes and buds and flowers. Once an extra-industrious garden boy of a tidying-up disposition cut off all the old brown ugly stems at housing time, and of course for the next two years we had only a few flowers that the stems of the year could provide for us. The variety I have is the larger one sometimes known as *Dietes Macleai*, whose flowers are as large as those of *Iris unguicularis*, and much like them in general appearance and shape, pure glistening white with rich yellow keel to the falls, and lilac style branches. Each flower lasts about twenty-four hours only, but they are freely produced if unattacked by garden boys.

In some seasons tall lanky Abutilons, and *Streptosolen Jamesonii*, come out here to be grouped among such permanent plants as species and forms of Agapanthus, Cotoneasters, and dwarf Berberis. Some are saved, lifted, and housed at Winter's first warning show of frost, but the lanky fellows that have done their best work in pots are left to take their chance, and after some mild winters old Abutilon stems have broken out into good growth.

But it is on the terrace when the Tulips have retired that we do our greatest deeds of bedding. I have already told how four out of the fifteen beds are filled with my beloved succulent plants in mixed groups. Most of the other beds we prefer filled with one kind of plant, so as to get a good mass of colour. Two of the beds are so placed that they are in a direct line with two of the straight paths that run from the bowling-green lawn down to the bank of the New River. Most of the paths in this garden were made at the period when it was considered sinful to walk in a direct line from any one point to another, so they are curved and twisted as though designed by drunken worms; and unless one rearranged them as an elaborate variation of the Greek Key Pattern it does not seem possible to alter them. However, I am truly grateful for two of these paths which I found ran fairly straight from lawn to river, and another which I made to do so, by giving it two new ends and taking a crick out of its neck

We have tried many things in the beds that show at the ends of these paths, but nothing is so satisfying to the eye as *Salvia splendens* Pride of Zurich, which goes out in June as nice bushy little plants with fiery scarlet heads, and flares away in ever-increasing, red-hot refulgence until a sharp October frost throws a pailful of cold water on its glowing cinders and puts out their glory. It is a magnificent bit of colour, and except when a heavy storm drenches it and knocks off many flowers and bruises the persistent scarlet calices, it seems to improve daily throughout the Summer. Heliotrope I must have for my nose's sake, so two beds are filled with it, one with a light-coloured and the other with a dark form, low spreading plants covering the soil and a few old standard specimens rising up among them ; and I don't know which enjoys them most, I or the White Butterflies. The two central beds on either side of my favourite of the stone vases, the Greek tripodal altar, are sacred to Pelargonium Paul Crampel, and in hot weather they rival the Salvias. We have tried many things in these terrace beds with varying success, and some of them are, I hope, gone for ever,

# Bedding Out

others we feel cannot be improved upon, and a few are still on trial. Pentstemons are among this last class, and I think a bed of a very fine deep scarlet one with large white throat, but still a well-shaped flower, will long continue to fill a bed, as it is just my idea of what a good Pentstemon should be, for I do not love the modern type of gaping, wide-mouthed monstrosities, with extra segments and an attack of tonsilitis, diphtheria, or some other disease that produces spots in the throat.

I was one of the first that received seeds of *Felicia petiolaris* from its generous introducer on the Continent, and I thought I should be right in devoting one of the terrace beds to this rosy-pink counterpart of *Agathaea coelestis*. It grew right enough, and soon filled its bed with long trailing growths, then it broke the bounds and trailed along the gravel path, and was nipped first by the gulls and then by me. It mounded itself up like a haycock, but never a bud did it show until October, when three flowers rather like lawn Daisies on long stalks decorated the whole bed of greenery. We decided it was not suit-able for bedding out in that manner. I had given away many youngsters of this newest treasure, and before long reproachful letters poured in, and I feared it needed a southern sky to make a good plant of it. Some plants I put out in the rock garden surprised us by keeping green and happy all through the Winter, and then we found out that in a roughish place on a dry sunny bank, *Felicia petiolaris* can be very pretty if allowed to root down and run about and make a tangle in one season and flower there in the next.

# My Garden in Summer

This year we filled a bed with the double white *Chrysanthemum frutescens*, Mrs. Sander; it was a fine snowy mound and provided a wondrous number of cut flowers, which I was rejoiced to find last more than a week, if cut in youth of course, and very pretty in wide-mouthed cut glass vases if you pick plenty so that they may hang out all round and be mounded up in the centre.

Fuchsias make an effective bed, but we somehow had all crimson and blue and none of my favourite white and pink, or crimson and white among them this season. The last beds at either end are large, and can be planted with miscellanies. In one the central object is always my large old specimen Pepper Tree, *Schinus Molle,* and this year it looks very well rising out of what sounds a trifle risky, a mixture of *Salvia patens,* pink and white Pentstemons, and *Ageratium mexicanum,* the old fluffy mauve fellow that smells so abominably of a dirty, soapy sponge. But the blue and mauve mixed with the Pentstemons was really very beautiful, and had a delightfully cool effect separated by the succulents from the glowing red Salvia. The other end had as a central specimen a fine old *Sparmannia africana* that summers out and gets strong and sturdy thereby; purple-leaved Cannas all round it made a fine dark mass against the Yew hedge background, and Henry Jacoby Pelargonium filled in the groundwork. These gay beds have a good effect here along the curve of the river, and particularly when reflected in it, and there would be no other way of treating the terrace beds among the stone vases that would be as satisfactory as the

# Bedding Out

alternation of Tulips in Spring and the bedding plants for Summer and Autumn.

Certain tender plants are grown on purpose to live for the Summer months in the rock garden, and though they are dotted about here and there still this is a form of summer bedding. The sweetest scented leaf I know is borne by one of them, *Cedronella triphylla.* Its flowers are not worth having and are better picked off, for they are small and dead-nettlish, and I have seen them described as pale purple, a colour one does not long for ; but the fresh green leaves are delicious to pick and sniff if they are only lightly bruised so that they do not give out too strong a turpentine scent. They act best if put into a button-hole, where as they fade they give out whiffs of a delightfully clean scent—I think it might be called a dry scent, to distinguish it from the hateful, cloying, nose-worrying, syrupy, sweet abominations that get into scent-bottles and soaps and annoy me nearly as much as does the odour of stinking fish or sewer gas. *Cedronella triphylla* is widely known as Balm of Gilead in spite of its coming from the Canary Isles, and after a mild Winter it will break up again from the root ; but it is never safe to rely on its doing so, therefore cuttings should be taken in Autumn and housed for the Winter.

*Matthiola tristis*, the old Night-scented Stock of one's great-grandmother, is another half-hardy indispensable, for I think its scent the sweetest of all those produced by the dingily coloured plants that wake up towards evening and advertise for moths to undertake their pollen dispersal in return for a supper of nectar, and so distil the most wonderfully alluring scents to attract them. This little perennial bushy Stock is not much to look at with its narrow grey leaves and spikes of small lilac and brown flowers ; but it beats all the rest of the family in its scent, which has more of Cassia-buds and Russia leather about it than the Cloves or Friar's Balsam I detect even in *Matthiola bicornis,* good as its evening offering of incense can be on a still summer night. I lost my *M. tristis* one Winter ; cuttings refused to strike, and moulded off in a way they have if not put in while the sun is still powerful and the air fairly dry, and very few winters spare the old plants outside, and that was not one of them. I tried hard to replace it, but could hear of it nowhere among the nurserymen. Then in Ireland, in a friend's garden, I pryed into the inmost corners of a small greenhouse in spite of being told, " Oh, there's nothing but rubbish in that old house," for many a time I have discovered hidden treasure in such half-deserted corners, and this time I saw three pots of fine old specimens of *Matthiola tristis,* a relic of my friend's grandmother and grown there ever since her day ; so cuttings from them have restored this sweetest of scents to my garden.

*Oxypetalum coeruleum* is an old plant but not often seen ; yet the blue of its flowers is as soft and pure as that of any flower of Summer, and it is as easy to grow as a Scarlet Pelargonium, and can be propagated by cuttings or from seeds. It should be pushed along a bit in a warm house in early Spring, hardened off in May, and then planted out to produce bunches of turquoise blue flowers till it is time to lift it back to shelter. I have left

# Bedding Out

plants out, but though they have lived through the Winter it took them so long to find out they were alive and to pluck up enough spirit to make fresh growth that they had not got to flowering strength before another attack of frostbites put them on the sick list again. It is sometimes called *Tweedia coerula* and came from Buenos Ayres, a name I always pronounced Bonyzares in the days of my youth until I was set right by some friends who had lived there, so now I call it Bwaynos Ires, and am so proud of my knowledge that I cannot resist showing it off phonetically here.

*Lavatera maritima grandiflora* makes a fine spring-flowering greenhouse bush, and then if hardened gradually and planted out will bloom till the frost comes, producing large Mallow flowers of a queer shade of greyish lilac with warmer rosy tints, very much like the colour of a bottle of lead lotion I used lately for an attack of Nettlerash, for it had been made attractive by the addition of a touch of Cochineal. But the Mallow flowers' real glory consists in a very conspicuous purple-blue eye that gives them a distinct appearance among the soft downy green leaves. It will grow into a fine bush on a wall in Southern Ireland, but I have never got it through a Winter in the open ground here. We generally group near the larger Mallow some little bushes of a smaller-flowered rosy red one that Dr. Lowe gave me as *Malvastrum grossulariae-folium,* a name there is some doubt about its rightly possessing, although it very well describes the foliage. This plant is also tender and flowers itself nearly to death, for it is so lavish with bloom first in the conservatory in

261

# My Garden in Summer

Spring and then out in the border, if it is kept clean and free from an aphis that loves to swarm all over it and to make it as sticky as treacle.

*Plumbago capensis* is delightful as a bedded-out specimen, and *Humea elegans* makes a good companion for it. When it does well its six-feet-high clouds of brownish-red flowers light up well in the sunlight, looking like spikes of some huge flowering grass instead of a plant of the Composite family. But the peculiar incense-like scent its leaves and flowers give out when touched at all times, and on the breeze in hot weather, is the chief charm of the plant ; it is something like the scent of Russia leather at times when a faint whiff reaches one, but at closer quarters is more like incense. The flowers keep their colour well when cut and dried, and will give out the scent for a long time, especially if slightly moistened now and then. For the last two years I have planted out pots of *Primula mala-coides* after they have become lanky and full of seed-pods in the houses, and some take a new lease and throw up fresh flower-stems, while others shed seeds which soon germinate and join the others in flowering, and I believe, if slugs would but leave them alone, they would battle through a fairly mild Winter,[1] for they have refused to be put seriously out of temper by eighteen degrees of frost.

Thus I find a place in the summer garden for many a plant that is either the better for a Summer in the open or has served its day inside, and so may as well be tried outside as thrown on the rubbish heap.

[1] A group of some dozen plants survived the Winter of 1913–14 and flowered freely in April.

# CHAPTER XV

## Flowers for Cutting

I SOMETIMES feel that cutting flowers to decorate one's rooms is a practice unworthy of the true lover of a garden, for I am convinced that most flowers look best when growing on the plant. Yet I could not be happy for long without cut flowers in the house, for there are so many dark hours and cold days when one can best enjoy their beauty indoors, and it gives me such pleasure to group and arrange them in vases for effects that are never produced by the plants themselves.

As I write I am enjoying the scent of a vase of Irises, and look up now and then to revel in the delicacy of their mingled shades of lilac, mauve, green, yellow, and creamy white, and on this stormy day, with a rough bullying wind that flings raindrops about like bullets, they would not long remain so fresh and unspotted out in the open. Artificial light brings out fresh and unsuspected charms in some flowers, even converting ferocious militant magentas into a saintly beneficent rose colour at times, and again with other flowers, Sweet Peas and *Centaurea montana* for instance, the more you cut the more you get. Shirley Poppies I have already praised for a similar good trait of character.

# My Garden in Summer

The scent of fresh flowers in rooms is one of the joys of life if sufficiently understood and controlled. I have been poisoned olfactorily, which means headache and a fearful longing for a whiff of the clean outdoor smell of greenery, by rooms with too many *Lilium auratum* or *Azalea mollis* in them; and I do not think I could be polite and good-tempered for long in a room with many bunches of Phloxes in it. A dinner-table decorated heavily with Sweet Peas spoils my dinner, as I taste Sweet Peas with every course, and they are horrible as a sauce for fish, whilst they ruin the bouquet of good wine. I once cut a quantity of Almond blossom for a centre-piece, and six smaller vases for the dinner-table, and quite smothered out the charms of a good dinner with its aroma. Violets, Mignonette, Wallflower, Roses, Hyacinths, Stocks, and many other flowers lose their sweet scent after about twenty-four hours in a room, and need carefully testing day by day as well for freshness of odour as for colour effect, and yet, again, some flowers are never agreeable to my fussy old nose. Phloxes smell to me like a combination of pepper and pig-stye, most Brooms of dirty, soapy, bath sponge, Hawthorn of fish-shop, and Meadow Sweet of curry powder, so I much dislike being shut up in a house with them; while *Philadelphus coronarius*, Elder, and *Spiraea Aruncus* simply drive me out, for they generally produce a violent attack of hay fever. But these are evils that are, for the most part, personal, many of them being peculiar to me and my fads and failings, but I believe there is a wider evil lurking in the apparently harmless practice

# Flowers for Cutting

of growing flowers chiefly for cutting. I mean that it tends towards regarding flowers merely as decorations, and plants are chosen because they will produce so many masses of colour of some particular shade, much as one would buy silks by the yard, and it seems to me a waste of energy, pelf, and intellectual powers to grow plants merely to fill a dozen large bowls with soft mauve or pale pink to place in the drawing-room because they go well with the curtains or wall-paper. The faculty for appreciating the habit and individuality of a plant is destroyed as one learns only to care for its decapitated heads in baskets, as some ancient tyrant might gloat over those of his enemies. I prefer to see pot plants in the house, and especially those that are flowering in their natural season, as that brings into use and notice many plants that can only be grown in pots and under glass, for I would far rather use my houses for growing tender plants that will not live in the open than for forcing plants that will be much better in form and colour when they appear a little later in the open ground.

I have ceased to care for forced Lily of the Valley now that, thanks to cold storage, it is so much like the poor, in being wan and pale and ever with us. When in May one can pick the real thing from the garden, I love its sweet scent and rich, deep green leaves as much as I dislike the anaemic, invalid creatures with sickly-yellow, parboiled leaves that have been first frozen and then forced ; indeed, I feel disposed to found a Society for the Prevention of Cruelty to Plants. Even the Winter Flowering Carnations that the last few years have brought to such perfection leave me as cold and indifferent as do the silk and velvet counterfeit blossoms, for wearing in hats, that I see in the shop windows. I do not want Carnations all the year round, nor do I admire half a yard of stem with scars at intervals where buds have been picked off in the fair promise of their youth, so that the one terminal flower may be as round and fringy and perfect as if it were made of pinked-out paper like a ham frill. But I do love Carnations in July, real ones, border varieties, and as I cannot grow them into yard-square clumps as people in softer climates can, I have to be content with layering them every season, and having some good long rows in the kitchen garden borders to cut from. Unless they can be grown on the top of a wall or in vases, so that the flowers may hang down in their natural way, I do not greatly care for the effect of them in the borders where they require staking. Those one sees growing in old biscuit tins, the remnants of a broken china jug or a wooden box, in Italian or Tyrolean window-sills and balconies, seem to me to be the most perfectly beautiful. I have seen them with stems thicker than my thumb (which is a sturdy and large one as thumbs go), and certainly no less than four years old, hanging down for quite a yard, and a mass of bloom above steely blue leaves, the picture of health, and I have longed to have a few like them. But alas! they do not grow old gracefully here, so I grow yearlings, and cut their long stems, buds and all. Trojan we think the best white for our purpose, as it produces such a harvest of large flowers on splendidly stiff, tall stems. Raby Castle, although it is poor in shape and often bursts

Border Carnation, " Renown."

(See p. 267.)

# Flowers for Cutting

its calyx, is such a delightfully soft, pure pink that I have never found any among the dozens I have tried that gives me such pleasure and such large basketfuls. Duchess of Wellington, a pinkish mauve, is also stout-stemmed and lavish in flowers, and goes wonderfully well with the white Trojans and pink Rabys, either all mixed in one vase, or each in a separate one, and stood together on a flower table. The pink of Raby Castle is charming, too, with the old red Cloves, but they are rather tiresome, as they require looking over daily and renewing so often, for aged blooms turn such a bad colour and curl up so miserably.

I have not yet found a pure yellow that is quite suitable to this garden and my requirements. Yellow Queen succeeds best, but it has rather thin stalks and a dangling habit. Miss Audrey Campbell does not grow here very freely, and the beautiful yellows of recent days are not hardy enough for us, needing protection and not getting it. Elizabeth Shiffner has disappointed me greatly, as she only wears a pale and sallow face here, instead of the fine orange buff one that beams at me from the show stands. Mrs. Reynolds-Hole we still grow, and in some seasons it does well and produces a fine supply of its deep apricot-coloured flowers for three weeks at a stretch, but in other seasons it is shy and peevish. Marigold is another useful variety that is orange and red in colouring, and reminds me of orange marmalade. Mrs. Cutbush and Renown give us a liberal supply of scarlet flowers. Ellen Willmott, though a better colour, requires disbudding and fussing over beyond our practice, but no doubt would be useful in gardens better suited for Carnation growing.

# My Garden in Summer

I grow the wild species in the rock garden, the *Dianthus Caryophyllus* from which the garden forms have been derived. Mr. Burbidge gave me the seed of my original plants, and told me he had brought it from the walls of Rochester Castle himself to Trinity College, Dublin. I have lately come across, and fallen desperately in love with, a dwarfer and better coloured race of single Carnations, called Grenadine, which are most suitable and lovely in the rock garden. Although I believe they originated in Southern France, they seem quite hardy. Of course these single-flowered forms are no good for cutting; all the same, I am always pleased to find a few singles among the seedlings each season, for they are useful to pull up by the roots to use all their buds and leafy shoots for placing in vases with the flowers of the double ones whose leaves and buds are too precious to pick in such a wholesale fashion. I am sure it is best to give cut Carnations their own foliage, but a large vase of *Gypsophila paniculata* and Carnations is effective, and when Carnation foliage has been scarce I have used Lavender leaves instead, with successful results.

I was pleasantly surprised this season by the lasting qualities when cut of the very fine Spiraea known as *Sorbaria arborea,* one of Wilson's Chinese introductions. It is a magnificent shrub in the garden, after the style of *Spiraea Lindleyana* or the newer *S. Aitchisonii,* with handsome, pinnate leaves, and growing about ten feet high; every shoot arches gracefully outwards, and bears at its tip a huge, flattened, pendant mass of pure white flowers; some of the largest bunches produced here this Summer

Spirea arborea. (See p. 268.)

were over eighteen inches in length and a foot across, and as the plant produces them over a period of several weeks it ought to become a popular and useful shrub. I never expected so large a mass of flowers borne on so slender a stem would last well in water, but most of them kept their full beauty for over a week. *Buddleia variabilis* is not so useful as a cut flower, for though it does not flag, yet the flowers that open indoors are not so richly coloured as those that develop under open-air treatment, and the spike fades into duller and weaker shades day by day. My idea of a really useful cut flower is one that will last for a week, so that once a week I may have a field day among the flower vases, and have them washed and filled with water for me to start afresh with on Saturday mornings. This works better in Spring and Autumn than in the hot summer months, when Sweet Peas, Mignonette, and Roses are only really good for two days.

*Chrysanthemum frutescens*, "Mrs. Sander," as I have already said, is a welcome discovery as a seven-day stayer, and a beautiful large-flowered form of *Myosotis palustris* that Mr. Robinson gave me, will root and grow, and flower beautifully in a china bowl in a light window, and last in full beauty for about ten days.

Of course there is a great deal in knowing when to cut your flowers, and I believe in bringing most of them into the house before they have attained their full size, and the pollen is shed. I would rather see a young flower, though rather small and pale, with a promise of fuller beauty in it than one I know has but a few more hours to last before curling at the edges if it is a Viola, turning transparent in the perianth if a Daffodil, or falling to bits after the manner of most other flowers. The gardener does not always realise this, but likes to bring his flower to the pitch of perfection before he can bear to pick it and part with it, and I can quite sympathise with him. It is doubtless the right moment to offer his treasure on the altar of sacrifice, but the only flower I know of that lasts best when cut in a fully matured condition is *Anthurium Scherzerianum*. I like to cut the flowers I am about to arrange myself, and even at times to take the vases out into the garden to make sure I get a sufficiency in one journey and of the right length of stem. I have learnt many little dodges and tricks for choosing those that will last the best, but which are difficult to impart in writing ; the most obvious is that in gathering Composite flowers one should choose those in which only a ring or two of the disc florets have opened. This is especially valuable advice for single Dahlias and Doronicums. In some Sweet Peas the buds if opened indoors come so much paler than their normal colour that they spoil the effect ; but in most self-coloured ones, which are to my idea the best of all, it only adds to the beauty of a large vaseful if some blooms are of a paler shade of the same colour. I have been inclined to grumble at the lack of really self mauves and lilacs in the newest and frilliest productions of the last few years, for I dislike bicolors, in which a cold and warm shade of lilac are blended in one blossom. Lady Grizel Hamilton is the shade I prefer, and Masterpiece also pleases me, but though I have tried to argue with myself, pointing out that as I like

# Flowers for Cutting

to mix a bright pink with a self lilac in a large bowl, so I ought to rejoice in a bicolor or shaded flower, I am not convinced, and I suppose it is because the two shades are too much alike. Those that I have enjoyed most of all this Summer are Moonstone, a delicate cool lavender grey, and endowed with the sweetest scent of any Sweet Pea known to me, not so strong that it becomes a burden, but always there in the flower even to its last moment of final collapse, whenever you like to apply your nose to it ; Tortoiseshell, for an orange-salmon, because it is the only one I know of that is not burnt and pied in hot weather if left unshaded ; and Seashell, as delicate a shaded pink as its name suggests. I believe all three were raised by Mr. Aldersey ; I know he raised Tortoiseshell, and I was greatly struck by its incombustible resistance to the sun when I saw tall bushes of glowing blooms in front of the south wall at Aldersey fully exposed to the fierce sunlight of 1911.

I like to place Mignonette in a cut glass bowl, it is so cool and fresh in its green and gold and a spangling of silver and a ruby here and there that brightens it at close quarters. It is a fitful thing to grow well, and here certainly does best in fresh ground. A newly made up vine border sown with Mignonette gives armfuls of joy, but is it good for the grapes ? I hope so, because I like both the grapes and the Mignonette, but even if it is not I should still wish to grow Mignonette there as the crop I prefer.

Various patches of flowering plants in corners of the kitchen garden provide something to cut all the year round, so that I need not rob my flower beds. *Iris*

# My Garden in Summer

*unguicularis* lines the foot of any bit of south wall I can commandeer for it, and with Hazel catkins from the nut walk and Winter Sweet from outside the span-roof vinery door supplies the darkest winter days. *Garrya elliptica* from the wall of the potting shed helps by the end of January, and spells of fair weather increase the supply of Irises until March brings the Daffodils among the Gooseberry and Currant bushes. The Tulips follow, and last until *Centaurea montana*, which edges one path, can fill a large basket twice or thrice a week. First Dutch and then Spanish and later still English Irises carry us on to the days of Mignonette, Shirley Poppies, Sweet Peas and Carnations. Later come Coreopsis, China Asters, Single Dahlias, early Chrysanthemums, and then the latest Michaelmas Daisies to complete the round, and each one seems to be the loveliest in its own season, wherefore I feel sure it is wiser to enjoy them when Nature gives them than to force hardy flowers to compete with the reigning beauty of the outdoor garden.

# CHAPTER XVI

## As July Ends

THERE comes a day in late July in each year when I realise that *Campanula lactiflora*, and *C. persicifolia* under its shelter, are no longer the beauties of the rock garden but a menace and danger, in that they are preparing to sow the whole place with their seeds. So I take off my coat and start to cut them down, and let in the light to other tall plants now anxious for a clear stage on which to display their charms. It is rather fascinating work, as it so thoroughly and rapidly alters the general appearance of that piece of ground ; the waving masses of the Campanula, which have almost covered the level portions, soon melt away, and the little Almond bushes form the thicket once more. Then *Phyteuma campanuloides* can show its long spikes of small, purple flowers, and here and there the tall, rust-coloured spires of *Digitalis ferruginea* tower up above everything else, unless a Mullein has invaded this semi-wild corner. A fine form of Verbascum that came to me as *V. pyramidalis* sows itself freely about the rock garden, and at weeding times I leave a few well-placed ones, chiefly trying to keep a row of them either in the edge of the bed or actually in the path itself, and in some seasons this line of their great branching golden candlesticks has a very fine effect, continuing that of the tall Eryngiums, that line the entrance to the rock garden out by the Cactus bank, a few of which are shown in the accompanying illustration. These are now so much hybridised and so variable that among the seedlings it is hard to find two just alike. A few remain true *E. serra* with its marvellous rosettes of saw-edged leaves, but others have the larger flower-heads of *E. agavifolium* combined with the tall, branching stems of *E. serra*, and leaves with a great variety of coarse or small teeth according to which parent they favour most. Some are very handsome, and seem to me better than either parent. The fall of the tall Campanulas shows up the rounded bushes of *Hypericum patulum*, now covered with large, waxy blossoms of purest yellow, but not so wonderfully thick in texture nor so rich in a central boss of stamens as *H. aureum*, a fine old bush of which lives in a sheltered bay where *Fuchsia bicolor* is its companion, and is now a mass of crimson and blue flowers, each of its blue petticoats having a central patch or pocket of crimson which perhaps entitles it to its specific name. I find it the hardiest of the Fuchsias here, recovering itself quicker and so blooming earlier than *F. Riccartonii* and *F. gracilis*, but in most Winters it is cut to the ground. On the opposite side of the path *F. pumila* nestles in a nook between the stones, and is charming now, full of bloom, and only six inches high. *F. retroflexa* has lived for many years in the next pocket, and is almost ready to open its first tiny crimson flowers. Even down this path a few Campanulas have found lodgment, and one is so large and such a good lilac in colour it must not

Eryngium serra by the Cactus bank.   (See p. 274.)

# As July Ends

be cut away with the rest, but left awhile for seed. By the time they have all fallen the paths have become choked up and resemble a newly-mown meadow, and the cutting fever having got hold of me, I call for a gardener to bring a barrow and clear away as I hack and hew, and I thoroughly enjoy myself, for many of the shrubs need a good trimming.

*Magnolia stellata* will block the path and smother the undergrowth unless a lower ring of boughs are sawn off, and *Aegle sepiaria* will poke out someone's eyes unless shortened, so one whole barrow-load this year was composed of Magnolia and Orange boughs, some of them so large that I should have been proud of them a few years ago if they had represented my largest specimen. A few days previously this season I filled a barrow with leaves from the hardy Palms, *Trachycarpus excelsus*, which looked even more cruel and sacrilegious a load to go to the rubbish heap. But I am rejoicing in the beautiful effect I have got in being able to see under them all, for with Magnolia, Orange, and Palms it adds to their apparent, and no doubt soon will to their actual, height, when the sap goes up all the better for the loss of these lower limbs. *Allium Ampeloprasum* var. *Babingtonii* now dominates the central range of the rock garden, as it is over six feet high, and in spite of the flower-heads being mostly composed of bulbils of various sizes forming a solid central mass, and the flowers being but few, the general outline of the giant is so good that I love to see it towering up here against the sky from behind the Orange tree and the large *Asparagus acutifolius*, its glaucous leaves and stems contrasting so well with their deep green tones. *A. sphaero-cephalum* is also in flower on a neighbouring mound, and much sought after by Bumble-bees. Its crimson globes of flowers are very beautiful, and coming so late in the year are very useful either in the mixed border or in the rock garden. *Epilobium hirsutum* is just out, and seems a fearfully coarse weed to admit to the rock garden, but you will not find any of the common form of it now I have had my day of cutting and chopping, for I have pulled up every one of the ordinary magenta seedlings, and have only left good forms, especially a pure white that one of my Sunday-school boys with a quick eye and a love of natural history found in the Cheshunt Marshes, and another from a neighbouring garden, with pink buds and anthers but white petals which give it a charming Apple-blossom effect of colouring. This form is the sinner which sows common red ones about if I do not cut its heads off before they are ready to do it. Yet another form grows in the rock garden, a beautifully variegated one, the white patches on its leaves being very clear and brilliant, and its pink stems helping the general effect. This I had from Glasnevin, where it was grown under the name of *E. angusti-folium*, but it is *E. hirsutum* right enough. I am fond of collecting all the forms I can get of a variable plant, and so in other borders you will see a very curious virescent form in which the petals are replaced by a succession of green, bract-like bodies, more interesting than beautiful, and best of all perhaps is a form Mrs. Robb gave me, telling me she got it from M. Correvon's garden at Geneva. In this the leaves are more silky than in our wild plant, and the

# As July Ends

flowers are quite a pleasing shade of red much warmer in tint than those of most Willow-herbs; it has a further charm in producing wonderfully white and silky tangles of seeds after flowering, which, especially with the evening light shining through them, show up well from a distance, and have a pretty, softening effect among the glare of the late summer flowers. I find these forms of *E. hirsutum* are more effective when grown in an ordinary border that is fairly dry, and in full sun, than when allowed to enjoy themselves according to their natural tastes in the bog garden, as in the dry ground they are less leafy and more floriferous, and moreover do not run underground quite so vigorously as in marshy ground, but even when thus well behaved they need a little curtailment, and are certainly the better for replanting every second or third year.

*Actaea spicata*, the Bane-berry, is now at its best and bearing ripe fruit; the flowers are so ineffective that one can only enjoy them with an eye to the future, when they shall have become berries. It is a pity this plant is so dreadfully poisonous, for my full enjoyment of its beauty is always spoilt by a fear lest one of the Sunday scholars may not have listened to me or disbelieved my warning lecture delivered annually on the first Sunday afternoon I notice its ripening charms, for if the old Adam should come out strongly, and an experimental tasting be made, I should soon have a writhing first-aid case to deal with. The wild native black-berried form is not the one I am afraid of, nor yet the ordinary bright sealing-wax red one, for it looks hard and no more inviting than a Holly-berry; but I have a fine tall form that bears large berries as semi-transparent and alluring in appearance as a Morello Cherry, and when ripe of just the same deep crimson colouring. The white-berried form I like best of all, but never can induce it to berry as freely as the others, and it ripens after the cherry-coloured beauty has shed its fruits. It is best to follow Miller, and regard it as a separate species, *A. alba*, its more finely cut leaves and curiously swollen pedicels being so distinct. The Bane-berry is one of the plants I should grow if only for its botanical interest, it is so original in its views even for such a large and versatile family as the *Ranunculaceae.* Thus it is the only one of its race that has but one carpel, and so forms a link with *Berberidaceae*, and again it imitates the Barberries, in ripening that carpel into a juicy berry.

Eryngiums of the Sea-holly type now claim notice. The best is *E. Oliverianum* and its good forms, as what one requires in a Sea-holly is that it should be perennial, free flowering, and blue. *E. Zabellii*, said to be of garden origin, seems to me only a very deeply-coloured, rather compact form of *Oliverianum*, and is the one I should choose if compelled to limit myself to one. The colour of its stems is marvellously blue when at its best, and is as successful an advertisement for suggesting a raging thirst to passing Bumble-bees as that seductive picture of a foaming glass of sparkling beer that I see so often on the hoardings is to frail humanity; I must confess it some-times make me wish for luncheon time.

*E. alpinum* does not flower freely here, otherwise its Honiton lace frill would attract me more than the coarser macramé pattern of *E. Oliverianum.* Although its lilac tint is not so brilliant, *E. amethystinum* is a beautiful thing, and its small flower-heads make up in quantity for their lack of size. The flowers of *E. campestre* are dull and green, and its running habit fits it only for rough places ; but in a good form its foliage is very ornamental, deeply cut, and a charming grey. *E. planum*, and its many allied forms or aliases, whichever way you regard them, according to your character as a splitter or lumper, are tall effective plants for groups in shrubbery borders, but not one of them is good enough for the choice borders. *E. creticum* should find a corner, though, as its late flowering and branching habit, which provides younger flower-heads to constantly replace the passée dowagers for some two months or more, make it a very useful plant. It seeds freely, and it is a good plan to raise seedlings and select and save the bluest, as it varies a good deal. A group of five plants will make a blue tangle from August to October. *E. Bourgatii* is good for the rock garden ; its leaves are prettily marked with white spots, and its habit neat. *E. glaciale* is even smaller and neater, and a gem for the sand moraine ; and the biennial *E. giganteum* is one of the best plants for a rough corner, or wild grass-covered place, where it may sow itself and colonise; its branching candelabra-like stems and silvery white bracts being wonderfully effective, even by night if the moonlight falls on them. Its bluish hybrid *E. hybridum* has failed to colonise here, and I do not care for it enough to struggle to satisfy its whims, for I believe a majority of the strain to be not only biennial, but sterile hybrids.

So many and so various are the plants in flower

now that even if I mention the more uncommon I fear there can be little connection between them save that of a synchronous florescence. *Crinum longifolium*, often called *C. capense*, is a striking object, especially towards evening, when its pure white flowers open out wider than in full daylight. It has a penchant for the bog garden, but has been wonderfully amiable over being placed on a shelf of the rock garden, and this season has sent up four strong heads of blooms which are worth having in spite of its rather straggly, long leaves. *Verbascum vernale* and *Achillea Ageratum* are two good, tall subjects for the rough and tumble of higher banks of the rock garden. The former must be a close relation of *V. Chaixii*, and like it is quite reliably perennial ; its branching stems bear innumerable flowers for a long period. I suspect it of hybridity, as it has never set any seeds here, but whatever the plant is, it has nothing to do with *nigrum*, which the *Kew Hand-list* declares to be the right name for *vernale*. The Achillea's flat heads of yellow flowers are very good when seen against the sky, giving an outline that is different from that of any other tall flower of the season. *Potentilla Friedrichsehnii* is also yellow, so has some right to be noticed next, and so preserve some idea of classification in my list. I have pruned an old specimen in the rock garden rather severely, insisting on its only increasing upwards, and have removed all spreading shoots save those that spring from somewhere above three feet, and it has made a charming specimen, its pillar-shaped lower growth improving the effect of the spreading upper half of the bush. Just now it is smothered in its sulphur-yellow

# As July Ends

flowers like small roses. It is said to be a hybrid between *P. fruticosa* and *P. davurica*, and the sulphur is certainly intermediate in colour between the rich yellow and white of the parents. *P. davurica* exists here in two forms; one is a congested, close-growing little bush in the rock garden, that has never yet flowered, and I rather fancy is a dwarfed, hump-backed, or twisty-tempered monstrosity that never will do much in flowers; the other grows in the pergola walk, and has made a fair-sized bush, considering it is sandwiched in between a large specimen of *Phormium tenax* and another of *Escallonia langleyensis;* and the picture facing p. 280 will show how good-temperedly it makes the best of it, and gives pure white flowers on every shoot, looking so happy among the great, stiff, flag leaves of the Phormium that I have never taken pity on it and moved it to freer quarters. Let us say, "How like the world, where the patient and cheery never get any pity!" and then we can all of us sigh and think we are one of those misunderstood treasures.

I should like to reserve a large bed for Potentillas, and I feel sure it would be attractive for the whole year; for when *P. nepalensis* gives up flowering, discouraged by December frosts, *P. alba* generally has a cluster of buds down in its heart, a few of which will open whenever a day of sunshine gives them encouragement. The bush forms have been so largely reinforced by the new Chinese introductions that one could make some effective groups of them in irregularly placed clumps, and there is a marvellous wealth of beautiful foliage and brilliant flowers to be found in the family and inherited by members of

281

# My Garden in Summer

all heights. *P. Tonguei*, a semi-double, flame-coloured form of garden origin, lies almost flat on the ground. Gibson's Scarlet is but little higher, but covers a great space when happy, and produces the most purely scarlet flowers of any. *P. McNabiana* is a great favourite, its orange-scarlet flowers being shaded with a yellow glow and backed with buff. *P. Hippiana* has fine, silvery pinnate leaves, but rather small, yellow flowers for such promising-looking foliage. *P. Hopwoodiana* is a garden hybrid, and one of the most distinct in colour, a creamy flesh tint brightened by bright rosy spots in the centre, showing *nepalensis* is one parent. Even the wild *P. Anserina*, rampant weed though it may be, is a very lovely plant, and I have a golden-leaved form that I only allow to grow in the gravel path, where it can be kept in check, that is surprisingly beautiful when newly arisen in Spring.

The many gorgeous florists' forms could be grouped together, and I should have more of La Vesuve than any other ; I so greatly admire its deep scarlet and buff double flowers, which always remind me, I suppose on account of the colour of their deepest red portion, of newly made strawberry jam. But here at present they are scattered all over the garden, so we must get back to realities. *Linum arboreum* is as real and pure a yellow as one can wish for, and just now is so thick with bloom that we hardly see the blue-green leaves that set off the flowers so well. It is undoubtedly the best hardy yellow Flax, but is not very often seen in good condition ; *L. flavum*, a lanky and less brilliant yellow one, often does duty for it beside a label inscribed *arboreum*. I do not despise

*flavum,* but it is only second best when *arboreum* is visible. I find *flavum* seeds itself about freely, and needs no care beyond keeping it in check lest it smother its neighbours, but *arboreum* needs striking afresh every third year, or else the old plants perish in Winter, or flower themselves to death. It is very pretty in the warm southern bank of the rock garden, hemmed in by the grey stones, as shown in the illustration facing p. 282. Then, not far from it, *Convolvulus mauritanicus* has begun its display, which will last until really sharp frosts destroy the buds. It is often called the Blue Convolvulus, but is far too red in tone to be truly called blue, and is really mauve with a white eye. It makes a fine curtain all over the rocks on this sunny bank, and comes pretty well through ordinary winters if the root is pushed under one of the stones when first planted. I have a rather smaller-flowered, deeper-coloured form for the first time this season, but I am rather afraid it is less hardy. *C. Cantabrica* is a gem, with narrow grey leaves, a neat, bushy habit, and soft, shell-pink flowers, but is rather hard to strike, as almost all the shoots turn their minds so early to flowering, and lately it has borne me but few seeds. *C. Cneorum* is still more silvery, and loves a hot, dry place such as we can give it, and its white flowers and pink buds are freely produced in late Summer. *C. althaeoides* exists here, but I fear will not prove hardy enough to flower as it does in Cornwall, for after four years my patch has not plucked up courage to produce even a bud. It is a fine thing, with very large flowers of a curious dull pink, as though one had stirred

# My Garden in Summer

up claret-cup and a strawberry ice together, and its greatest charm is the rich purple eye. The plant that generally does duty for it in gardens, and always, so far as I know, in nursery lists, is *C. tenuissimus*, a hardier thing and even more beautiful, for its finely-cut leaves are silvery and the flowers a lovely bright rose colour. It has taken possession of one mound of the rock garden, but replaces the bulbous plants of Spring very pleasantly in Summer. It is all the happier if provided with a pea-stick or two to scramble up, but beware of planting it where it could run among plants that would dislike its smothering embraces. *Campanula Tommasiniana* is a distinct member of its family, with fine wiry growths and a multitude of narrow, tubular bells of a pale lavender colour. They are of a peculiarly stiff, firm texture, so that if you shake them they make quite a rustling sound, and are, perhaps, the only Harebells that can really ring a chime. It is a good plant for a chink in the rock garden, and once settled down should need no further care. My oldest clump has been in its place for twenty years, and except for having its dead stems cut off in Spring, and a few rooted shoots pulled out for friends now and then, has been left to its own devices, and has spread into a large plant. It is sometimes confused with *C. Waldsteiniana*, but differs in having hanging bells instead of upright ones.

My most beautiful flowering shrub of mid-July is a Privet, a form of *Ligustrum ovalifolium*, called very fittingly variety *multiflorum*. I have a standard specimen of this Privet on one of the lawns backed by a large Yew, and

Ligustrum ovalifolium multiflorum.   (See p. 284.)

# As July Ends

when it is one mass of white flowers, almost hiding its leaves, it is a fine sight. It was discovered by Mr. George Paul one lucky day in France. He saw it among the ordinary kind in a hedge, and having an eye for a good plant if anyone has, he soon noticed that it flowered more profusely than any Privet he knew, and so induced the owner to part with it, I think he told me, for ten francs, which must have seemed a large sum for a bit of a hedge that one franc would replace. And now that the flowering form has been allowed to grow freely and unshorn, it has shown the beauty that Mr. Paul detected promise of so cleverly. Every year I think it must flower itself to death—look at its picture facing p. 284, and see if you would not—but it manages to make a bit of growth and another crop of buds before the following July comes round.

There are several good blue-flowered things at their best now—*Ceanothus Gloire de Versailles* for one, especially two old bushes that I have short-coated so that they might be called standards, their round heads a mass of pale blue that looks wonderfully well contrasted with the tall spikes of *Lilium testaceum* just beneath one of them. The soft apricot and cream colouring of this easily grown Lily could never clash with anything, but is especially beautiful against the grey-blue of the Ceano- thus. Both are backed by some large, old tree Ivies, whose darker leaves show them up well, and the second brood of Holly Blue Butterflies skipping about over the Ivies visit the Ceanothus a good deal, and when settled are absolutely lost in the silvery-blue flower mass which so closely resembles their own colouring. *Agapanthus intermedius* is a really good hardy border plant that is not so well known as it deserves. It is quite cheap—I think fivepence a plant from Dutch nurseries—and its deep blue flowers are much larger than those of *A. minor Mooreanus*, and I believe it is quite as hardy. For a good purple, one should grow *Verbena venosa*, quite hardy in a warm corner in fairly light soil, also *Delphinium vestitum*, for, even though it has narrower spikes than the florists' Larkspurs, it has many good points, such as a later flowering period, a graceful, self-supporting habit, rich purple flowers with black eyes and stalks, handsome leaves, and a general air of well-bred dignity about it that I greatly admire. *Cistus purpureus* I consider the best of the many red-flowered members of its family. It has narrow greyish leaves and very large, rosy-purple flowers, and can be known at sight by the handsome, deep crimson spots at the base of each petal, which it inherits from one of its parents, *C. ladaniferus*, for it is a hybrid, and so never sets seed, and therefore take a hint from me and never buy seed if it is listed as *C. purpureus*, or even a plant, without first seeing its spotted face. Of late it has been fashionable, but none the less iniquitous, to call *C. creticus*, *C. purpureus Sunset*. This is a very good plant, and the brightest rose carmine of any Cistus I know, but quite old enough to be left alone under its own name of *Creticus*.

Of *Montbretia rosea* I never get enough, as it is not a running, ramping, rapid increaser, like other Montbretias, but more bulbous in character ; a delicate-looking, slender

Convolvulus mauritanicus.   (See p. 283.)

plant, with pale, rose-coloured flowers, and suitable for a warm corner among really choice plants. I am also fond of a totally different plant, a large, coarse I might almost say, annual Balsam, I used to imagine was an albino form of *Impatiens Roylei*, but when I sent it to Kew and then to the late Sir Joseph Hooker, it was declared to be something new and unnamed. This was not long before Sir Joseph's death, and I have never found out if he described or named it to be published presently. It came to me from Mr. Bonney, of Rugeley, who has grown it for some years, but its origin is a mystery at present, as he can only trace it as far as a station-master who gave him his first plant. It grows some six feet high, like the ordinary Balsams that are so amusing to pinch to make the seedpods fire off, but the flowers are pure white and very distinguished in appearance, looking rare and exotic, somehow far beyond the possi-bilities of the old pink ones, but like them they have a pleasant scent of ripe plums. I can see *Buddleia nivea* is in flower, but chiefly because the bees are thronging to it, otherwise its dingy little purple flowers would pass un-observed in the mass of white felt they grow among. The flowers are very inconspicuous, and, except for pleasing the Bumble-bees, there is not much object in allowing it to flower at all, for, if it is kept cut over two or three times during the Summer, we get a much better silvery effect from the great column it has grown into.

*Malva Alcea* var. *fastigiata* is one of the best rosy-pink things out now ; it forms a large but very shapely, bushy plant, smothered with satiny, pale rose-coloured flowers,

and will sow itself with a profuse generosity. Its greatest
charm is its colour—a soft pink, good enough to compare
with a La France Rose. Another member of its order
just misses being a magnificent plant—I mean *Kitaibelia
vitifolia*—for, with its handsome leaves and stately six-feet
high stems, it wants flowers just three times larger than
they are in reality. They are pretty and pure white,
but too much overpowered by the many large leaves.
There is a very interesting and beautiful form of it known
as variety *Lindemuthii*, which has its leaves finely spangled
with golden yellow. It is said to have been produced
as a graft hybrid when Professor Lindemuth was experimenting with grafting shrubby plants on herbaceous ones.
He grafted the variegated form of *Abutilon Thompsonii* on
to the ordinary Kitaibelia. After a time the scion died,
but a shoot came forth from the root of the stock,
which had, in some mysterious way, caught the variegation of the Abutilon, and this has been propagated
and distributed fairly widely. The known graft hybrids
are so few that this handsome, easily grown one
is worth having. It only wants a single Hollyhock's
flower on it to make a superb plant. I have a great
weakness for single Hollyhocks and a dislike for earwiggy
double ones, and a row of the former type, at the back
of one of the Iris beds by the river, is a very fine sight,
and is confirming me in my opinion that they are
better than the double ones for this garden. They sow
themselves, and provide endless variation of colour, and,
if an especially beautiful one appears, it can be propagated by division. I will not say they are quite as

Hollyhocks, Sunflowers, and Eryngiums.

(See p. 274.)

immune to the rust as I at one time hoped, but they are certainly freer from it than any double forms I have tried.

If ever you want to provide an unending struggle for a brother gardener, and perhaps make a lifelong enemy of him, give him a morsel of the Blue Sowthistle, *Lactuca alpina*. It is so beautiful, and seems to grow so pleasantly for its first two seasons, making a compact carpet of handsome leaves and giving tall stems of lovely blue flowers, that anyone who knows not its wicked ways is sure to let it make itself at home—then he must spend the rest of his life striving to keep the trespasser from running over his whole garden ; but other members of the family have pleasanter manners, and for a reliable and handsome plant I recommend *L. Bourgaei*. Listen to its good qualities : no running gadabout habits, but it sits as tight as a brooding hen—tighter in fact, for my oldest plant has sat in the same place for fifteen years, and I hope will continue there for another fifteen ; next, stiff stems that need no stake until the many flowering heads are beaten by violent rains, and even then a girdle of tarred twine to bind them to one another will keep the seven-foot-high clump as it should be ; the flowers are a soft bluish-lavender, and very freely produced on over a foot of stem, and form large branching heads ; and if a few stems are shortened early in June, they will branch out and flower at a lower level and a little later than the others, so if I remember it I like to nip the tops off the outer ring of stems of one or two of my plants. Its only failing is that it seeds about rather freely, but my visitors

# My Garden in Summer

consider that more as a virtue than a vice. *L. Plumieri* is also good, but for a rougher place, as its leaves are very large and rather coarse; but the stout stem runs up for four or five feet and bears large, grey-blue flowers, and it makes a tap root instead of runners. *L. perennis* is as dainty and lovely a thing as one could wish for in the wilder part of the rock garden, to recall the rocky places by the roadside where one sees its blue stars in its alpine homes. *Escallonia pulverulenta* on the wall is very effective and unusual in appearance, its grey leaves go so well with the pale coral-pink flowers, the whole plant looking almost too much of an exotic to be so happy in the open. Close by it we have our first flowers on *Tricuspidaria dependens*, though it has only reached five feet in height, and older and larger specimens I know of in Cornwall were much slower in beginning to flower. In spite of its being a newcomer and a bit of a rarity still, I would exchange it any day for as healthy and hearty a plant of *T. lanceolata*, which is not so hardy here, but whose lovely red flowers are much more satisfactory than the pallid, not very clear white ones of *T. dependens*. Further along, in a cooler and more shady bed, *Mimulus Lewisii* is very pretty among some good Shield-ferns, its clear, rose-coloured flowers looking well among the fern's green lace flounces, and *Viola canadensis* is flowering for the second time, and its summer flowers are even larger than the first crop that came in Spring. They are Violets, not Pansies, in shape; but very large and very white, with a bright lemon-yellow eye and a rosy-purple back to the petals that deepens as they age. It is a beau-

# As July Ends

tiful plant, but very seldom seen in gardens, the one that generally does duty for it being *V. striata*, a smaller cream-coloured one that never flowers before July and then continues till frost comes, an unusual flowering period for a Violet. My *V. canadensis* came to me as a delightful gift from a friend I have made through my wanderings into print, but whom I have never yet met. In a Virginian wood he thought of me and the kind of plants I liked, got a wooden box from the hotel, and filled it with moss and plants and posted it to me, and I don't think I ever more perfectly enjoyed a box of plants. They arrived rather dry, so I sprinkled them and turned them all into my vasculum, and left them closed up there all night. When I opened it next morning ferns and flowers, moss and leaves, were as fresh as though only gathered a few hours before, and I sorted them over with the aid of Britton & Brown's *Flora*, and could make out what most of them were though they were quite new to me ; and except *Silene virginica* and the Walking Fern, *Camptosorus rhizophyllus*, since devoured by slugs, all are growing well.

# CHAPTER XVII

## August

AUGUST is always supposed to be a bad month for gardens, a breathing-space for the flowers between the rush of summer Roses and the best herbaceous plants and the final flare-up of Asters and Sunflowers and Dahlias and the other gorgeous things of early Autumn ; so I have made a practice when in gardens or nurseries of noting plants that are good in August and trying them here, therefore my garden has something good to show throughout the month, unless the Clerk of the Weather refuses us any rain. *Anomatheca cruenta* will brighten up a shady but sheltered corner during August. I learnt the tip about shade from seeing a fine colony of it at Bitton beneath a large Palm, so I copied it here, and between the house and the conservatory, and behind my large Palm, it has increased as it never did elsewhere in the garden. I have just added the albino form to it, hoping it will thrive as well as the type, and will some day give us offspring with white ground and the crimson patches on it that add so much to the beauty of the red-flowered original form. *Kniphofia Northiae* is flowering further along by the conservatory; but its spike is a clumsy and dull-coloured affair, not so good as that borne by *K. caulescens* earlier in the season, but the wide, handsome, dark-green leaves of *K. Northiae* make it one of the most tropical-looking of plants that are hardy enough to be left out with no more protection than a wall to cut off N.E. winds. *Cuphea ignea* grows at its feet, and has reappeared here very satisfactorily after the last two mild winters; but its orange and scarlet flowers are worth having, even if one has to house it for the winter. The old specimen of *Salvia Grahamii* is, of course, still full of bloom, and this narrow bed looks its best in August with so much going on in it. The large herbaceous bed is gay with Daisy-flowered plants, most of which have been already praised, but other families deserve mention. *Hydrangea paniculata,* var. *grandiflora,* produces a fine sight with its large white heads, and a good form of *Veratrum album* is also very striking, towering up almost six feet, and bearing hundreds of really white flowers, instead of the greenish ones more often seen in this species. *Hemerocallis Kwanso,* fl. pl., is a wonderfully effective neighbour for it, but I wish each of the great double orange flowers would last more than its allotted day. Several Alliums are helping to fill the dull period with a bright display. *A. sativum,* the garlic of the cook, is quite worth growing in the mixed border to provide large, pale lilac balls on yard-high stems, beautiful from their first appearance when wrapped in their pointed green nightcaps, but more so when the time comes for a split and the escape of the flower-buds, to be followed by six weeks of flowering, and even late in the Winter the seed-heads are attractive, as they have such a bold outline. *A. pulchellum* is one of the prettiest of the smaller members of the family; its flowers are of so

# My Garden in Summer

bright a shade of mauve and hang gracefully on their remarkably thin foot-stalks, and are prettily bell-shaped. The variety *flavum* is equally good, only a great contrast in colour, being a really good clear yellow. *Zygadenus elegans* is an unusual-looking plant, with tall spikes of green, white, and yellow flowers, something like those of an Ornithogalum in shape. It is a Liliaceous plant from America, perfectly hardy and very well suited for a semi-shady spot in the rock garden to keep up the interest late in the season when its neighbouring Primulas and Ramondias are taking it easy.

The double white form of *Saponaria officinalis* is a prettier flower than the old pink one, but like it a terrible devourer of space, and should be hemmed up in a corner from which it cannot escape. *Sutherlandia frutescens* is doubtfully hardy, but occasionally gets through the Winter here, and then makes a fine specimen and bears many bunches of its curiously shaped orange flowers; they are something like those of the closely allied Bladder Sennas, Colutea, but hang down and are longer and more pointed, and always remind me of the picture in the *Nonsense Book* of *Shoebootia utilis*, for they are shaped rather like Turkish slippers. This year I have a fine tall two-year-old bush in the rock garden, but in most seasons I have to be content with young six-months-old seedlings. *Hyoscyamus aureus* in a crevice just beside Sutherlandia is full of long spikes of bright yellow, black-eyed flowers. My plants of it came from one given me by Mr. Frederick Hanbury, who gathered the seed from a plant growing in the wall of the house of Simon the Tanner at Joppa.

# August

*Sphaeralcea canescens* is a recently arrived treasure here, brought by a good friend from British Columbia. Its grey leaves contrast charmingly with the rich, orange-red flowers, and it seems hardier than the more rosy *S. Munroana*, which I generally lose outside in Winter, and have to take a potful of cuttings to keep inside. *S. coccinea* is a fine scarlet, and has lived for many years here, but is rather a sprawly, weak grower, so I think highly of the freely-branching *S. canescens* and its generous supply of blossoms. Close beside it is a group of a very pretty double *Silene inflata*. I like it better than the well-known double form of *S. maritima*, whose flower-heads are so large that they flop about and burst their calices. This one stands upright, and its branching stems bear a plentiful supply of fully double flowers like tiny Roses. I found it growing wild on the edge of a ploughed field at Wretham, in Norfolk ; had no trowel with me to dig it up with, but felt certain that if I left it I should have great difficulty in finding the place again, so, as the soil was sandy, I set to work with my fingers and dug about eight inches down, and then came to a harder layer of soil, almost a sandstone ; the root showed no signs of branching at that depth, so I continued work with a half-crown until I deemed it safe to pull the root, and so, at last, extracted enough to pot up and coax into growth.

*Jasminum floridum*, one of the newer Chinese plants, makes a delightful bush, and fulfils the promise of its name in the wealth of flowers it bears. They are a good yellow, but not so sweetly scented as a Jasmine should be.

# My Garden in Summer

*Heliotropium anchusaefolium* is the selfsame plant as *Tournefortia heliotropioides;* it makes a large sprawling mat of green leaves and has pretty mauve flowers that look so much like Cherry-pie that it is disappointing to find they have none of its sweet scent. Once established in light soil it is fairly hardy, and a handful of bracken has been enough to protect it during several winters here. *Fuchsia gracilis* is a glowing show of crimson flowers and buds ; *Solanum jasminoides*, on the roof of the shelter-house, is just beginning to flower ; and *Clematis Armandii* has given us a second flowering this year: these summer blooms are larger and whiter than those of April.

Flowering shrubs that will come to one's help in mid-August are none too plentiful, so those that make a bright display are of great price ; *Genista aethnensis* is one of the best, for an old specimen has so many good points—among them I reckon a trunk that is a veritable tree, graceful pendant branches, slender twigs of a rich green, a delightful habit of bearing its bunches of flowers scattered evenly over the whole plant, and a delicious scent to crown all.

*Spartium junceum*, the well-known Spanish Broom, if sheared over in Spring, though contrary to the treatment required by most of its near relations, should be a solid mass of its great yellow flowers just at this period ; I am sure they are finer and more effective for an annual Spring pruning than if left to straggle, and if one nips the tell-tale sharp-nosed keel out of a spike of extra large ones for a button–hole, it is possible to excite a

Genista aethnensis (See p. 296 )

# August

Sweet Pea enthusiast into the belief that you are wearing a yellow variety of his favourite flower.

*Hybiscus syriacus*, alias *Althea frutex*, in its many single varieties, gives good things for a sunny position with soil conditions that are moist and cool—their feet in a well and their heads in a furnace, in fact, as the Arabs describe the best conditions for Palms. I find the double-flowered ones only make a show in very sunny seasons here, and even then I do not like any of them so well as the more reliable single ones, the best of which, to my idea, is a Japanese form known as Hamabo. It was imported from Japan by the late Mr. Chambers, and was so much admired in his beautiful garden at Haslemere that cuttings were soon given by his generous hand to many friends, and most of the older bushes in this country, mine included, can be traced to him or to Bitton, where a similar centre of distribution was soon established. It has very large, perfectly-shaped, flesh-coloured flowers, with magnificent deep maroon eyes and a few radiating red veins, and seems to be one of the first to flower. The variety called *totus albus* is pure white and very beautiful, but has a rival in Snowdrift, with rather larger flowers, which, I expect, will surpass the older form when it has had time to make large specimens. The best red one I know is var. *rubis*, with flowers of a pleasant, softened purplish-crimson, and var. *coelestis* is so nearly the colour of cobalt in parts that it gives one the effect of a blue rather than of a purple flower, and is a remarkably beautiful shrub when flowering well. *Nandina domestica* grows, as it should with such a

# My Garden in Summer

specific name, close to the house, and as it does in Japan, where every garden, however small, possesses a specimen close by the door. One would like to think it was so favoured on account of its beauty, but I have been told that it produces wood with an aromatic flavour that is valued by the Japanese as being the most tasty and suitable for a toothpick. If this be true the poetry of the name *domestica* vanishes, so let us hope it is false. Anyway, I grow the plant for its beauty, and like to remember that Celestial Bamboo is one of its old names. It does well here, I believe, chiefly because it is shaded by a screen of Ivy from the southern sunshine, and it is practically evergreen, only losing its leaves after severe winters. My plant is five feet high and beautiful all the year, perhaps most especially so when the young leaves are every imaginable shade of crimson, copper, and bronze, and contrast with the deep green old ones; but now, in August, with its large bunches of white flowers, it is quite worthy of a place so near to the morning-room window. The fine red berries that are produced freely in warmer countries, and especially in the gardens round Pau, where they are largely used for Christmas decorations, are never ripened here, or it might well be at its best in Winter.

*Yucca filamentosa* var. *flaccida* is one of the best of its family for flowering generously, and I am disappointed of my lust if I have not some scores of flower-spikes each August. But then I have dabbled rather largely in this particular floral investment, having learnt to love it and its kindly ways in my earliest gardening days, buying a

# August

plant now and then for eighteenpence from a local nurseryman who had a very large stock of it. Then he retired from business, and at his sale I was able to buy the greater part of his Yucca beds at a very comfortable figure. So here they are, some in a large, irregular planting on a lawn, others forming ends to beds of shrubs, but all of them delightful whether in or out of flower. It is not such a handsome plant as the true, wide-leaved *Y. filamentosa*, the real Adam's Needle-and-Thread, for the effect of its rosettes of leaves is not so bold, and its flowers are smaller, but it is far better tempered, and produces offsets so freely round the central rosette that by the time it is ready to flower and die, there are generally two or three others to replace it. The leaves are slightly glaucous, and have a curious habit, that I have not noticed in any other Yucca, of producing horny and spiral outgrowths from their edges when the plant is growing vigorously. A large group of it is very pleasing, as the deep blue-green leaves make a dense mass about two feet high ; the flower-stems rise to about four feet, and I think it is the hardiest of all Yuccas, only needing a well-drained situation quite in the open.

Sidalceas, especially the white form of *S. candida* and the pale pink *S. Listeri*, flower in August, and of course where Phloxes do well, which means where the soil is not too dry, they now make a fine show. My favourites here are the well-known Coquelicot, so nearly a scarlet ; General van Heutsz, so seldom spelt rightly, and no wonder with such a final arrangement of consonants, a

# My Garden in Summer

lovely warm salmon with a cool grey centre ; Fiancée and Mrs. Jenkins, good whites ; and then for quite another part of the garden, so that the two groups cannot clash with each other, I like a few purple and lilac varieties. Le Mahdi is a fine purple and Dr. Charcot rather bluer, and an old plant from our grandmothers' gardens, the wild type of *P. paniculata*, which they called the *Carolina Lychnidea*, very tall and rosy lilac, though its flowers are not so large as those of the newer varieties, fits in well with this group as to colour. *Crinum Powellii*, both the pink, white, and intermediate forms, are throwing up their strong crimson stalks, and have many flowers open, and *Lilium Henryi* is at its best. This is a very well-behaved Lily here, and a group at the end of the Eremurus bed makes a fine show. One should be careful, if staking is necessary, to allow the stick to reach no higher than half-way up the stem, so that the upper half may take its natural curving habit, which makes it look like a giant Solomon's Seal. Then the flowers are spread out in a grand wide head, and the poise is delightful, each one hanging over in its natural way : if the stem is held stiffly upright half the charm is destroyed. *Antirrhinum majus* is a most useful thing to poke in here and there in Spring, where one knows bulbous plants will leave gaps later on, and if some of the glorious shades of colour now at our disposal are chosen, the late summer borders can be filled with rich colouring, for I know nothing that will stand our droughts so cheerfully ; long centuries of life on dry walls has doubtless left this good trait in their character. I like the tall

Antirrhinums (Snapdragons).   By E. Fortescue Brickdale

(See p. 300.)

# August

varieties best, and can be kind to medium ones if they are of lovely colouring, but I cannot tolerate the hunchbacks that form the dwarf race. The larger florists' Clematis do not do well here, I am sorry to say; that mysterious fate, a sudden blasting, overlooking, the Evil Eye, or whatever it is that causes a healthy-looking plant to flag and die as suddenly as though struck by lightning, over-takes many a Clematis as well as *Daphne Mezereum* much too frequently in this garden. The *viticella* group thrives best, and that lovely climbing form of *integrifolia* known as *Durandii* is fairly reliable. I am hoping that a discovery I have lately made of an English nursery in which they are all grown on their own roots, will help me to once more have the masses of mauve Lady Northcliffes and purple *Jackmaniis* I have loved and lost so often—that is if the evil practice of grafting on *C. vitalba* stock is the cause of previous failures. *C. viticella alba* has been grand some seasons on the trellis, and has a curious way of pro-ducing a number of quite green flowers at times, and then green-tipped ones perhaps for a week or so, and after that will steady down into a supply of purest white ones like large butterflies. The real butterflies I see have transferred their affections from the purple Buddleias, now failing in their supplies of honey, to *Aster acris*, one of the plants whose advent points out that Summer is almost finished, and ushers in the real Michaelmas Daisies; so also in the rock garden I see the rains of last week have brought up the leafless flowers of *Crocus Scharojanii*, so richly orange in their shade of yellow, and so reminiscent of Spring, and more autumnal still are the red stems and hanging

# My Garden in Summer

bells of *Leucojum autumnale* which have suddenly appeared from the bare ground. So I go to look for other signs of the times, and sure enough here is *Scilla autumnalis*, both the ordinary blue, and a very lovely pure white form I found on the Start, just below the Lighthouse, many years ago, opening their first blossoms, and *Cyclamen neapolitanum* has a flower or two out. So I must close this chapter and volume before the first Colchicum and *Crocus zonatus* appear, or I shall be robbing Peter to pay Paul, and giving to Summer plants what should be reserved for a future account of My Garden in Autumn and Winter.

Clematis.　By Hugh L. Norris.

(See p. 301.)

# INDEX

*Abutilon*, 255
— *Thompsonii*, 288
*Acacia Baileyana*, 144, 254
*Acanthus Caroli-Alexandri*, 117
   *longifolius*, 117
   *mollis*, 117
   *Schottii*, 117
   *spinosus*, 117
   — var. *spinosissimus*, 117
*Acer californica aurea*, 124
— *Negundo*, 169
*Achillea*, 238
— *Ageratum*, 280
— *Clavennae*, 238
— *moschata*, 238
— *umbellata*, 238
*Aconitum Anthora*, 200
*Acorus Calamus*, 173
*Actaea alba*, 278
— *spicata*, 277
Adam's Needle and Thread, 299
*Adenocarpus anagyrus*, 143
— *decorticans*, 143
— *foliosa*, 144
*Aegle sepiaria*, 275
Aestivation, 55 *et seq.*
*Agapanthus*, 255
— *intermedius*, 286
— *minor Mooreanus*, 286
*Agathaea coelestis*, 257
Agave, 181, 182, 194
   *americana*, 191
   *applanata*, 191
   *Parryi*, 190, 191
   *utahensis*, 191
*Ageratum, mexicanum*, 258
*Aira caespitosa*, 222, 223
— *flexuosa*, 223
— *vivipara*, 223
*Alchemilla grandiflora*, 153

Aldersey, Mr., 271
Allen, Grant, *The Colours of Flowers*, 65
*Allium Ampeloprasum*, var. *Babingtonii*, 275
— *Ostrowskianum*, 152
— *pulchellum*, 293
-   — var. *flavum*, 294
— *sativum*, 293
- *Schoenoprasum*, var. *sibiricum*, 118
— *sphaerocephalum*, 276
Almond blossom, 264
-  dwarf, 207, 273
— purple, 169
Aloe, 182, 195
- *abyssinica*, 197
- *arborescens*, 193
- *ferox*, 197
- *Hanburyana*, 197
- *mitraeformis*, 198
- *saponaria*, 198
— *variegata* [Partridge Breast], 198
Alpine heights in June, 202
— meadows, 219, 220
*Althaea frutex*, or *Hybiscus syriacus*, q.v., 297
Anderson, Miss, 208, 210
Andrews' *Geraniaceae*, 94
*Anemone alpina*, 135, 220
*Anomatheca cruenta*, 292
*Anthemis*, 242
— E. C. Buxton, 240
— *tinctoria*, var. *Kelwayi*, 239
*Anthurium Scherzerianum*, 270
*Antirrhinum majus*, 300
*Apera arundinacea*, 235
*Aphyllanthes monspeliensis*, 222
*Apocynaceae*, 56

303

# My Garden in Summer

Aquatics, 157–179
*Arenaria balearica*, 96, 115
Aroids, 18
*Arrhenatherum bulbosum*, 230
Arrowheads, 165. *See* Sagittaria
Artemisias, 125
Arum, White, 168
*Arundo conspicua*, 228
— *Donax*, 35, 227
— *Phragmites*, 166
*Asparagus acutifolius*, 145, 275
— — var. *orientalis*, 145
*Aster acris*, 301
   *alpinus*, 238
   *incisifolius*, 245
   Mesa grande, or Erigeron
*speciosus*, 245
   *Thompsonii*, 244
   — var. Winchmore Hill, 244
   *Tradescantii*, 238
Asters, treatment of, 244
*Astilbe Davidiana*, 176
— *grandis*, 176
— *sinensis*, 175
*Atragene alpina*, 73
*Atraphaxis Billardieri*, 217
— *buxifolia*, 218
— *lanceolata*, 218
*Atriplex Halimus*, 125
August, 292–302
*Azalea mollis*, 264
*Azolla caroliniana*, 162, 165

BAKER, Hiatt, 206
Balm of Gilead, 259
Balsam, annual, 287
Bamboos, 38, 219, 228
— the Celestial, 298
Bane-berry, 277, 278
Barbary Ragwort, 254
Barberries, 278. See also *Berberis*
Bauhin's *Pinax*, 68
Bean, Bog, 160
— Buck, 161
Bedding out, 252–262
*Bellis perennis*, 238
— *rotundifolia coerulescens*, 238
Berberidaceae and Ranunculaceae, 278.
*Berberis*, dwarf, 255
Beschornerias, 195
*Bidens dahlioides*, 241

Bieberstein, 210
*Bilbergia nutans*, 193
Bistort, 220
Bladder Senna, 294
Bocconia, 135
Bog Bean, 160
— Myrtle, 172
Boissier, *Flora Orientalis*, 210
Bonney, Mr., 287
*Botanical Magazine*, 94, 98
*Boussingaultia baselloides*, 144
*Bouteloua oligostachya*, 229
Bramble, a New Zealand, 147
*Briza maxima*, 133, 226, 229
— *media*, 229
Britton and Brown's *Flora of the
United States*, 168, 291
Bromeliads, 192
Broom, scent of, 264
— Spanish, 296
Brown, Mr. N. E., 215
— Sir Thomas, 54, 57
Buck Bean, 161
*Buddleia*, butterflies on, 151
— *globosa*, 150
— *nivea*, 287
— *variabilis*, 150, 269
Bulrush, 158
*Buphthalmum salicifolium*, 245
Burbidge, F. W., 268
Burman, *Plantarum Africanarum*,
94
Burnet Rose, Wild, 51, 63, 64
Burning Bush, 43
Bush Lawyer, 148
Butcher's Broom, 107
*Butomus umbellatus*, 160
Butterflies on Buddleias, 151
Buxton, E. C., 240

CABBAGE moths on Romneyas, 206
Cactuses, 182, 183, 184, 185
Caesalpinus, 68
Calceolarias, 252, 253
*Calibanus caespitosus*, 200
*Calla palustris*, 174
Calthas, 169
Camerarius, 68
Campanula, 210
   *abietina*, 154
   *alliariaefolia*, 211
— *barbata*, 155

Campanula, *caespitosa Miranda*, 211
  *celtidifolia*, 209, 210
  *cenisia*, 23, 214
  *excisa*, 214, 215
  *Grossekii*, 210
  *lactiflora*, 207, 209, 210, 273
  *lamiifolia*, 211
  *latifolia*, 211
  — var. *macrantha*, 211
  *linifolia*, 212
  *Loreyi*, 155
  *patula*, 154
  *persicifolia*, 273
  *pulcherrima*, 210
  *rapunculoides*, 210
  *Rapunculus*, 155
  *rhomboidalis*, 214
  *sibirica*, 210
  *tomentosa*, 211
  *Tommasiniana*, 284
  *Waldsteiniana*, 284
*Camptosorus rhizophyllus*, 291
Canadian Osmunda, 170
Candle-plant, 199
Cannas, 258
  — purple-leaved, 254
Caparne, Mr., 26
*Carex baldensis*, 232
  *Buchananii*, 232
  — *Fraseri*, 231
  — *Gaudichaudiana*, 233
  — *montana*, 232
  — *pyrenaica*, 231
  *scaposa*, 231
  *strictus*, 176
  *Vilmorinii*, 232
Carnations, 266
  clove, 267
  Duchess of Wellington, 267
  Elizabeth Shiffner, 267
  Ellen Willmott, 267
  Grenadine single, 268
  Marigold, 267
  Miss Audrey Campbell, 267
  Mrs. Cutbush, 267
  Mrs. Reynolds Hole, 267
  Raby Castle, 266, 267
  — Renown, 267
  — Trojan, 266, 267
  — wild species, 268
  — winter-flowering, 265
  Yellow Queen, 267

*Carolina Lychnidea*, 300
Caroways, 114
Cassias, 38
Castellar, collecting at, 213
Cattleya, 22
*Ceanothus Gloire de Versailles*, 285
*Cedronella triphylla*, 259
Celandine Poppy, 137
Celosias, 22
*Centaurea babylonica*, 248
  · *Clementii*, 254
  · *macrocephala*, 248
  — *montana*, 263, 272
  — *ruthenica*, 249
  · *Scabiosa*, 249
*Cerastium tomentosum*, 125
*Cereus*, 180, 182, 183, 184, 188, 194
  — *grandiflorus*, 193
  — *paucispinus*, 187
Chambers, the late Mr., 297
Cheeseman, Mr., 215, 216, 232
*Chelidonium*, 138
  — *majus*, 135
Chenault of Orleans, 242
Chionodoxa, 76
Chives, 118
*Chrysanthemum frutescens*, Mrs. Sander, 258, 269
  — *leucanthemum*, 237, 240
  — *maximum*, 131, 240, 242
  — — King Edward VII, 243
  — — King Edward VII Improved, 243, 244
  — — Princess Henry, 243
  — — *vomerense*, 243
*Cineraria maritima*, 254
*Cistus creticus*, or C. *purpureus* Sunset, 286
  — *ladaniferus*, 286
  — *purpureus*, 286
Citranges, hybrid, 143
*Cladium mariscus*, 233
*Clematis*, 301
  — *Armandii*, 145, 296
  — *integrifolia*, 120
  — — *Durandii*, 301
  · *Jackmanii*, 301
  · Lady Northcliffe, 301
  — *montana rubens*, 10
  — *vitalba*, 301
  — *viticella*, 301
  · — *alba*, 301

# My Garden in Summer

Clusius, 20
Cock's-foot, 230
Colchicum, 302
Colletia spinosa, 143
Colouring of flowers, 64, 65
Colutea, 294
Convallaria, 149
Convolvulus althaeoides, 283
— Cantabrica, 283
— Cneorum, 283
— mauritanicus, or Blue Convolvulus, 283
— tenuissimus, 284
Coreopsis Drummondii, 242
Corokia Cotoneaster, 217
Cotoneaster multiflora, 208
Cotoneasters, 255
Cotton Grass, Tyrolean, 229
Cotyledons, 180, 182, 189, 197
— farinosa, 189
— (Echeveria) Purpusii, 189
— gibbiflora, 197
— metallica crispa, 197
Coxcombs, 22
Crambe cordifolia, 116
Crane's-bill, 94. See also under Geranium
blue, 99
Dusky, 106
Pencilled, 92
Wood, 98
Crassula arborescens, 193
— (Rochea) falcata, 199
— perfossa, 199
— portulacea, 193
— sarcocaulis, 189
Crataegus Oxyacantha inermis, 217
Crinum, 20
— longifolium, or capense, 280
— Powellii, 300
Crithmum maritimum, 114
Crocus Imperati, 22
— longiflorus, 22
— Scharojanii, 301
— zonatus, 302
Cuphea ignea, 293
Cure-all, 246
Cyclamen europeum, 212
— neapolitanum, 302
Cyperus alternifolius, 169
— longus, 168, 169, 233
— vegetus, 233

Dactylis glomerata, 230
Daffodils, acclimatisation of New Zealand bulbs of, 4
— the last, 4
— twisted leaves of Narcissus maximus, 38
Dahlias, Collerette, 22
— single, for cutting, 270
Daisies, 237–251. See under Chrysanthemum
— Blue, 238
— New Holland, 247
— treatment of, 244
Damp bed, the, 118
Daphne Mezereum, 301
Dasylirion, 191
— Hookeri, 192
— longifolium, 192
Delphinium, 130
— vestitum, 286
Dianthus Caryophyllus, 268
Dicranostigma Franchetianum, 138
Dictamnus Fraxinella, 43
Dietes Macleai, 255
Digitalis ferruginea, 273
Dillenius, 200
— Hortus Elthamensis, 94
Diospyros Kaki, 147
Dog Daisies, 237
— Rose, 51, 53, 55, 57
Doronicums, for cutting, 270
Douglasia, 221
Duckweed, Ivy-leaved, 162
Dunington, Miss, 139
Dykes, W. R., 27, 30, 33, 37, 41

Echeverias, 189. See Cotyledon
Echinocactus, 184
Echinopsis, 183, 188, 195
Echinops horridus, 249
— persicus, 249
— Ritro, 249
— Tournefortei, 250
Edelweiss, 42, 229
Elder, golden-leaved, 124
— scent of, 264
Elecampane, or Cure-all, 246
Ellacombe, Canon, 35, 88, 113, 251
Elwes, H. J., 179
Elymus giganteus, 227
— glaucus, 226
Enfield Market Cross, 85

# Index

*Epilobium hirsutum* and varieties,
  276, 277
*Eremurus Bungei*, 123
  *Elwesianus*, 123
  *grandiflorus*, 245
  *Olgae*, 123
  *Shelfordi*, 123
  *Warei*, 123
*Erigeron*, 239, 242
  *mucronatus*, 247
  *multiradiatus*, 245
  Quakeress, 239
  *salsuginosus*, 239
  *speciosus*, 239, 245
  *Tournefortei*, 250
*Erodium*, 110, 112 *et seq.*
  *absinthioides*, 114
  *amanum*, 113
  *carvifolium*, 113
  *chamaedryoides*, or *Reichardii*,
    115
  *corsicum*, 114
  *gruinum*, 110
  *guttatum*, or *cheilanthifolium*,
    114
  *hymenodes*, 112, 113
  *macradenum*, 114
  *Manescavii*, 112, 113
  — var. *luxurians*, 112
  origin of name, 94
  *pelargoniflorum*, 112, 113
  *romanum*, 113
  — seeds of, 110
  — *Semenovii*, 110
  — *supracanum*, 114
*Eryngium*, 136, 274
  *agavifolium*, 274
  *alpinum*, 278
  *amethystinum*, 279
  *Bourgatii*, 279
  *campestre*, 279
  *creticum*, 279
  *giganteum*, 279
  *glaciale*, 279
  *hybridum*, 279
  *Oliverianum*, 278
  *planum*, 279
  Sea-holly types, 278
  *serra*, 274
  *Zabellii*, 278
*Erythrochaete palmatifida*, 170
*Escallonia langleyensis*, 281

*Escallonia pulverulenta*, 290
Esparto Grass, 226. See *Stipa*
Eucalyptus trees, 47
  — *pulverulenta*, 146
*Eucommia ulmoides*, 44
*Euphorbia*, 198
  — *antiquorum*, 198
  — *cereiformis*, 198
  — *pendula*, 198
Evening Primroses, 56

FARRER, Reginald, 140, 207, 211,
  213
*Felicia abyssinica*, 247
  — *petiolaris*, 257
Ferns, 170 *et seq.*
  — Marsh, 174
  — Royal, 170
  — Walking, 291
Fescues, dwarf, 230. See also
  *Festuca*
*Festuca elatior*, 222
  — *glauca*, 230
  — *viridis*, 230
Flaxes, 282. See Linum
  — New Zealand. See *Phormium*,
    43
Flowering Rush, 160
Flowers for cutting, 263–272
  — succession of, 271, 272
  — when to gather, 270
Foliage, spotted, 37, 38
  — vases of, 169
Ford, J. W., 171
Foster, Sir Michael, 27, 34, 35
Fuchsia, 258
  — aestivation in, 56
  — *bicolor*, 274
  — *gracilis*, 274, 296
  · *pumila*, 274
  · *retroflexa*, 274
  — *Riccartonii*, 274
*Funkia Fortunei*, 152
  · *undulata variegata*, 131
Furcraeas, 191

GALE, Sweet, or Bog Myrtle, 172,
  173
Galingale, 168, 169
Garden House, the, 152
Garlic, 293
*Garrya elliptica*, 272

# My Garden in Summer

Gasteria, 194
— *disticha*, 195
— *verrucosa*, 195
*Gaya Lyallii*, 146
*Genista aethnensis*, 296. *See also*
  Broom
*Gentiana Kurroo*, 3
— *verna*, 214
Gentianaceae, 56
Geranium, 92–115
  *aconitifolium*, or *rivulare*, 106
  *albanum*, or *cristatum*, 105
  *anemonaefolium*, 103
  *angulatum*, 98, 99
  *argenteum*, 95, 96
  *armenum*, 98
  *asphodeloides*, 106
  blue, 99 *et seq.*
  *bohemicum*, 106
  *cinereum*, 95, 96
  — var. *subcaulescens*, 95
  differentiation from Pelargoniums, 108
  *Endressii*, 102
  *eriostemon*, 100
  *Fremontii*, 105
  *grandiflorum*, 99
  *ibericum*, 100
  *intermedium*, 95
  Lowei, 104
  *nepalense*, 97
  *nodosum*, 105
  origin of name, 93
  *palustre*, 99
  *phaeum*, 106
  *platyanthum*, 100
  *platypetalum*, 100
  *polyanthes*, 105
  *pratense*, 93, 101
  — double, 101, 102
  — var. *striatum*, 101
  *psilostemon*, 98
  *pyrenaicum*, 105
  *reflexum*, 107
  *Richardsonii*, 105
  *sanguineum*, 97
  — *album*, 96
  — *lancastriense*, 96, 97
  — *prostratum*, 96, 97
— *sessiliflorum*, 103
— *striatum*, 92, 102
  *sylvaticum*, 98

Geranium, *Traversii*, 103
— *Wallichianum*, 101, 105
— *Webbianum*, 96
— *Wlassovianum*, 105
— *yesoense*, 105
Gerard, 68, 94, 132, 200
*Geum reptans*, 23
Ghost Tree, foliage of, 169
*Gladiolus brenchleyensis*, 32
Globe-flowers, 169
— Thistles, 249
Goats' Beard, 220
Godetias, 22
Golden-leaved plants, 124
Gough Park, Garden ornaments
  from, 147
Grasses, 219–236
— golden, 230
— large, 219–228
— smaller, 228
*Grevillea rosmarinifolia*, 143
Groundsel family, 200
— Giant, 246
Gumbleton, W. E., 91, 243
*Gunnera arenaria*, 178
— *chilensis*, or *manicata*, 178, 179
— *dentata*, 178
— *monoica*, 178
— *scabra*, 178, 179
*Gypsophila paniculata* and carna-
  tions, 268

*Habenaria chlorantha*, 178
Hanbury, Frederick, 294
Haworthias, 182, 194, 195
Hawthorn, prickles of, 53
— scent of, 264
Hazel catkins, 272
*Helenium*, 24
— *autumnale*, 247
— *Bolanderi*, 246
— *cupreum*, 241, 242
— *grandicephalum*, Riverton Gem,
  247
— *pumilum magnificum*, 246
*Helianthus*, 242, 247
*Heliopsis*, 247
Heliotrope, 256
*Heliotropium anchusaefolium*, or
  *Tournefortia heliotropioides*, 296
*Hemerocallis Kwanso*, fl. pl., 293
Henry, Augustine, 87

# Index

Herb-Robert, 104
Hermann, 68
Heron's-bills, 94, 112. See *Erodium*
Hollyhocks, 288
Honeysuckle, 19
Hooker, Sir Joseph, 287
House leeks, 229
*Humea elegans*, 262
Hyacinths, scent of, 264
*Hybiscus*, 297
— syri*acus*, or *Althea frutex*, 297
  *coelestis*, 297
— — *Hamabo*, 297
  *rubis*, 297
  Snowdrift, 297
— — *totus albus*, 297
*Hydrangea paniculata*, var. *grandiflora*, 293
*Hylomecon japonica*, 138
*Hyoscyamus aureus*, 294
*Hypericum aureum*, 274
— *Hookeri*, 124
— *patulum*, 274
— *triflorum*, 124

*Inula crithmoides*, 114
  *Helenium*, 246
Iris beds, the, 14–29
Iris, Albert Victor, 21
  *albicans*, 26
  *albopurpurea*, 39
  *amoena* varieties, 14, 16, 18
  Ariadne, 33
  *aurea*, 35, 36
  Bacchus, 25
  Bearded, 20, 32
  Beardless, 30
  Black Prince, 25
  *Boissieri*, 30
  Chrysolora, 32
  Coeleste, 24
  De Bergh, 16
  distinction between natives of
dry and wet soil, 37
  Donna Maria, 18
  Duchesse de Nemours, 18
  Dutch, 30
  dwarf, 14, 15, 16
  English, 32
  *filifolia*, 30
  *flavescens*, 26
  *florentina*, 14, 17

Iris, *foetidissima*, 224
— *fulva*, 37
— *germanica*, 14, 28, 37
-   — *aurea*, 15
-   Golden Fleece, 14
-   Gracchus, 15
-   Innocenza, 16
-   Intermediate, 26
-   *Jacquiniana*, 16
-   Japanese, 20, 38, 39, 159
-   Julius, 33
-   *Kaempferi*, 38, 169
-   *kaskmiriana*, 27
-   *Kochii*, 28
-   La Prestigieuse, 16
-   *laevigata*, 39
-   Leander, 14
-   Leonidas, 25
-   Madonna, 27
-   Maori King, 15
-   Mer de Glace, 33
-   *Milesii*, 41, 45
-   Mme. Chereau, 25
-   *Monnieri*, 35
-   *Monspur*, 35
— Mont Blanc, 33
— Morning Mist, 39
-   Mr. Veen, 33
-   Mrs. H. Darwin, 16
-   Mrs. Neubronner, 16
-   *neglecta*, 25
-   *ochraurea*, 34
-   *ochroleuca*, 33, 35
-   *orientalis*, 36
-   *pallida*, 14, 20, 24, 35
-   — *dalmatica*, 21, 22, *et seq.*
-   — guide to identity of, 24
-   *plicata*, 16, 25
-   Princess of Wales, 26
-   *Pseudacorus*, 37, 39, 40, 41
-   — var. *Bastardii*, 40
-   Psyche, 33
-   Purple King, 28, 29
-   Queen of May, 24
-   Regelio-cyclus, 18
-   Rembrandt, 31
-   *sibirica*, 36
-   Snow Queen, 36
-   Spanish, 30, 32
-   *spuria*, 33, 34, 35, 36
-   — *alba*, 35
—. *squalens* varieties, 14

Iris, *tectorum*, 41, 42, 44, 45
  Thorbeck, 18
  Thunderbolt, 32
  *tingitana*, 30, 31
  *unguicularis*, 20, 271
  *variegata*, 15
  — *aurea*, 15
  *versicolor*, 37, 40
  Victorine, 18
  *xiphioides*, 32
  *Xiphium*, 30
Isham, Sir Charles, 104
Ivy timber, 17
— tree, 107, 285
Ivy-leaved Duckweed, 162

JACQUES, M., 77
*Jasminum floridum*, 295
— white, 147
*Juncus acutus*, 233

KING Crabs, 152
Kingsmill, Andrew, 231
*Kitaibelia vitifolia*, 288
— — var. *Lindemuthii*, 288
*Kleinia*, 199
— *Anteuphorbium*, 199
— *articulata*, 181, 199
— *tomentosa*, 200
*Kniphofia caulescens*, 254, 292
— *Northiae*, 292, 293
— *Tysonii*, 254
Knuth, *Das Pflanzenreich*, 94, 96, 98, 101, 106, 109

*Lactuca alpina*, 289
— *Bourgaei*, 289
— *perennis*, 290
— *Plumieri*, 290
Lady's Mantle, 153
*Lastrea Thelypteris*, 174
*Lavatera maritima grandiflora*, 261
Lavenders, 139
Leichtlin, Max, 99
*Lemna trisulca*, 162
*Leucojum aestivum*, 158
— *autumnale*, 301
— *Hernandezii*, 158
*Lewisia Howellii*, 211
L'heritier, 93, 94
*Ligustrum ovalifolium*, var. *multiflorum*, 284

Lilies, 121, 132. See *Lilium*
— Martagon, 132
— mountain, 132
— St. Bruno's, 220
*Lilium auratum*, 264
— *bulbiferum*, 121, 122
— *colchicum*, or *monadelphum*, 132
— *croceum*, 121, 122
- *Harrisonii*, 132
- *Henryi*, 300
- *monadelphum*, 132
- — var. *Szovitzianum*, 132
— *pyrenaicum*, 132
— *testaceum*, 285
— *Washingtonianum*, 204
Lily of the Valley, 265
*Limnanthemum nymphaeoides*, or *Villarsia*, 161
Lindemuth, Prof., 288
Linnaeus, 20, 55, 68, 93
*Linum arboreum*, 282, 283. See also Flax
— *flavum*, 282
Lobel, 68
Lobelia, Blue, 252, 253, 254
Loddiges, 214
*Lonicera tragophylla*, 204
Lowe, Dr., 88, 120, 134, 135, 261
— Miss, 48, 86
Lunatic Asylum, the, 15
*Luzula lutea*, 234
— *marginata*, 234
— *maxima*, 234
— *nivea*, 234
*Lychnis Floscuculi*, 119
*Lygeum spartium*, 226
Lynch, R., 189

MADAGASCAR Reed, 169
*Magnolia stellata*, 275
Mallows, 261. See also Malva
*Malva Alcea*, var. *fastigiata*, 287
Malvaceae, 56
*Malvastrum grossulariaefolium*, 261
*Mammillaria*, 181, 182, 198, 201
— *elongata*, 198
*Manettia bicolor*, 144
Maple, Silver, 169
March Fern, 174
Marigolds, African, 22
Martagon Lilies, 14
*Matthiola bicornis*, 260

# Index

*Matthiola tristis*, 259, 260
Meadow Sweet, scent of, 264
*Meconopsis*, 76
— *integrifolia*, 216
— *Wallichii*, 204
*Melianthus major*, 254
*Melica altissima*, 222
— *papilionacea*, 228
— *uniflora*, 228
*Mentha Pulegium*, 178
*Menyanthes trifoliata*, 160
*Mertensia paniculata*, 118
— *pulmonarioides*, or *virginica*, 118
*Mesembryanthemum*, 195, 201
— *barbatum*, 198
— *Bolusii*, 201
— *stellatum*, 198
— *tigrinum*, 201
*Mibora verna*, 221
Michaelmas Daisies, 247
Mignonette, 269
— for cutting, 271
— scent of, 264
Miller, 34, 278
Mimicry in plants, 114, 119, 120
*Mimulus Lewisii*, 290
*Miscanthus*, 219, 228
— *japonicus, fol. var.*, 230
— *saccharifer*, 224
*Molinia coerulea, fol. var.*, 230
*Moltkea petraea*, 96
*Montbretia rosea*, 286
Moorhens, 158
*Moraea bicolor*, 254
— *Huttonii*, 254
— *iridioides*, 254
Mulleins, 131, 187, 273
Müller, Dr., 218
Munichoven, Everard, 20
*Mutisia Clematis*, 144
*Myosotis palustris*, 269
— *versicolor*, 65
*Myrica Gale*, 172
Myrtle, Bog, 172
*Myrtus tarentina*, 145

NAMING of plants, 244
*Nandina domestica*, 297
*Narcissus*, acclimatisation of New Zealand bulbs, 4
— *poeticus*, 5

New River, 157
Night-scented Stock, 259
Norfolk Meres, 158
*Nymphaea*, 166
— *Leydekeri*, 166
— *Marliacea* group, 166
— — *albida*, 166
*Nymphoides peltatum*, 161

*Olearia insignis*, 145
— *stellulata*, 131
*Onagraceae*, 56
*Onobrychis*, 220
*Onoclea sensibilis*, 170
*Ononis fruticosa*, 217
*Opuntia*, 182, 183, 185, 186, 187, 189, 194
- *camanchica*, 189
- *cantabrigiensis*, 189
— *cylindrica*, 196
— *glauca*, or *robusta*, 189
— *subulata*, 183, 184
- *Tuna*, 185
Orange-trees, 275
Orchids, Marsh, 178
*Orchis latifolia*, 178
*Oreocome Candollei*, 119
Oriental Poppies, 125
*Orontium aquaticum*, 174
*Oryzopsis miliacea*, 225
*Osmunda*, Canadian, 170
— *regalis*, 170
*Othonnopis cheirifolia*, 254
*Oxypetalum coeruleum*, 260

*Paeonia albiflora*, or *Whitleyi*, 120
- *lutea*, 3, 124
- *officinalis*, 124
- *Riverslea*, 124
— Single, 120
- *Veitchii*, 152
- Water Lily, 120
Palms, hardy, 275
Pampas Grass, 219, 228
*Panicum clandestinum*, 225
—· *maximum*, 224
— *virgatum*, 225
Pansy, aestivation of, 58
*Papaver aculeatum*, or *horridum*, or *gariepinum*, 127. See also Poppy
— *alpinum*, 129
— — var. *laciniatum*, 130

311

*Papaver arenarium*, 127
Carington-Lee, 125
*caucasicum*, 127
*glaucum*, 128
*Heldreichii*, 126
Jenny Mawson, 125
Lady Roscoe, 125
— Mrs. Perry, 125
— *nudicaule*, 129
— *orientale Silberblick*, 122
*pavonium*, 127
*pilosum*, 125, 126
— Queen Alexandra, 125
— *rupifragum*, 125, 126
— Salmon Queen, 125
— *sinense*, 126
— *somniferum*, 125, 126
*umbrosum*, 120
Parkinson, quoted, 20
*Passiflora coerulea*, Constance, Elliott, 144
Paul, Mr. George, 285
Peacock Poppies, 127
Pelargonium, 107 *et seq.*, 252, 253
— *apiifolium*, 109
— *australe*, 109
— differentiation from Geranium, 108
— *Endlicherianum*, 107
— Henry Jacoby, 258
— *inodorum*, 109
— King of Denmark, 253
— origin of name, 94
— Paul Crampel, 253, 256
*saniculaefolium*, 110
— *triste*, 109
*Pennisetum macrourum*, 226
Penny Royal, 178
Pentstemons, 257, 258
Pepper Tree, 43, 258
Pereskia, 183
Periwinkle, 56
Perry, Amos., 126, 177, 241, 244, 245
*Petasites japonica gigantea*, 153
— *palmata*, 168
Pheasant's tail grass, 235
*Philadelphus coronarius*, scent of, 264
*Phleum pratense*, 230
Phlox, 131, 264
— Coquelicot. 299

Phlox, Dr. Charcot, 300
· Fiancée, 300
· General van Heutsz, 299
· Mahdi, 300
· Mrs. Jenkins, 300
· *paniculata*, 300
· treatment of, 244
*Phormium tenax*, 43, 159, 281
Phyllocacti, 193
Phyllody, 90
Phyllotaxy, 55, 59, 183
*Phyteuma campanuloides*, 273
Pillar, the brick, 140
Pincke-needle, 94
*Pinguicula grandiflora*, 178
Pinwill, Captain, 106, 233
*Piper nigrum*, 43
Plum, purple, 169
*Plumbago capensis*, 144, 262
*Poa alpina*, 202
— — *vivipara*, 229
*Polemoniaceae*, 56
*Polyanthus*, 31
— Primroses, 31
Polygonatum, 149
*Polygonum baldschuanicum*, 217
Pond, the, 157
Pools, in rock garden, 173
Poppies, 125–130. See *Papaver*
— Celandine, 137
— hybrid, 125, 126
— Oriental, 125
— Peacock, 127
— Shirley, 128, 263
— Welsh, 140
Potentilla *alba*, 281
- *anserina*, 282
- *davurica*, 281
- *Friedrichsehnii*, 280
- *fruticosa*, 281
- Gibson's Scarlet, 282
- *Hippiana*, 282
- *Hopwoodiana*, 282
- La Vesuve, 282
- *McNabiana*, 282
- *nepalensis*, 281
- *Tonguei*, 282
- *Tormentilla*, 62
Pots for garden, 195
Prickles of Roses, 51–53
Prickly Pear, 181
Primrose, aestivation in, 57

# Index

Primrose, Polyanthus, 31
Primulas, 178
— *Auricula*, 31
*Bulleyana*, 132
*malacoides*, 262
*minima*, 221, 229
*Poissonii*, 178
*rosea*, 178
Privet, 284. See *Ligustrum*
Purple-leaved plants, 130
— Plum, 169
*Pyrethrum roseum*, 237
Solfaterre, 237
*Tchihatchewii*, 238

QUAKING Grass, 133, 229

RAGWORT, Barbary, 254
Ranunculaceae and Berberidaceae,
278
*Ranunculus pyrenaeus*, 203
— *Thora* and antidote, 200
Redouté's *Les Roses*, 87, 88
Reeds, 166
— Giant, 227, 228
— Madagascar, 169
Rhipsalis, 198
Rhododendron, 18, 47
*fastuosum, fl. pl.*, 19
*ponticum*, 19
Sappho, 19
*Rhodostachys*, 194
*andina*, 192
*littoralis*, 192
*pitcairniaefolia*, 192
*Ribes*, 124
Rice, Wild, 167
*Richardia africana*, 168
Robb, Mrs., 276
*Robinia pseudacacia aurea*, 124
Robinson, Mr., 97, 269
Rocket, Double White, 122
*Romneya*, 180
*Coulteri*, 205, 206
*trichocalyx*, 205
Roses, 46 *et seq.*
Adelaide d'Orleans, 78, 277
*Alberti*, 65
— var. *ochroleuca*, 65
*alpina*, 52, 71
— *pendulina*, 52
— *pyrenaica*, 72

Roses, *altaica*, 63, 64, 75
— *anemonaeflora*, 82
— Anna Maria de Montravel, 49
— Ariel, 79
— Ash-leaved, 83
— Austrian Brier, or *Rosa foetida*,
67, 68, 69, 70
· Banksia, 146
· *Beggeriana*, 83
· Bengal, 86
— Blanche Double de Courbet, 74
— *blanda*, 83
— Blush Rambler, 77
— Boursault, 52
— *bracteata*, 79
— Bramble, 81
— Brier, 49
· *Brunonii*, 74
· Burnet, or *spinosissima*, 51,
63, 64, 65, 66
· Cabbage, Double Yellow, 70
— Canarien Vogel, 48
— *canina*, 53
— var. *Andersonii*, 73
— Carmine Pillar, 75, 84
— Caroline Testout, 48
— China, or *chinensis*, 86
· — *grandiflora*, 88
· — *minima*, 89
· — single, 48
· — *viridiflora*, 90
· Copper Austrian, 75
· Cramoisie Supérieure, 49
— Crimson Rambler, 49, 76
— Dog, 51, 53, 55, 57
— Dorothy Perkins, 76
· *Dupontii*, 83
— dwarf, 49, 73
· *Ecae*, 66
— Fairy, 79, 86, 89
— *Fedtschenkoana*, 51, 75
— Félicité Perpétue, 77, 78
— *foetida*, 67, 68, 69, 70
— *foliosa*, 83
— Frau Karl Druschki, 47
— *fraxinifolia*, 83, 90
— *gallica*, 76, 83
· — *pumila*, 73
— green, 86, 90
— *gymnocarpa*, 91
— H.P., climbing, 74
· *Harrisonii*, 70

# My Garden in Summer

Roses, Hiawatha, 76
  hibernica, 75
  hips of, 51, 62, 71, 82, 84
  hispida, 63, 64
  Hugonis, 67
  humilis, 75
  indica, 86, 87
  — fragrans, 88
  Irish Beauty, 76
  Irish Glory, 76
  Irish Singles, 48, 76
  Jersey Beauty, 76
  Joseph Billiard, 80
  La France, 47, 49
  La Mesch, 48
  Lady Curzon, 73
  Lady Gay, 76
  Lady Penzance Sweet Brier, 75, 80
  laevigata Anemone, 85
  Liberty, 49
  lucida, 75
  Lyons, 48
  macrophylla, 71
  Maharajah, 75
  Malyi, 71
  microphylla, 84
  Mignonette, 49
  Miss Jekyll's arvensis, 74
  Mme. Abel Chatenay, 49
  Mme. Georges Bruant, 74
  Mme. Levavasseur, 49
  Mme. Ravary, 48
  Monthly, 86
  moschata, 83
  — nasturana, 79
  — nepalensis, 74, 82
  Moyesii, 71
  Mrs. Cutbush, 49
  multiflora, 80
  Musk, or R. Brunonii, 74, 82
  — myriacantha, 83
  — nitida, 51, 75
  — nivea, 83
  — nutkana, 83
  — Paul's Single White, 74
  pergola for, 77
  Perle d'Or, 48
  — Pharisäer, 49
  — pillar, 79
  — Pissartii, 78
  — prickles of, 51–53

Roses, Prince de Bulgarie, 49
  Ramblers, 76, 80
  Rayon d'Or, 47, 48
  — reversa, 51
  — Richmond, 49
  — rubrifolia, 72, 75
  — rugosa, 74, 75, 83, 84
  - scabrata, 73
  - scent of, 264
  - Scotch, 75
  - Scotch Briers, 64
  — sempervirens, 77
  — sepals of, 38, 53
  . — Seraphinii, 82
  — sericea, 51, 62, 75
  — — var. denudata, 52
  — — var. pteracantha, 52, 63
  — Simplicity, 79
  — single, 49, 62–91
  . Soulieana, 81
  — spinosissima, or Burnet, 72, 83
  — standard, 47
  - Sulphurea, 48
  - Sweet brier, 68
  - Tea-scented, 86, 88
  - — — single, 48
  - Trier, 79
  - Watsoniana, 91
  - Webbiana, 83
  - Wichuriana, 73, 74, 76, 83
  — Willow-leaved, 86
  - Woodsii, 83
  — xanthina, 66, 75
  Rostrum Ciconiae, 94
  — gruis, 94
  Rouy, 112
  Royal Fern, 170
  Rubber plant, 44
  Rubus bambusarum, 148
  — cissoides pauperatus, 147
  — parvus, 147
  Rudbeckia nitida, Herbstone, 241
  Rushes, 219
  — Flowering, 160
  — Scented, 174

  Sagittaria, 165
  — gracilis, 166
  — japonica, 165
  — sagittifolia, 165
  — variaeformis, 165
  St. Bruno's Lily, 220

# Index

St. John's Wort, 124. See *Hy-pericum*
*Salvia argentea*, 125
    *Grahamii*, 123, 293
    — *patens*, 254, 258
    — *pratensis*, 220
    — *splendens*, Pride of Zurich, 256
Samphire, Marsh, 114
*Saponaria officinalis*, 294
Sawflies, 149
*Saxifraga* (*Megasea*) *cordifolia*, 133
Scarlet Runners, 76
Scent of Flowers, 264
*Schinus Molle*, 43, 258
*Schoenus nigricans*, 233
Scilla, 76
    — *autumnalis*, 302
    — *peruviana*, 20
*Scirpus Holoschoenus*, 233
    — *lacustris*, 158
    — *maritimus*, 168
Scopoli, 34
Scots Pines, 138
Sea Hollies, 278
Sedges, 160, 176, 219, 231
*Sedum dendroideum*, 193
*Selinum tenuifolium*, 119
*Sempervivum*, 195, 196
    *arachnoideum*, 250
    *arboreum*, 198
    *holochrysum*, 197
*Senecio*, 200
    — *Clivorum*, 246
    — *compactus*, 254
    — *Doronicum*, 122
    — *Greyi*, 254
    *japonicus*, 170
Senna-producing Cassias, 38
*Sesleria coerulea*, 234
    — *nivea*, 234
Shamrock, four-leaved, 44
Shield-ferns, 290
Shirley poppies, 128, 263
Shrubs, flowering, in August, 296
*Sidalcea candida*, 299
    — *Listeri*, 299
*Silene fimbriata*, 130
    *inflata*, 295
    *maritima*, 295
    *virginica*, 291
Silver-leaved plants, 124
Silver maple, 169

Sloe, prickles of, 53
Smith of Worcester, 107
*Solanum jasminoides*, 145, 296
Solly, Mrs., 92
Solomon's Seals, 149
*Sorbaria arborea*, for cutting, 268
Sow-thistle, Blue, 289
*Sparmannia africana*, 258
*Spartium junceum*, 296
Spearwort, 173
*Sphaeralcea canescens*, 295
    — *coccinea*, 295
    ·  *Munroana*, 295
*Spiraea Aitchisonii*, 268
    ·  *Aruncus*, 264
    ·  *digitata*, or *lobata*, 176
    — for cutting, 268
    — hybrids, 175
    — *japonica*, 175
    — *laevigata*, 120
    ·  *Lindleyana*, 268
    ·  *opulifolia* var. *aurea*, 119
    — *palmata*, 175
    ·  — var. *purpurea*, 176
    — Peach Blossom, 175
    ·  Queen Alexandra, 175
    ·  *ramschatica*, or *gigantea*, 175
    ·  *venusta*, 175, 176
Sprenger, Herr, 243
Spring, merging with Summer, 1
Stinking Johnny Moons, 237
*Stipa gigantea*, 224
    — *pennata*, 224
    — seed-sowing apparatus of, 111
Stock, Night-scented, 259. See *Mattheola*
    — scent of, 264
Stork's-bill, 94, 107
*Stratiotes aloides*, 161
*Streptosolen Jamesonii*, 255
*Stylophorum*, 138
    — *diphyllum*, 135
    — *lasiocarpum*, 137
Succulents, 180–201
    — grouping of, 193–196
Summer, merging with Spring, 1
Sündermann, Herr, 112, 122
*Sutherlandia frutescens*, 294
Sweet Peas, 263, 264, 269
    — the first, 4
    — Lady Grizel Hamilton, 270
    — Masterpiece, 270

# My Garden in Summer

Sweet Peas, Moonstone, 271
  Seashell, 271
  to gather, 270
  Tortoiseshell, 271
Sweet's *Geraniaceae*, 94, 97, 99, 105, 109
Symphytum, 136

TABERNAEMONTANUS, 68
*Telekia speciosissima,* or *cordatum,* 245
*Thalictrum aquilegifolium,* 227
Thistles, Globe, 249
Thornless Thorn, 217
Tom Tiddler's Ground, 18, 124
Tournefort, 93
*Tournefortia heliotropioides,* 296
*Trachycarpus excelsus,* 38, 275
*Tricuspidaria dependens,* 290
  — *lanceolata,* 290
*Trifolium repens,* 44
*Trollius sinensis,* 204
*Tweedia coerula,* 261
*Typha minima,* 170

*Uniola latifolia,* 226

VAN TUBERGEN, Messrs., 30
Vase of foliage, 169
*Veratrum album,* 293
*Verbascum Chaixii,* 280
  — hybrid, 187
  — *phoeniceum,* 130
  — *pyramidalis,* 273
  — *vernale,* 280
*Verbena venosa,* 286
*Veronica parviflora,* 140
*Viburnum tomentosum plicatum,* 148
*Villarsia nymphaeoides,* 161

*Viola calcarata,* 203, 221
  — *canadensis,* 290, 291
  — *scabriuscula,* 135
  — *striata,* 291
Violets, American Yellow, 135
  — scent of, 264
*Villadenia trilobata,* 247

WAHLENBERGIA, 210, 215
  — *gracilis,* or *vincaeflora,* 216
  — *saxicola,* or *albomarginata,* 215
Walking Fern, 291
Wallflower, scent of, 264
Water beds, 168, 169
Water Lilies, James Brydon, 166. See Nymphaea.
Water Soldier, 161
Water voles, 159
Welsh Poppy, 76, 140
Wilks, Rev. W., 128
Willmott, Miss, 52, 79, 82, 86, 127
Willow-herbs, 277
Wilson, E. H., 71
Winter Sweet, 272
*Wistaria brachybotrys,* 12
  — *chinensis,* 10–13
  — *multijuga,* 5–7, 9, 12, 13, 77

YELLOW Martagon, 132
Yews, 15, 17, 19
Yuccas, 194, 254
  — *filamentosa,* 299
  — — var. *flaccida,* 298

*Zizania aquatica,* or *latifolia,* 168
  — *canadensis,* 167
*Zizaniopsis Miliacea,* 168
*Zygadenus elegans,* 294

Printed by BALLANTYNE, HANSON & Co.
at Paul's Work, Edinburgh

CPSIA information can be obtained at www.ICGtesting.com
Printed in the USA
BVOW02s1323280815

415592BV00022B/332/P